P9-EDK-177

Books by Hermann Hesse

POEMS

AUTOBIOGRAPHICAL WRITINGS

PETER CAMENZIND

BENEATH THE WHEEL

GERTRUDE

ROSSHALDE

KNULP

DEMIAN

STRANGE NEWS FROM ANOTHER STAR

KLINGSOR'S LAST SUMMER

WANDERING

SIDDHARTHA

STEPPENWOLF

NARCISSUS AND GOLDMUND

THE JOURNEY TO THE EAST

THE GLASS BEAD GAME

IF THE WAR GOES ON . . .

AUTOBIOGRAPHICAL WRITINGS

Autobiographical Writings

HERMANN HESSE

EDITED, AND WITH AN INTRODUCTION,
BY THEODORE ZIOLKOWSKI

TRANSLATED BY DENVER LINDLEY

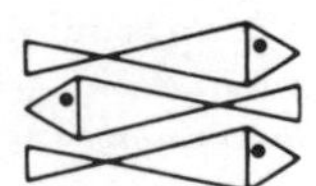

Farrar, Straus and Giroux

NEW YORK

FIRST NOONDAY PRINTING, 1973

Library of Congress catalog card number: 75-165401
Published simultaneously in Canada
by Doubleday Canada Ltd., Toronto
Printed in the United States of America

DESIGNED BY HERB JOHNSON

Contents

The year of composition follows each title. In most cases, first publication in German also occurred that year

Introduction

IN the Pedagogic Province that provides the scene for Hermann Hesse's last novel, *The Glass Bead Game* (1943), the students are required each year to submit a "Life"—a fictitious autobiography set in any period of the past the writer may choose. Through writing these Lives the students learn "to regard their own persons as masks, as the transitory garb of an entelechy." These compositions, in which the students enjoy complete freedom of invention and expression, often afford "astonishingly clear insight into the intellectual and moral state of the authors." Accordingly, the fictional narrator of Hesse's novel includes three such Lives composed by the Magister Ludi, Joseph Knecht, suggesting that they represent "possibly the most valuable part of our book."

A precise analogy can be established between Knecht's Lives and Hesse's own novels. While Hesse never wrote a single comprehensive account of his life, in several senses all his works are—in Goethe's well-known phrase—"fragments of a great confession." Whether the setting is the ancient India of *Siddhartha,* the medieval Europe of *Narcissus and Goldmund,* or the utopian Castalia of *The Glass Bead Game,* the principal characters of his novels always turn out to be transformations of Hesse himself, adapted to the circumstances of the fiction. In the autobiographical sketch "Childhood of the Magician," Hesse confides that it was his most fervent wish, as a child, to possess the magical ability to disappear or to change his shape. The adult equivalent of this magical power, he continues, was the gift of concealing himself playfully behind the figures of his fictional world. This aesthetic dissimulation is exemplified by the fact that so many of his fictional surrogates—from Hermann Heilner in *Beneath the Wheel* (1906) to Harry Haller in *Steppenwolf* (1927) and H.H., the narrator of *The Journey to the East* (1932)—share the author's initials. In his novels Hesse does not so much attempt to deal objectively with the real world as embark on adventures in self-discovery or, in the terms of *The Glass Bead Game*, create fictitious Lives in which the author's "entelechy" is displayed in a variety of transitory garbs.

It is not only the protagonists in whom this autobiographical tendency of the author is evident. Whether the novels are set in the past, present, or future, the settings and secondary figures are often taken directly from Hesse's own experience. In such disparate works as the schoolboy novel *Beneath the Wheel*, the medieval tale *Narcissus and Goldmund*, and the futuristic *Glass Bead Game*, the settings are based in considerable detail on the former Cistercian monastery at Maulbronn, where Hesse spent one of his school years. In many other stories and novels, his home town, Calw, is described in such detail that it can be charted by an attentive reader. Hesse's friends regularly turn up in his narratives in various guises: Pistorius, the organist with antiquarian interests in *Demian*, is modeled after Hesse's psychoanalyst, Josef B. Lang; Carlo Ferromonte in *The Glass Bead Game* owes his names as well as his musical talent to Hesse's nephew, Karl Isenberg (both surnames mean "iron mountain"); and through a similar onomastic trick Hesse introduces his wife Ninon into *The Journey to the East*, where she is called "Ninon the Foreigner" (a play on her maiden name, Ausländer, which in German means "alien").

Now, while Hesse's novels emerge and are shaped from

autobiographical reality, a reverse movement is simultaneously at play: for his autobiographical writings often tend to blend back into fiction. At several points in "Childhood of the Magician," Hesse's account of his early years moves beyond autobiographical "fact" into a magical realm of the imagination, which—factual or not—assumed greater significance than external reality (e.g., the "little man" who functioned as the daemon of Hesse's childhood). Similarly, the encounter with the boisterous Dutchman in "A Guest at the Spa" as well as the interview with the Dostoevskian young man in "Notes on a Cure in Baden" are molded through the power of fictional imagination into episodes that might have come right out of such a novel as *Steppenwolf*. The most startling example of this playful bending of reality occurs at the end of "Life Story Briefly Told," where Hesse, after recapitulating the events of his life up to the time of writing (1925), speculates on its course in the future. It would be inevitable, he surmises, that a man of his non-comformist disposition should sooner or later come into conflict with the law. Late in his life, presumably, he would be arrested—say, for the seduction of a young girl by means of magic. During his extended stay in prison he amuses himself by painting on the wall of his cell an elaborate mountain landscape in which a train is shown entering a tunnel. The "conjectural biography" ends when Hesse, weary of the interrogations and the tedium of jail, climbs into the painted train and disappears with it into the tunnel of his own creative imagination, leaving a prison-like reality behind, along with its consternated guards.

The point is simply this. Whether Hesse is writing "fiction" or "autobiography," he almost invariably ends up in what he has called the "timeless realm of the spirit," which is located just outside time and space—beyond the painting on the prison wall or, to take the title of one of his earliest works, *An Hour beyond Midnight*. The essential distinction in Hesse's mind and work obtains not between life and art or between fact and fiction, but rather between the meaningful reality of the spirit and the transitory world of everyday that he terms "reality" (with the quotation marks of disparagement) or "so-called reality." Once we understand how vividly *real* this spiritual realm was for Hesse, we are in a position to comprehend the frequent disappearance in his works of the arbitrary barriers conventionally maintained between autobiography and fiction. For Hesse it is more than a private joke when, in the autobiographical account of his "Journey to Nuremberg," he records that he saw his old friend Pistorius. By referring to Dr. Lang by the name he is given in *Demian*, Hesse manages to imply two things: first, that the essential relationship between the writer and the psychoanalyst is most adequately adumbrated by the somewhat ambivalent friendship between Pistorius and Emil Sinclair; and, second, that he prefers to encounter his friends on this shared spiritual plane rather than on the level of everyday reality that is delimited by official names and titles. For the same reason, the painter Louis Moilliet shows up in these pages under the name he bears in *The Journey to the East*, Louis the Terrible. And Hesse himself, several years before the publication of the novel that popularized the image, begins referring to himself as a "wolf" from the steppes. The effect of all this mystification—the appearance of "real" people in the fiction followed by their reappearance, in fictional guise, in the world of "reality"—is to blur the boundaries between Poetry and Truth (to borrow the title of Goethe's autobiography) and to force us, as readers, to enter that "timeless realm of the spirit" where Hesse felt most at home and which he has mapped out as his most characteristic literary province.

Although Hesse's entire *oeuvre* is autobiographical in this large sense, it is no accident that he was in his forties before, suddenly and for the first time, he began producing frankly autobiographical pieces. We have Hesse's own word for the fact that for years he did not realize how subjectively dependent his works were upon the circumstances of his life. In 1921, asked to prepare a selected edition of his works, he reread much of his earlier fiction. "And all these stories were about myself, they reflected my chosen path, my secret dreams and wishes, my own bitter anguish!" he noted to his surprise. "Even those books in which, when I wrote them, I had honestly thought I was portraying alien destinies and conflicts remote from myself, even these sang the same song, breathed the same air, interpreted the same destiny, my own." For years, in other words, Hesse had been so close to his works that he was unable to comprehend how unerringly they revolved around the common center of his own consciousness. It was the experience of psychoanalysis in the years following 1916 that afforded him the detachment necessary to look objectively at his earlier works and, in addition, inspired him to scrutinize his life once more—*consciously* and without the mediation of fiction.

It is important for at least two reasons to remember that the turn to autobiography was the direct product of psychoanalysis. First, the autobiographical pieces represent not so much an attempt to set down the record of his life for others as they do the endeavor to understand the meaning of his own tormented present in the light of his past. In other words, he is interested less in providing a dispassionate account of outer events—"reality"—than in undertaking an agonizing reappraisal of his inner growth—spiritual reality. But, second, the exposure to analytical psychology did not simply produce the incentive for self-analysis: it also provided Hesse with the tools of analysis. If Hesse, examining his past, is now able to detect archetypal patterns in his own life, it is due to the influence of Jung, whom he had come to know personally and through his writings. For instance, one of the recurrent leitmotifs in "Childhood of the Magician" is the paradise image: "For a long time I lived in paradise." This is anything but conventional or decorative. According to one of Hesse's basic beliefs, raised to consciousness by his study of Jung, each individual reenacts in his life an archetypal myth: born into a paradisiacal state of innocence and childlike unity with all being—what Hesse calls "magic"—the individual is plunged by growing consciousness into crisis and despair as he is made aware of the traditional polarities through which commonly accepted morality has shattered that natural unity. Hesse's accounts of his journey to the East Indies in 1911—especially the epiphany on Mount Pidurutalagala in Ceylon—make it clear that he set out rather naïvely to recover in the Orient the paradise that modern European man had lost. Realizing belatedly that the loss of innocence is not a social and geographical phenomenon, but individual and psychological—the crucial insight described in "Life Story Briefly Told"—Hesse concluded that each individual must undertake a "journey through the hell" of his own consciousness in order to acknowledge the "chaos" of his own soul. At times, notably at the end of "A Guest at the Spa," the dualism between the two poles of life (Right and Wrong, Good and Evil, Spirit and "Reality") seems to be discouragingly irreconcilable. Two years later in "Journey to Nuremberg," he describes how he developed a subtle sense of irony, so greatly admired by André Gide and Thomas Mann, as one means of dealing with the conflict. By looking at "reality" ironically we are capable of liberating ourselves from its constraints, at least spiritually, for we no longer take them seriously. The most fortunate individual, however, can transcend the conflict and move into a new state of innocence, the "timeless realm of the spirit" that lies beyond the painting on the prison wall. This triadic rhythm of human development—from innocence through despair to irony or, at best, to a higher consciousness—underlies all of Hesse's major fiction: it is most paradigmatically clear in such novels as *Demian* and *Siddhartha*, written shortly after Hesse's first experience with psychoanalysis. But it is equally plain that Hesse also recounts the story of his own life in such a way as to bring out its generally human or "mythically" valid aspects: he himself is unmasked as the archetype of man fallen from innocence; the journey to the East turns into a mythic quest for the lost paradise; his grandfather takes on characteristics of the "Wise Old Man" of myth and legend; the trip to Nuremberg becomes both a voyage into the past and an exploration of the present.

If Hesse began by contemplating his life, unconsciously, in the refracting mirrors of his fictional world, he progressed, under the impact of Jungian psychology, to manipulating the microscopic lens of the autobiographical reminiscence in order to investigate hitherto hidden contours of his own life. It is a logical development when he arrives at the heightened objectivity of the reflective essay, in which—to pursue the optical analogy—the life is no longer examined microscopically in isolation but viewed telescopically as one point in a larger constellation. These late essays, written mostly in the forties and fifties, are "occasional" pieces in the finest sense of the word, precipitated by such events as the move into a new house, the twenty-fifth anniversary of his first visit to Baden, the death of a sister, the chance rediscovery of a poem written by his grandfather. The impulse, in other words, is no longer purely internal and self-analytical but external and more generally reflective. The focus has shifted from the author's own subjectivity to the reality of the world surrounding him. We acquire more biographical facts from these essays than from the ostensibly "autobiographical" works, but this information is actually a by-product. Since Hesse's own *persona* is no longer the obsessive center of interest, his life is reflected indirectly—through the people he knew, through the houses in which he lived.

It is symptomatic of this new objectivity that Hesse wrote memorial essays for both of his sisters as well as his brother Hans, all of whom died before him. In all three essays—represented in this book by "For Marulla"—we become acquainted with the writer as a member of a family. The autobiographical writings of the twenties, which dwelled with a feverish intensity upon the individuality of the writer who was just beginning to explore his own consciousness, virtually neglected these family relationships: the family is portrayed primarily as the bearer of outmoded values against which the child and young man rebelled. Depicting only those aspects of his childhood that were important for the growth of the writer, the earlier pieces barely suggest that Hesse grew up in a family with five brothers and sisters: after all, magicians don't have siblings. In the late reflections, the author has achieved such a degree of assurance and such a firm sense of self that he can regard himself, once again, as a member of a social unit—the family—rather than as threatened by it and in opposition to it. Having attained this equanimity, Hesse is able to look back at his life in "reality" from a point in the "timeless realm of the spirit." This pronounced shift in focus that is evident in the later autobiographical writings—away from the self in the narrow sense and outward to the individual in his broader social function—corresponds precisely to a development that is familiar from Hesse's novels. *Demian* (1919), *Siddhartha* (1922), and *Steppenwolf* (1927) are intensely subjective books, obsessed with the problems of their heroes. In *The Journey to the East* (1932) and *The Glass Bead Game* (1943), in contrast, the individual is subordinated to the whole and portrayed in his relationship to such human institutions as the League and the Pedagogic Province of Castalia.

Every period of Hesse's life, from the magic of childhood through the crisis of maturity to the serenity of age, is covered in the autobiographical writings collected here. But since Hesse was for the most part more concerned with patterns and meanings and relationships than with biographical detail, the external framework of names, dates, and circumstances is often missing. Readers who turn to these autobiographical pieces are no doubt interested primarily in the development of the author's consciousness. But it will perhaps serve a useful purpose if we supply the basic information that Hesse either omits or includes quite allusively.

Hesse spent most of his formative years—up to the age of seventeen—in the town of Calw in Württemberg, where he was born on July 2, 1877, with Sagittarius on the ascendant, as he frequently reminds us. Although the family lived in Basel from 1881 to 1886, it was Calw, an almost absurdly picturesque town at the edge of the Black Forest, that Hesse regarded as his home town and that is portrayed repeatedly in his stories and novels. Calw can also be taken as a symbol for a more general aspect of Hesse's experience. He often remarked that spiritually he felt most at home in the German literature and culture of the period from 1750 to 1850, and its influence is everywhere evident in his works. (Note, for instance, the favorite music and reading matter of Harry Haller in *Steppenwolf.*) Hesse's most immediate access to this culture was provided by thinkers and writers from his own region—the Swabian Pietists, the poets Hölderlin and Mörike, the philosophers Schelling and Hegel—who had grown up in neighboring towns, attended the same schools, and studied at the same universities. This lifelong allegiance to classical German culture should not be thought of as provincial or restrictive, however, for Hesse's Calw impressions were qualified and enlarged, from childhood on, by an unusual family.

Hesse's father, Johannes Hesse, was a Baltic German from Estonia, who continued to the end of his life—in the midst of the local Alemannic dialect—to speak a pure High German that his son recalled with fondness and that no doubt influenced Hesse's own literary style. After spending four years as a missionary on the Malabar Coast of India, Johannes Hesse was compelled for reasons of health to return to Europe. There he was reassigned by the Basel Missionary Society to assist Dr. Hermann Gundert, the director of the Calw Missionary Press. In Calw he met Gundert's widowed daughter, Marie Isenberg, whom he soon married. Marie brought two sons, Theo and Karl, into the marriage; and of the children born to her and Johannes Hesse in the following years, four survived: Adele, Hermann, Hans, and Marulla. It was therefore a generation of six children that grew up in this South German household dominated by the wizard-like old grandfather, who was fluent in many European languages and an authority on Indian culture and languages. Hermann Gundert, who had spent over twenty years on the Malabar Coast, was one of the most distinguished missionaries of the nineteenth century and, in addition, a noted scholar. Among the many works that he produced, the major contribution was a Malayalam-English dictionary, which occupied him even during his years as director of the publishing house in Calw. Through his own monumental personality—reflected in several of the autobiographical pieces, notably in "About Grandfather"—and through the exotic visitors who often came to his house, Gundert added to South German culture a cosmopolitan dimension that became increasingly important to his grandson: a fascination with the Orient, its philosophy, and its literature. German classical culture, Orientalism, and a broadly ecumenical Christianity that grew into an interest in religion generally—these are the three principal elements of Hesse's childhood experience that developed into the major themes of his subsequent works.

The richly documented family history—the Hesses and Gunderts were compulsive correspondents and diarists—suggests that for a time during his childhood young Hermann was a family tyrant, an irrationally temperamental child who plagued his parents and teachers alike. These episodes might well have foretold Hesse's later academic troubles as well as his lifelong resistance to authority. But such disruptive elements have been filtered out of Hesse's own recollections of the "Childhood of the Magician," where these years have been toned down to a soft golden hue of magic and paradise. It was taken for granted that Hesse, who despite his headstrong nature was a talented student, would follow the path expected of the scion of a missionary family and enter a learned profession. In 1890, accordingly, he was sent off to the Latin School at Göppingen to study with the famous Rector Bauer, who is fondly depicted in the essay "From My Schooldays." (The year in Göppingen is also recalled in several novels, notably *Beneath the Wheel* and *Demian*.) Here Hesse prepared for the state board examinations that provided admission to one of the famous "seminaries" of Württemberg, which in turn funneled the most gifted students into the university at Tübingen. In the summer of 1891 Hesse passed the examinations and was admitted to the seminary at Maulbronn, a former Cistercian monastery where Hölderlin had studied a century earlier.

Although Hesse seemed at first to be enchanted with his new status as student at Maulbronn, within half a year he ran away from school and had to be brought back by officers of the local constabulary. From March until May of 1892 his health deteriorated and he slumped into a mood of such abject depression that his parents finally removed him from Maulbronn. If we can believe "Life Story Briefly Told," Hesse's school problems can be explained in part by his decision, at age thirteen, to become a writer—a calling, he notes, for which there is no prescribed curriculum. For a year and a half he was sent from school to school, but the changes produced only suicide attempts and increasingly severe attacks of headache and vertigo. In the fall of 1893 Hesse begged his parents simply to take him out of school, and thus at age sixteen he ended his formal education. For six months he lounged around Calw, working in the family garden plot, helping his father (who had become director of the press after Gundert's death in 1893), and reading in his grandfather's library. In the summer of 1894, rebelling against any sort of academic career, Hesse signed on as an apprentice in Heinrich Perrot's tower-clock workshop in Calw. This experience provided the material for many of Hesse's early stories, which often deal with tradesmen, apprentices, and tramps in rural Germany (e.g., *Knulp*), and it left him with such respect for his resourceful and ingenious boss that, fifty years later, Perrot turned up in Hesse's last novel as the inventor of the first, primitive "Glass Bead Game."

In 1895 the pattern of Hesse's life was changed again. On his own initiative he acquired a position as apprentice in a Tübingen bookstore, and for the next eight years —first in Tübingen, then in Basel—he advanced in the profession of bookdealer while, on the side, he read widely, giving himself the education he had resisted at school. At the same time he was writing: 1899 saw the publication of a collection of poems, *Romantic Songs*, as well as the volume of brief prose sketches entitled *An Hour beyond Midnight*. These unabashedly romantic works were followed in 1901 by *The Posthumous Writ-*

ings and Poems of Hermann Lauscher and, in 1902, by a second volume of poems. Hesse's bohemian existence during these years, in rented rooms decorated by pictures of Nietzsche and Chopin, is recaptured in the essay "On Moving to a New House."

Although Hesse attracted a certain amount of critical attention with these early books—both Rilke and the publisher S. Fischer praised him—it was not until 1904 that he achieved, with the novel *Peter Camenzind*, his first broad acclaim as well as a measure of financial independence. That year Hesse married Maria Bernoulli, an intensely introspective and musically gifted woman who was nine years his elder. Giving up his position as bookdealer, Hesse moved to the village of Gaienhofen on the German shore of Lake Constance, determined to earn his living as a writer. The deceptive tranquillity of the following eight years, during which three sons were born, is depicted in "On Moving to a New House." It was in Gaienhofen that Hesse wrote some of his most popular stories and novels (e.g., *Beneath the Wheel* and *Gertrude*). His growing reputation involved him increasingly in the paraliterary life of the successful man of letters. Co-founder of one liberal-oppositional journal, *März*, he was also much in demand as a contributor to other fashionable periodicals of the pre-war years. In addition, he reviewed scores of books and edited several anthologies and works of German romantic literature. By all external standards of measurement, Hesse was a successful young writer. But this surface bliss merely masked the emotional dissatisfaction lurking underneath—a situation of family tension depicted quite precisely in the novel *Rosshalde* (1914), which concludes that a successful artist can never be a successful husband and father.

In 1911 Hesse journeyed to the East Indies with the painter Hans Sturzenegger, but his expectations of discovering an intact paradise in the Orient were, as we noted, disappointed. It was only ten years later, in the novel *Siddhartha* (1922), that Hesse finally managed to objectify and come to terms with his experiences in the East. In the meantime, he still sought to compensate for inner turmoil through external mobility. In 1912 he moved his family from Gaienhofen to Bern, and it was therefore in Switzerland that World War I overtook him. Unlike many of his contemporaries in Germany and France, Hesse was appalled by the war from the start. Through a number of widely circulated pacifist essays—collected in the volume *If The War Goes On . . .*—Hesse attacked this war mentality that had permeated Europe, and in doing so, antagonized many of his former friends and readers, who now turned against him with vile denunciations. This grave psychic jolt was exacerbated by family difficulties: in 1916 his father died, his youngest son became seriously ill, and his wife was afflicted with an emotional disturbance that soon made it necessary for her to enter a mental institution. It was as a result of these pressures that Hesse made up his mind, toward the end of that same year, to put himself in the care of Dr. Josef B. Lang, a disciple of Jung, in the Sonnmatt sanatorium near Lucerne.

It must not be imagined that Hesse suffered such a severe nervous breakdown that he was in any sense incapacitated. As a matter of fact, during the entire war he worked actively for Swiss relief organizations, editing a biweekly Sunday journal and a series of literary editions for German prisoners-of-war, as well as a newspaper for German internees in Switzerland. It should also be understood that the experience of psychoanalysis struck Hesse less as a revelation than as a systematized confirmation of insights he had gleaned implicitly from the great works of literature. Nevertheless, the sessions with Lang, which extended into 1917 and led to Hesse's acquaintance with Jung, produced a definite sense of spiritual liberation. Hitherto oppressed by feelings that conflicted with conventional notions of right and wrong, Hesse learned to acknowledge their existence in his own soul and in the world. Instead of forcing his thoughts and emotions into patterns prescribed by society, he decided to accept the "chaos" of his own consciousness, where the boundary between good and evil did not seem nearly so sharp and clear as in Judaeo-Christian ethics. The immediate product of this psychic release was the novel *Demian*, which Hesse wrote in a few weeks in 1917. The radical ethical ideas of the novel were formulated more systematically in his two essays about Dostoevsky published in *In Sight of Chaos* (1920). These two essays caught T. S. Eliot's attention and he cited the book in his Notes on *The Waste Land*.

When the war ended and Hesse had wound up his affairs in Bern, he determined to make a radical break with the past. Early in 1919, leaving his family behind, he moved to Ticino in southern Switzerland. Here, in the village of Montagnola above Lugano, Hesse spent what he later regarded as his happiest and most productive year. To symbolize the new beginning, he published much of his work that year—the novel *Demian* as well as several essays—under the pseudonym Emil Sinclair. It was at this time, in addition, that Hesse wrote his two finest novellas—*Klingsor's Last Summer* and *Klein and Wagner*—and began the novel *Siddhartha*. In 1919, finally, he also toyed seriously with the idea of giving up writing and becoming a painter. (Though he remained primarily a writer, water-color painting became an increasingly important avocation and, indeed, source of income.)

The euphoria of 1919 did not last. This blissful year was followed by what Hesse said was the most unproductive and despondent year of his life. In addition, the post-war inflation had depleted his savings and virtually wiped out his German royalties. In order to eke out his precarious financial situation, he began accepting commissions for hand-illustrated editions of his poems and fairy tales. In 1923, the year he became a Swiss citizen, Hesse was driven by the rheumatic pains that plagued him increasingly for the rest of his life to make the first of his autumnal visits to the spa at Baden, where he always stayed in the same room at the Hotel Verena-Hof. (As a matter of record, in 1924 Hesse was married for a second time; but this marriage to Ruth Wenger lasted only a few months and was formally dissolved in 1927.) From 1925 to 1931 Hesse interrupted his hermit's existence in Montagnola by spending the winters in Zurich. It was during these years that he also undertook reading tours such as the one that produced "Journey to Nuremberg."

The last thirty years of Hesse's life, inaugurated by his marriage to Ninon Dolbin (née Ausländer) in 1931 and their move into the new house in Montagnola built for Hesse by his friend Hans C. Bodmer, differed very much in temper and structure from the preceding fifty years. To be sure, Hesse continued to spend a few weeks each fall at the spa in Baden as well as frequent summers at Sils Maria in the Engadine. But these sojourns, described in autobiographical sketches included here, were little more than a gentle syncopation in the smooth rhythm of his new life. Hesse's first forty years had been marked by frenetic external motion—flights from school, flights from home, flights across Europe and Asia, flights from his family. The years from 1919 to 1931 were, externally at least, somewhat calmer, but the writer was torn inwardly by the violent process of spiritual revaluation that he called "the journey through the hell of myself." His last years, in contrast, seem radiant with inner peace and outer tranquillity. The permanence of this settled existence is best caught in the late reflective essays, such as "Events in the Engadine," that stress the sameness and the recurrent quality of life.

During the thirties and early forties, to be sure, Hesse was still involved in the world outside: he wrote letters to friends protesting National Socialism in Germany; he continued to review books by the score, notably books by writers banned in Germany; and he assisted many friends and colleagues in their flight from the Nazis. (He set aside the income from his water-color editions specifically for this purpose.) Immediately after the war a new kind of recognition—exemplified by such honors as the Nobel Prize and the Goethe Prize—came to him: for it became apparent to many readers that Hesse's works had preserved intact many of the values (the "timeless realm of the spirit") that had been lost in the literary and cultural vacuum produced in Germany by twelve years of National Socialism. Despite all the turmoil in the world below, however, Hesse's life in Montagnola moved according to certain invariable, almost mythic patterns. And it is these patterns—too sacred to Hesse to be upset by trips to Germany or Sweden to accept awards!—that are reflected in the autobiographical essays of the last years. It is characteristic that after the publication of *The Glass Bead Game* in 1943 Hesse wrote virtually no more fiction and no more analytical autobiography. His needs for self-expression, until his death on August 9, 1962, were most adequately filled by such public forms as the circular letter and the reflective essay.

The present volume includes twelve of the most important and representative autobiographical pieces, arranged so that Hesse narrates his own life in roughly chronological sequence. Hesse's readers in the United

States and Great Britain know very little about the author of the novels to which they have often given their unreserved admiration. This ignorance is due in part to the circumstance that few of his personal documents —essays, letters, autobiographical writings—have been available in English. But it can surely be explained as well by the paradoxical fact that Hesse's pronounced tendency to lead us away from "reality" to the "timeless realm of the spirit" discourages interest in personality as such. Yet the reader of Hesse's novels who turns to his *Autobiographical Writings* will soon discover that the appeal of the novels lies not so much in their fictionality as in the qualities which are an expression of the author's own life. The pattern of Hesse's early life turns out to be—more than *Demian* or *Siddhartha*—a paradigm of alienated youth who, unable to accept outmoded values and unwilling to sell out to the establishment, drop out of structured society in search of themselves. The spiritual crisis of Hesse's maturity reflects, even more clearly than *Steppenwolf*, the *crise de conscience* of many over-thirties in this country who have been forced by events of the past decade—war, poverty, technologization—to reassess their values, often at the risk of antagonizing friends and associates not yet shaken by the glaring discrepancy between the American "reality" and the American Dream. And the older Hesse, like one of those serene sages from *The Glass Bead Game*, represents a mode of life toward which still other readers might wish to aspire. So secure in his own beliefs that he is no longer troubled by the frantic pursuit of individuality, Hesse created in Montagnola his own Castalia and, in the midst of "reality," lived in the realm of the spirit where values are preserved intact and where life goes on according to immutable, timeless patterns. In these pages we encounter once again Emil Sinclair, Siddhartha, Harry

Haller, Goldmund, and Joseph Knecht—all in the *persona* of Hesse himself. Or, to take Hesse's own analogy from *The Glass Bead Game*, the autobiographical writings reveal the "entelechy" of which Hesse's fictional characters are but the transitory garb.

Theodore Ziolkowski

AUTOBIOGRAPHICAL WRITINGS

Childhood of the Magician
(1923)

Again and yet again, lovely and ancient saga,
I descend into your fountain,
Hear your golden lieder,
How you laugh, how you dream, how softly you weep.
As a warning from your depths
Comes the whispered word of magic;
Drunken and asleep, so I seem,
And you call me forth and away . . .

NOT by parents and teachers alone was I educated, but by higher, more arcane and mysterious powers as well, among them the god Pan, who stood in my grandfather's glass cabinet in the guise of a little dancing Hindu idol. This deity, and others too, took an interest in me during my childhood years, and long before I could read and write they so filled me with age-old Eastern images and ideas that later, whenever I met a Hindu or Chinese sage, it was like a reunion, a homecoming. And yet I am a European, was, in fact, born with the sign of the Archer on the ascendant, and all my life have zealously practiced the Western virtues of impetuosity, greed and unquenchable curiosity. Fortunately, like most children, I had learned what is most valuable, most indispensable for life before my school years began, taught by apple trees, by rain and sun, river and woods, bees and beetles, taught by the god Pan, taught by the dancing idol in my grandfather's treasure room. I knew my way around in the world, I associated fearlessly with animals and stars. I was at home in orchards and with fishes in the water, and I could already sing a good number of songs. I could do magic too, a skill that I unfortunately soon forgot and had to relearn at a very advanced age—and I possessed all the legendary wisdom of childhood.

To this, formal schooling was now added, and it came easy to me, was amusing. The school prudently did not concern itself with those important accomplishments that are indispensable for life, but chiefly with frivolous and attractive entertainments, in which I often took pleasure, and with bits of information, many that have remained loyally with me all my life; for instance, today I still know beautiful, witty Latin sayings, verses, and maxims and the number of inhabitants in many cities in all quarters of the globe, not as they are today, of course, but as they were in the 1880's.

Up to my thirteenth year I never seriously considered what I should one day become or what profession I should choose. Like all boys, I loved and envied many callings: the hunter, the raftsman, the railroad conductor, the high-wire performer, the Arctic explorer. My greatest preference by far, however, would have been to be a magician. This was the deepest, most profoundly felt direction of my impulses, springing from a certain dissatisfaction with what people call "reality" and what seemed to me at times simply a silly conspiracy of the grownups; very early I felt a definite rejection of this reality, at times timorous, at times scornful, and the burning wish to change it by magic, to transform it, to heighten it. In my childhood this magic wish was directed toward childish external goals: I should have liked to make apples grow in winter and through magic to fill my purse with gold and silver. I dreamed of crippling my enemies by magic and then shaming them through my magnanimity, and of being called forth as champion and king; I wanted to be able to find buried treasures, to raise the dead, and to make myself invisible. It was this art of making oneself invisible that I considered most important and coveted most deeply. This desire, as for all the magic powers, has accompanied me all my life in many forms, which often I did not immediately recognize. Thus it happened later on, long after I had grown up and was practicing the calling of writer, that I frequently tried to disappear behind my creations, to rechristen myself and hide behind playfully contrived names—attempts which oddly enough were frequently misunderstood by my fellow writers and were held against me. When I look back, it seems to me that my whole life has been influenced by this desire for magic powers; how the objects of these magical wishes changed with the times, how I gradually withdrew my efforts from the outer world and concentrated them upon myself, how I came to aspire to replace the crude invisibility of the magic cloak with the invisibility of the wise man who, perceiving all, remains always unperceived—this would be the real content of my life's story.

I was an active and happy boy, playing with the beautiful, many-colored world, at home everywhere, not less with animals and plants than in the primeval forest of my own fantasies and dreams, happy in my powers and abilities, more delighted than consumed by my burning desires. I exercised many magic powers at that time without knowing it, much more completely than I was ever able to do later on. It was easy for me to win love, easy to exercise influence over others, I had no trouble playing the role of ringleader or of the admired one or the man of mystery. For years at a time I kept my younger friends and relations respectfully convinced of my literally magic power, of my mastery over demons, of my title to crowns and buried treasures. For a long time I lived in paradise, although my parents early made me acquainted with the serpent. Long enduring was my childish dream that the world belonged to me, that only the present existed, that everything was disposed about me to be a beautiful game.

If on occasion discomfort or yearning arose in me, if now and then the happy world seemed shadowed and ambiguous, then for the most part it was easy for me to find my way into that other freer, more malleable world of fantasy, and when I returned from it, I found the outer world once more charming and worthy of my love. For a long time I lived in paradise.

There was a wooden shed in my father's small garden where I kept rabbits and a tame raven. There I spent endless hours, long as geological ages, in warmth and blissful ownership; the rabbits smelled of life, of grass and milk, of blood and procreation; and in the raven's hard, black eye shone the lamp of eternal life. In the same place I spent other endless epochs in the evenings, beside a guttering candle with the warm, sleeping animals, alone or in the company of a friend, and sketched out plans for discovering immense treasures, finding the mandrake root and launching victorious crusades throughout the world, which was so much in need of deliverance, crusades on which I would execute robbers, free miserable captives, raze thieves' strongholds, have traitors crucified, forgive runaway vassals, win kings' daughters, and understand the language of animals.

There was an enormously big heavy book in my grandfather's large library; I often looked through it and read here and there. This inexhaustible book contained marvelous old pictures—sometimes you could find them when you first opened the book and leafed about, there they were bright and inviting; sometimes you could search for a long time and not find them at all, they were gone, magicked away as though they had never existed. There was a story in this book, exceedingly beautiful and incomprehensible, that I read again and again. It too was not always to be found, the hour had to be favorable, often it had completely disappeared and would keep itself hidden, often it seemed as though it had changed its residence and address; sometimes when you read it, it was strangely friendly and almost understandable, at other times it was all dark and forbidding like the door in the attic behind which at times in the twilight you could hear ghosts chattering or groaning. Everything was full of reality and everything was full of magic, the two grew confidently side by side, both of them belonged to me.

Then too the dancing idol from India which stood in my grandfather's fabulous glass cabinet was not always the same idol, did not always have the same face, did not dance the same dance at all hours. Sometimes he was an idol, a strange and rather droll figure such as are made and worshipped in strange, incomprehensible countries by strange and incomprehensible people. At other times he was a magical object, full of meaning, infinitely sinister, avid for sacrifices, malevolent, harsh, unreliable, sardonic—he seemed to be tempting me to laugh at him in order afterward to take vengeance on me. He could change his expression although he was made of yellow metal; sometimes he leered. Again at other times he was all symbol, was neither ugly nor beautiful, neither evil nor good, laughable nor frightful, but simply old and inscrutable as a rune, as a lichen on a rock, as the lines on a pebble, and behind his form, behind his face and image, lived God, the Infinite lurked there, which at that time as a boy, without knowing its name, I recognized and revered not less than in later days when I called it Shiva, Vishnu, named it God, Life, Brahman, Atman, Tao, or Eternal Mother. It was father, was mother, it was woman and man, sun and moon.

And around the idol in the glass cabinet and in other of Grandfather's cabinets stood and hung and lay many other beings and objects, strings of wooden beads like rosaries, rolls of palm leaves inscribed with ancient Hindu writing, turtles carved out of green soapstone, little images of God made of wood, of glass, of quartz, of clay, embroidered silk and linen covers, brass cups and bowls, and all this came from India and from Ceylon, from Paradise Island with its fern trees and palm-lined shores and gentle doe-eyed Singhalese, it came from Siam and from Burma, and everything smelled of the sea, of spice and far places, of cinnamon and sandalwood, all had passed through brown and yellow hands, been drenched by tropic rains and Ganges water, dried by the equatorial sun, shaded by primeval forests. All these things belonged to my grandfather, and he, the ancient, venerable, and powerful one with the white beard, omniscient, mightier than any father and mother, he possessed other things and powers as well, his were not only the Hindu idols and toys, all the carved, painted, magically endowed objects, the cocoanut-shell cups and sandalwood chests, the hall and the library, he was a magician too, a wise man, a sage. He understood all the languages of mankind, more than thirty, perhaps the language of the gods as well, perhaps that of the stars, he could write and speak Pali and Sanskrit, he could sing the songs of the Kanarese, of Bengal, Hindustan, Senegal, he knew the religious exercises of the Mohammedans and the Buddhists though he was a Christian and believed in the triune God; for many years and decades he had lived in hot, dangerous, Oriental countries, had traveled in boats and in oxcarts, on horses and donkeys, no one knew as well as he that our city and our country were only a very small part of the earth, that a thousand million people had other beliefs than ours, other customs, languages, skin colors, other gods, virtues, and vices. I loved him, honored him, and feared him, from him I expected everything, to him I attributed everything, from him and his god Pan disguised in the likeness of an idol I learned unceasingly. This man, my mother's father, was hidden in a forest of mysteries, just as his face was hidden in the white forest of his beard; from his eyes there flowed sorrow for the world and there also flowed blithe wisdom, as the case might be, lonely wisdom and divine roguishness; people from many lands knew him, visited and honored him, talked to him in English, French, Indian, Italian, Malayalam and went off after long conversations leaving no clue to their identity, perhaps his friends, perhaps his emissaries, perhaps his servants, his agents. From him, from this unfathomable one, I knew, came the secret that surrounded my mother, the secret, age-old mystery, and she too had been in India for a long time, she too could speak and sing in Malayalam and Kanarese, she exchanged phrases and maxims with her aged father in strange, magical tongues. And at times she possessed, like him, the stranger's smile, the veiled smile of wisdom.

My father was different. He stood alone, belonging neither to the world of the idols and of my grandfather nor to the workaday world of the city. He stood to one side, lonely, a sufferer and a seeker, learned and kindly, without falseness and full of zeal in the service of truth, but far removed from that noble and tender but unmistakable smile—he had no trace of mystery. The kindliness never forsook him, nor his cleverness, but he never disappeared in the magic cloud that surrounded my grandfather, his face never dissolved in that childlikeness and godlikeness whose interplay at times looked like sadness, at times like delicate mockery, at times like the silent, inward-looking mask of God. My father did not talk to my mother in Hindu languages, but spoke English and a pure, clear, beautiful German faintly colored with a Baltic accent. It was this German he used to attract and win me and instruct me; at times I strove to emulate him, full of admiration and zeal, all too much zeal, although I knew that my roots reached deeper into my mother's soil, into the dark-eyed and mysterious. My mother was full of music, my father was not, he could not sing.

Along with me, sisters were growing up, and two older brothers, envied and admired. Around us was the little city, old and hunchbacked, and around it the forest-covered mountains, severe and somewhat dark, and through its midst flowed a beautiful river, curving and hesitant, and all this I loved and called home, and in the woods and river, I was well acquainted with the growing things and the soil, stones and caves, birds and squirrels, foxes and fishes. All this belonged to me, was mine, was home—but in addition there were the glass cabinet and the library and the kindly mockery in the omniscient face of my grandfather, and the dark, warm glance of my mother, and the turtles and idols, the Hindu songs and sayings, and these things spoke to me of a wider world, a greater homeland, a more ancient descent, a broader context. And high up in his wire cage sat our grave parrot, old and wise, with a scholar's face and a sharp beak, singing and talking, and he too came from afar, from the unknown, fluting the language of the jungles and smelling of the equator. Many worlds, many quarters of the earth, extended arms, sent forth rays which met and intersected in our house. And the house was big and old, with many partly empty rooms, with cellars and great resounding corridors that smelled of stone and coolness, and endless attics full of lumber and fruit and drafts and dark emptiness. Rays of light from many worlds intersected in this house. Here people prayed and read the Bible, here they studied and practiced Hindu philology, here much good music was played, here there was knowledge of Buddha and Lao-tse, guests came from many countries with the breath of strangeness and of foreignness on their clothes, with odd trunks of leather and of woven bark and the sound of strange tongues, the poor were fed here and holidays were celebrated, science and myth lived side by side. There was a grandmother, too, whom we rather feared and did not know very well because she spoke no German and read a French Bible. Complex and not understood by everyone was the life of this house, the play of light here was many-colored, rich and multitudinous were the sounds of life. It was beautiful and it pleased me, but more beautiful still was the world of my wishful thinking, richer still the play of my waking dreams. Reality was never enough, there was need of magic.

Magic was native to our house and to my life. Besides the cabinets of my grandfather there were my mother's cabinets as well, full of Asiatic textiles, cloths and veils. There was magic too in the leering glance of the idol, and mystery in the smell of many ancient rooms and winding stairways. And there was much inside me that corresponded to these externals. There were objects and connections that existed only within me and for me alone. Nothing was so mysterious, so incommunicable, so far removed from commonplace actuality as were these, and yet there was nothing more real. This was true even of the capricious comings and goings of the pictures and stories in that big book, and the transformations in the aspect of things which I saw occurring from hour to hour. How different was the look of our front door, the garden shed, and the street on a Sunday evening from on a Monday morning! What a completely different face the wall clock and the image of Christ in the living room wore on a day when Grandfather's spirit dominated than when my father's spirit did, and how very completely all this changed again in those hours when no one else's spirit but my own gave things their signature, when my soul played with things and bestowed on them new names and meanings! At such times a familiar chair or stool, a shadow beside the oven, the headline in a newspaper, could be beautiful or ugly and evil, significant or banal, could cause yearning or fear, laughter or sadness. How little there was that was fixed, stable, enduring! How alive everything was, undergoing transformation and longing for change, on the watch for dissolution and rebirth!

But of all the magic apparitions the most important

and splendid was "the little man." I do not know when I saw him for the first time, I think he was always there, that he came into the world with me. The little man was a tiny, gray, shadowy being, a spirit or goblin, angel or demon, who at times walked in front of me in my dreams as well as during my waking hours, and whom I had to obey, more than my father, more than my mother, more than reason, yes, often more than fear. If the little one were visible, he alone existed, and where he went and what he did I had to imitate. He showed himself in times of danger. If a bad dog or an angry, bigger boy was plaguing me and my situation became critical, then at the most dangerous moment the little man would appear, running before me, showing me the way and bringing rescue. He would show me the loose board in the garden fence through which in the nick of time I could escape, or he would demonstrate for me just what I was to do—drop to the ground, turn back, run away, shout, be silent. He would take out of my hand something I was about to eat, he would lead me to the place where I could recover lost possessions. There were times when I saw him every day, there were times when he remained absent. These times were not good, then everything was tepid and confused, nothing happened, nothing went forward.

Once the little man was running in front of me in the market square and I after him, and he ran to the huge fountain with its more than man-high stone basin into which four jets of water fell, he wriggled up the stone wall to the edge and I after him, and when from there he sprang with a vigorous leap into the water I sprang too, there was no choice—and I came within a hairsbreadth of drowning. However, I did not drown but was pulled out by a pretty young woman, a neighbor of ours whom I had barely known up to then and with whom for a long time I had a happy, teasing sort of friendship.

Once my father had to lecture me for a misdeed. I halfway exonerated myself, suffering once more from the fact that it was so hard to make oneself understood by grown-ups. There were a few tears and a mild punishment and in the end my father gave me, so that I should not forget the occasion, a pretty little pocket calendar. Somewhat ashamed and dissatisfied with the whole affair, I went away and was walking across the river bridge, when suddenly the little man ran in front of me. Springing onto the bridge railing, he ordered me with gestures to throw my father's gift into the river. I did so at once; doubt and hesitation did not exist when the little man was there, they existed only when he was not there, when he had disappeared and left me abandoned. I remember one day when I was out walking with my parents and the little man appeared. He walked on the left side of the street and I followed him, and whenever my father ordered me back to the other side the little one refused to come with me and insisted on walking on the left side, and every time I had to go across to him again. My father got tired of the business and finally let me walk where I liked. He was offended and later, at home, asked me why I had been persistently disobedient and had insisted on walking on the other side of the street. At such times I was in serious embarrassment, indeed in real distress, for nothing was more impossible than to say a word about the little man to anyone at all. Nothing would have been worse, viler, more of a deadly sin than to betray the little man, to name him, to breathe a word about him. I could not even think of him, not even call on him or wish him by my side. If he was there, it was good and I followed him. If he was not there, it was as if he had never existed. The little man had no name. The most impossible thing in the world, however, would have been, once the little man was there, not to follow him. Where he went I went after him, even into the water, even into the fire. It was not as though he ordered or advised me to do this or that. Not to imitate something he did was just as impossible as it would have been for my shadow in the sun not to follow my actions. Perhaps I was only the shadow or mirror image of the little one, or he of me; perhaps when I thought I was imitating him I was acting before him or simultaneously with him. Only he was not, alas, always there, and when he was absent then my actions lost all naturalness and necessity, then everything could be otherwise, then for every step there was the possibility of acting or not acting, of hesitation, of reflection. But the good, happy, lucky steps in my life at that time all occurred without reflection. The realm of freedom is also the realm of illusions, perhaps.

What good friends I became with the merry woman from next door who had pulled me out of the fountain! She was lively, young, pretty, and dumb with an amiable dumbness that bordered on genius. She let me tell her stories about robbers and magicians, believing sometimes too much, sometimes too little, and considered me at least one of the wise men from the East, something I readily agreed to. She admired me greatly. If I told her something funny, she laughed loudly and immoderately long before she understood the point. I chided her for this, saying: "Listen, Frau Anna, how can you laugh at a joke if you haven't understood it at all? That's very stupid, and besides it's insulting to me. Either you get my jokes and laugh or you don't—then you shouldn't laugh and act as though you understood." She went on laughing. "No," she cried. "You are the cleverest youngster I've ever seen. You're great. You will be a professor or an ambassador or a doctor. But laughing, you know, is nothing to take amiss. I laugh just because I enjoy you and because you're the wittiest one there is. And now go ahead and explain your joke to me." I explained it circumstantially, she still had to ask this and that, finally she really understood it, and if she had laughed heartily and generously beforc, now she really laughed for the first time, laughed quite madly and contagiously, so that I was forced to laugh too! There were difficult tongue twisters that I sometimes had to repeat to her, very fast, three times in a row. For example: "Wiener Wäscher waschen weisse Wäsche."* Or the story of Kottbuser Postkutschkasten. She had to try them too, I insisted on that, but she started laughing first and could not bring out three words right, nor did she want to, and each sentence that she began ended in renewed roars of laughter. Frau Anna was the most joyous person I have ever known. In my boyish cleverness I considered her incredibly dumb, and actually she was, but she was a happy human being, and I am sometimes inclined to consider happy human beings the secret wise men, even if they seem stupid. What is stupider and makes people more unhappy than cleverness!

Years passed, and my friendship with Frau Anna had fallen into abeyance, I was already an older schoolboy and subject to the temptations, sorrows, and dangers of cleverness when one day I encountered her again. And once more it was the little man who led me to her. For some time I had been desperately struggling with the question of the difference between the sexes and the origin of children, the question became more and more burning and tormenting, and one day it tormented and burned me so much that I would have preferred not to go on living unless this terrifying riddle was solved. Angry and sullen, I was returning from school across the market square, my eyes on the ground, unhappy and morose, and there suddenly was the little man! He had become a rare guest, for a long time he had been untrue to me, or I to him—and now I suddenly saw him again, small and nimble, running along the ground in front of me; he was visible for only an instant and then dashed into Frau Anna's house. He had disappeared, but already I had followed him into the house and already I knew why, and Frau Anna screamed

---

* Viennese laundrymen wash white linens.

as I burst unannounced into her room, for she was just in the act of undressing, but she did not send me away, and soon I knew almost everything that was so painfully necessary for me to know at that time. It would have turned into an affair had I not been still much too young.

This merry, silly woman was unlike most other grownups because, though she was stupid, she was natural and open, always aware, never deceitful or embarrassed. Most grownups were the opposite. There were exceptions—my mother, epitome of liveliness, of mysterious effectiveness, and my father, embodying all uprightness and intelligence, and my grandfather who was now hardly human, the hidden one, the many-sided, laughing, inexhaustible one. By far the largest number of grownups, however, although one had to honor and fear them, were decidedly gods of clay. How comic they were with their awkward play-acting when they talked to children! How false their voices, how ridiculous their smiles! How seriously they took themselves, with their appointments and their busynesses, how exaggeratedly solemn their posture when you saw them crossing the streets with their accouterments, portfolios, books clamped under their arms, how eager they were to be recognized, saluted, and honored! Sometimes people came on Sunday to my parents' house "to pay a call," the men with high hats in their awkward hands encased in stiff, kid gloves, impressive, full of dignity, men embarrassed by the degree of their own dignity, lawyers and judges, ministers and teachers, directors and inspectors, with their timorous, browbeaten wives. They sat stiffly on chairs, one had to prompt them at every turn, be helpful to them at every move, while they were taking off their coats, entering the room, sitting down, asking questions and answering them, taking their leave. It was easy for me not to take this petty-bourgeois world as seriously as it demanded because my parents did not belong to it and they themselves found it comic. But even when they were not play-acting, were not wearing gloves and paying calls, most grownups seemed to me hugely strange and ludicrous. How self-important they were about their work, about their trade guilds and official positions, how great and venerable they seemed to themselves! If a conductor, a policeman, or a bricklayer barricaded the street, that was a sacred matter, it was assumed that you should get out of the way, make room, or give assistance. But children with their work and their play weren't important at all, they were pushed aside and roared at. Did they therefore do less that was right, that was good, that was important than the grownups? Oh no, on the contrary, but the grownups just happened to be powerful, they gave orders, they ruled. But at the same time they had their games just like us children, they played at being firemen and at being soldiers, they went to clubs and to taverns, and all this with an air of importance and authority as though everything had to be just that way and there was nothing more beautiful or more holy.

Granted, there were some clever people too, even among the teachers. But wasn't it a strange and suspicious thing that among all those "big" people, who after all had been children themselves not long ago, there were so very few who had not completely unlearned and forgotten what a child is, how it lives, works, plays, thinks, what it likes and what it hates? Few, very few, who still knew this! There were not only the tyrants and vulgarians who were mean and hateful toward children, repulsed them, looked at them askance, full of hate—yes, who sometimes apparently felt something like fear of them. Even the others who meant well, who sometimes liked to condescend to converse with children, for the most part no longer had any idea what was important. They too, almost all of them, if they wanted to communicate with us, had laboriously and embarrassedly to reduce themselves to children, not to real children but rather to invented, silly caricatures of children. All these grownups, almost all of them, lived in a different world, breathed a different kind of air from us children. They were frequently no cleverer than we were, often they had no advantage over us except the mysterious one of strength. They were stronger, yes; they could, unless we willingly obeyed them, compel and beat us. But was that true superiority? Wasn't every ox and elephant much stronger than any of those grownups? But they had the power, they commanded, their world and their way were judged to be right. Nevertheless, and this was especially remarkable to me and on some occasions almost frightening, there were many grownups who seemed to envy us children. Sometimes they would even express it quite naïvely and openly and say, perhaps with a sigh: "Yes, you children are really the lucky ones!" If this was not pretense—and it was not, as I knew whenever I heard such remarks—then the grownups, the mighty ones, the dignified and commanding ones, were by no means happier than we who had to obey and show them deep respect. In a music album from which I was being taught, there actually was a song with the astounding refrain: "How blessed to be a child once more!" Here lay a mystery. There was something that we children possessed and that the big folk lacked, they were not simply bigger and stronger, they were also in some respects poorer than we were! And they whom we often envied for their imposing stature, their dignity, their apparent freedom and matter-of-factness, for their beards and long trousers, they at the same time envied us little ones, even in the songs they sang!

Well, for the time being, despite everything, I was happy. There was a great deal in the world and even in school that I would have liked to see otherwise; but nevertheless I was happy. It is true that I was assured and instructed from many sides that man does not tread the earth simply for his own pleasure and that true happiness comes only in the beyond to those tested and proven worthy; this was expressed in many maxims and verses which I learned and which often seemed to me beautiful and touching. But these themes, which also much engaged my father's attention, did not greatly impress me, and if things went badly with me, if I were sick or suffered from unfulfilled desires or from conflicts with and defiance of my parents, then I seldom sought refuge in God but had other byways that led me back again into the light. If my customary games failed, if railroads, toy store, and fairy-tale book were exhausted or boring, just then the finest new game would very often occur to me, even if it were only closing my eyes in bed at night and losing myself in the glorious sight of colored circles appearing before me—how happiness and mystery blazed up anew, how meaningful and full of promise the world became!

The first years at school went by without changing me so very much. I learned through experience that trust and openness can bring us to grief, I learned under a few indifferent teachers the most necessary arts of lying and disguising oneself; from then on, I made out. Slowly, however, the first bloom faded, slowly I too learned, without being aware of it, that false song of life, that compromise with "reality," the world "as it happens to be." By then I knew why the songbook of the grownups contains such verses as: "How blessed to be a child once more," and for me there were many hours in which I envied those who were still children.

In my twelfth year, when the question of my taking Greek arose, I answered yes without hesitation, for to become in time as learned as my father, and if possible my grandfather, seemed essential. But from that day on, a life plan was laid out for me; I was to study and become either a preacher or a philologist, for there were scholarships for these professions. My grandfather too had once followed this path.

On the surface there was nothing wrong with it. Only

now all of a sudden I had a future, signposts lined my road, and every day and every month brought me closer to the prescribed goal, everything pointed toward it, everything led away, away from the playfulness and awareness that had filled my days hitherto, qualities that had not been without meaning but without a goal and without a future. The life of the grownups had caught me, at first by a lock of hair or a finger, but soon it would have caught and bound me completely, the life lived according to goals, according to numbers, the life of order and of jobs, of professions and examinations; soon the hour would strike for me too, soon I would be undergraduate, graduate student, minister, professor, would pay calls with a high hat and leather gloves to go with it, would no longer understand children, would perhaps envy them. But actually in my heart I didn't want any of this, I did not want to leave my world where things were good and precious. There was, to be sure, a completely secret goal for me when I thought about the future. The one thing I ardently wished for was to become a magician.

This wishful dream remained true to me for a long time, but eventually it began to lose its omnipotence; it had enemies, opposing forces stood against it—the real, the serious, that which was not to be denied. Slowly, slowly, the blossom withered, slowly out of the unlimited, something limited was coming toward me, the real world, the world of grownups. Slowly my wish to be a magician, although I continued to hold it passionately, became less worthy in my own eyes, in my own eyes it turned into childishness. There was already something in which I was no longer a child. Already the infinite, many-splendored world of the possible was limited for me, divided into fields, cut up by fences. Gradually the primeval forest of my days was altered, paradise congealed around me. I no longer remained what I was, prince and king in the land of the possible, I was not becoming a magician, I was learning Greek, in two years Hebrew would be added, in six years I would be at the university.

Imperceptibly this contraction took place, imperceptibly the magic faded around me. The marvelous story in my grandfather's book was still beautiful, but it was on a certain page whose number I knew and it was there today and tomorrow and at every hour, there was no further miracle. The dancing god from India smiled indifferently, and was made of bronze, I seldom looked at him any more, he never again leered at me. And—worst of all—less and less often did I see the gray one, the little man. I was surrounded by disenchantment on every hand, much became narrow that once had been open, much became tawdry that once had been golden.

But I perceived this only obscurely, under my skin; I was still cheerful and ambitious, I learned to swim and to skate, I was first in Greek, it seemed all was going splendidly. But everything had a somewhat paler color, a somewhat emptier sound, I had become bored with going to see Frau Anna, imperceptibly something was lost from all that I experienced, something unnoticed, unmissed, but it was nevertheless gone, wanting. And now if sometimes I wished to feel altogether myself and full of ardor, then I needed stronger stimuli, I had to shake myself and take a running start. I acquired a taste for highly spiced foods, I nibbled sweets often, sometimes I stole groschen in order to indulge myself in some special pleasure, for otherwise things were not lively and lovely enough. Then, too, girls began to attract me; this was shortly after the occasion when the little man had appeared to me one more time and one more time had led me to Frau Anna.

From My Schooldays
(1926)

Twice during my years at school I had a teacher whom I could honor and love, in whom I could freely recognize the highest authority and who could direct me by a wink. The first was called Schmid, a teacher at the Calw Latin School, a man much disliked by all the other pupils as being severe and bitter, evil-tempered and terrifying. He became important to me because in his class (we students were twelve years old) instruction in Greek began. In this little half-rural Latin school we had grown accustomed to teachers whom we either feared and hated, avoided and deceived, or laughed at and despised. They possessed power, that was unalterably true, an overwhelming power completely undeserved, often frightfully and inhumanly exercised—it frequently happened in those days that the paddling of hands or the pinching of ears was carried to the point of drawing blood—but this pedagogic power was simply a hostile force, dreaded, hated. That a teacher might possess power because he stood high above us, because he represented intellect and humanity, because he instilled into us inklings of a higher world, this was something we had not yet experienced with any of our teachers in the lower classes of the Latin school. We had encountered a few good-natured teachers who lightened the boredom of school for themselves and for us by indifference and by gazing out the window or reading novels while we busily copied one another's written exercises. We had also encountered evil, dark, raging, maniacal teachers and had had our hair pulled by them and been hit over the head (one of them, a particularly ruthless tyrant, used to accompany his lectures to bad students by rhythmically thumping them on the head with his heavy latchkey). That there might also be teachers whom a student would follow gladly and with enthusiasm, for whom he would exert himself and even overlook injustice and bad temper, to whom he would be grateful for the revelation of a higher world and eager to render thanks —this possibility had remained hitherto beyond our ken.

And now I came to Professor Schmid in the fourth form. Of the approximately twenty-five students in this form, five had decided upon humanistic studies and were called "humanists" or "Grecians," and while the rest of the class were engaged in profane subjects such as drawing, natural history, and the like, we five were initiated into Greek by Professor Schmid. The professor was by no means beloved; he was a sickly, pale, careworn, morose-looking man, smooth-shaven, dark-haired, usually solemn and severe in mood, and if on occasion he was witty it was in a sarcastic tone. What really won me over against the unanimous judgment of the class I do not know. Perhaps it was a response to his unhappiness. He was frail and looked as if he were suffering, had a delicate, sickly wife who was almost never visible, and he lived like all our teachers in shabby poverty. Some circumstance, very likely his wife's health, prevented him from increasing his small income as the other teachers did, by taking in boarders, and this fact gave him a certain air of distinction in contrast to our other teachers. To this was now added Greek. We five chosen ones always seemed to ourselves like an intellectual aristocracy in the midst of our fellow students. Our goal was the higher studies, while the others were destined to be hand workers or tradesmen —and now we began to learn this mysterious, ancient language, much older, more mysterious, and more distinguished than Latin, this language that one did not learn for the purpose of earning money or to be able to travel about in the world but simply to become acquainted with Socrates, Plato, and Homer. Certain features of that world were already known to me, for Greek scholarship had been familiar to my parents and grandparents, and in Schwab's *Myths of the Classical World* I had long since made the acquaintance of Odysseus and Polyphemus, of Phaëthon, Icarus, the Argonauts, and Tantalus. And in the reader which we had recently been using in school there was amid a crowd of most prosaic pieces, lonesome as a bird of paradise, a marvelous poem by Hölderlin which, to be sure, I only half understood, but which sounded infinitely sweet and seductive and whose secret connection with the world of Greece I dimly perceived.

This Herr Schmid did nothing to make our school year easy. Indeed, he made it extra hard, often unnecessarily hard. He demanded a great deal, at least from us "humanists," and was not only severe but often harsh and frequently ill-tempered as well; he would have attacks of sudden anger and was then feared, with reason, by all of us, including me, very likely as the young fish fry in a weir fear the pursuing pike. Now I had become acquainted with this under other teachers. With Schmid I experienced something new. I experienced, besides fear, respect, I discovered that you can love and honor a man even when he happens to be your enemy. Sometimes in his dark hours, when his haggard face beneath the black hair looked so tragic, oppressed, and malicious, I was forced to think of King Saul in his periods of gloom. But then he would recover, his face would grow smooth, he would draw Greek letters on the blackboard and say things about Greek grammar and language that I felt were more than pedagogic rigmarole. I fell deeply in love with Greek, although I was terrified of the Greek class, and I would draw in my schoolbook certain Greek letters such as upsilon, psi, omega, quite entranced and obsessed, as though they were magic signs.

During this first year of the humanities, I suddenly fell ill. It was a sickness that so far as I know is unknown and unregarded today, but that the doctors at that time called "growing pains." I was given cod-liver oil and salicylic acid, and for a while my knees were massaged with ichthyol. I enjoyed my sickness thoroughly, for despite my humanistic idealism I was far too accustomed to hate and fear school not to regard a halfway bearable illness as a gift of grace and a release. For a long time I lay in bed, and since the wall beside my bed was of wood painted white I began to work on this convenient surface with water colors, and at the level of my head I painted a picture that was supposed to represent the Seven Swabians and was heartily laughed at by my brothers and sisters. But when the second and third weeks had gone by and I was still sick abed, some concern was felt lest, if this were to last much longer, I might be left too far behind in Greek. One of my classmates was summoned to keep me in touch with what went on in class, and then it became apparent that Herr Schmid with his humanists had by that time got through a formidable number of chapters in the Greek grammar. These I must now make up, and under the eyes of the Seven Swabians I struggled through many lonesome hours against my own indolence and the problems of Greek conjugation. At times my father helped me, but when I was well again and allowed to be up and around I was still very far behind, and some private lessons from Professor Schmid were thought necessary. He was willing to give them, and so for a short period I went every other day to his dim and cheerless apartment where Schmid's pale, taciturn wife was fighting a mortal illness. I seldom got to see her, she died shortly thereafter. The hours in this oppressive apartment were as though bewitched; the moment I crossed the threshold I stepped into a different, unreal, terrifying world; I found the honored wise man, the feared tyrant whom I had known in school, strangely and uncannily changed. Intuitively I began to understand his tormented expression, I suffered for him, suffered under him, for his mood was usually very bad. But twice he took me out for walks, strolled about with me in the open air unburdened by grammar or Greek, and on these short walks he was gracious and friendly to me; without sarcasm, without attacks of temper, he asked about my hobbies and about my dreams for the future, and from then on I loved him, although, as soon as I was back in his classroom once more, he seemed to have forgotten the walks completely. After his wife was buried I remember that he made his characteristic gesture of pushing his long hair back from his forehead more often and more abruptly. As a teacher he was very difficult at that time, and I believe I was the only one of his pupils who loved him, despite his harshness and his unpredictability.

Not long after I finished Schmid's class I left my home town and its school for the first time. This happened for disciplinary reasons, for at that time I had become a very difficult and wayward son and my parents did not know what to do with me. In addition to that, however, I had to be as well prepared as possible for the "district examination." This official examination, which was held every summer for the whole province of Württemberg, was very important, for whoever passed it was granted room and board in a theological "seminary" and could study there on a scholarship. This course had been decided upon for me. Now there were certain schools in the district in which preparation for this examination was a specialty, and so to one of these schools I was sent. It was the Latin school in Göppingen, where for years the old rector, Bauer, had been cramming students for the provincial exam; he was famous for it in the whole district, and year after year a throng of ambitious students flocked around him, sent there from all parts of the province.

In earlier years Rector Bauer had had the reputation of being a harsh pedagogue, fond of caning; an older relation of mine who years before had been his pupil had been severely beaten by him. Now an old man, Bauer was regarded as a marvelous eccentric and also as a teacher who demanded a great deal from his students but could be nice to them. Nevertheless, it was with no little dread that I, after the first painful farewell to my family's house, waited, holding my mother's hand, outside the famous rector's study. I believe my mother was not at first enchanted by him as he came toward us and invited us into his den, a bent, aged man with tangled gray hair, somewhat protuberant eyes marked with red veins, dressed in an indescribably old-fashioned garment stained with greenish discolorations, wearing spectacles low on his nose and holding in his right hand a long pipe with a porcelain bowl reaching almost to the floor, from which he continuously blew mighty clouds of smoke into the already smoke-filled room. Even in class he would not be parted from his pipe. This strange old man with his bent, careless posture, his untidy old clothes, his sad, moody expression, his shapeless slippers, his long fuming pipe, seemed to me like an aged magician into whose custody I was now to be given. It would perhaps be terrifying with this dusty, gray, otherworldly ancient; also conceivably it could be pleasant and enchanting—in any case, it would be something strange, an adventure, an experience. I was ready and willing to meet him halfway.

But first I had to endure the moment at the station when my mother kissed me and gave me her blessing and got into the train and the train moved off, and for the first time I stood outside and alone in "the world," in which I must now find my way and defend myself—I have not yet been able to do so even up to the present moment when my hair is beginning to grow gray. Before the parting, my mother had prayed with me, and although at that time my piety was no longer anything to boast about, nevertheless during her prayer and her blessing I had solemnly resolved in my heart to behave myself here, away from home, and not to disgrace my mother. In the long run I did not succeed! My later school years brought her and me severe storms, trials, and disillusionments, much sorrow, many tears, much strife and misunderstanding. But at that time in Göppingen I remained completely true to my resolve and behaved well. This, to be sure, was not discernible to the model students or, for that matter, to the house mother with whom I and four other boys lived, and ate, and by whom we were cared for, but whom I could not respect and obey in the manner she expected from her charges. No, I never stood very high in her regard, and although there were many days when I could turn charmer and divert her to smiles and good will, she was a judge in whom I acknowledged neither power nor importance, and when on a bitter day after some small boyish misdeed she once summoned her big, powerfully muscled brother to inflict corporal punishment on me, I rebelled most stubbornly and would sooner have thrown myself out the window or sunk my teeth into the man's throat than allow myself to be punished by someone who in my opinion did not have the right to do it. He did not dare touch me and had to withdraw without accomplishing his purpose.

I did not like Göppingen. The "world" into which I had been thrust did not appeal to me, it was barren and bleak, coarse and impoverished. At that time Göppingen had not yet become the manufacturing city it is today, but there were already six or seven tall factory chimneys there, and the little river, in comparison with the one at home, was a proletarian, creeping shabbily between piles of rubbish, and the fact that the outer surroundings of the city were very beautiful was hardly known to us since we had only brief periods when we could be away, and I got onto the Hohenstaufen only a single time. Oh no, this Göppingen displeased me completely, this prosaic manufacturing city could not really compare with my home town, and if I told my schoolmates, all of whom like me were languishing in a strange land and in durance vile, about Calw and the life there, then I laid the colors on thick and created romances out of yearning and love of boasting for which no one could call me to account, since I was the only one from Calw in our school. Almost all sections of the province and all the provincial cities were represented in the school, barely six or seven in the class being from Göppingen, all others having come from afar to make use of the approved springboard for the provincial examination.

And the springboard continued to be effective with our class as it had been with so many others. At the end of our Göppingen stay an impressive number of students had passed the examination, and I was among them. Göppingen was not to blame if nothing good ever came of me.

Now, although the dull, industrial city, the imprisonment under the supervision of a strict house mother, and the whole exterior side of my life in Göppingen were highly unpleasant for me, this period (it was almost a year and a half) was nevertheless extraordinarily fruitful and important in my life. That relationship between teacher and pupil of which I had had an inkling in Calw with Professor Schmid, that infinitely rewarding and yet so subtle relationship between an intellectual leader and a gifted child, came to full bloom in the case of Rector Bauer and me. That strange, almost frightening-looking old man with his countless eccentricities and whimsies, who stared out, watchful and moody, from behind his small, greenish eyeglasses, who constantly filled the crowded schoolroom with smoke from his long pipe, became for a time in my eyes leader, exemplar, judge, demigod. We had two other teachers too, but as far as I was concerned, they did not exist; they receded like shadows behind the beloved, feared, honored figure of the old man, as though they had one less dimension. And just so the unappealing life in Göppingen disappeared for me, and even my friendships with fellow students, they too dwindled to nothing beside this looming figure. At that time when my boyhood was in full flower and when even the first intimations and premonitions of sexual love began to stir, school, a generally so despised institution, was for more than a year the central point of my life around which everything else revolved, even my dreams, even my thoughts during vacation time. I, who had always been a sensitive and critical pupil used to defending myself tooth and nail against every form of dependence and subjugation, had been completely caught and enchanted by this mysterious old man, simply because he called upon my highest efforts and ideals, seemed not to see at all my immaturity, my awkwardness, my inferiority, assumed the best in me and regarded the highest accomplishment as natural. He did not need many words to express his praise. If he commented on a Latin or Greek exercise: "You have done that quite nicely, Hesse," then for days I was happy and filled with enthusiasm. And if just in passing he happened to whisper without looking at me: "I'm not entirely satisfied with you, you can do better," then I suffered and went to mad lengths to propitiate the demigod. He often talked to me in Latin, translating my name as Chattus.

Now there was no way for me to tell how far this experience of a completely special relationship was shared by my fellow students. Certain favored ones, to be sure, my closest friends and rivals, were obviously, just like me, under the spell of the old catcher of souls and, just as I had been handed the boon of vocation, felt themselves initiates on the bottom step of the sanctuary. If I attempt to understand my youthful psyche, I find that the best and most productive part of it, despite many rebellions and many negations, was the ability to feel reverence, and that my soul prospered most and blossomed most beautifully when it could revere, adore, strive for that highest goal. This happiness, the beginnings of which my father had earlier recognized and cultivated in me, and which under a series of mediocre, lackluster teachers had almost withered away, which had burgeoned a bit once more under the dyspeptic Professor Schmid, came into full flower, for the first and last time in my life, under Rector Bauer.

Had our rector been able to do nothing except cause some of his better students to fall in love with Latin and Greek and inspire in them a belief in an intellectual vocation and its responsibilities, even that would have been a great and praiseworthy accomplishment. However, the unique, the extraordinary thing about our teacher was his ability not only to nose out the more intelligent of his pupils and to supply their idealism with nourishment and support but to give proper due to the age of his pupils, to their boyishness and passion for play. For Bauer, an honored Socrates, was also a clever, a highly original schoolmaster who again and again found ways to make school attractive to thirteen-year-old youngsters. This sage, able with such wit to teach us Latin syntax and the rules of Greek accent, had constant pedagogic inspirations too, and they delighted us boys. One must have some inkling of the severity, stiffness, and boredom of a Latin school at that time to be able to imagine how fresh, original, and inspired this man seemed in the midst of the usual crowd of dry bureaucrats. Even his exterior, the fantastic appearance which at first made you want to laugh, soon became the instrument of his authority and discipline. Out of his oddities and hobbies, which seemed by no means suited to support his authority, he made new aids for education. For example, his long pipe, which had so horrified my mother, in the shortest time was no longer for us pupils a laughable or annoying appanage but rather a kind of scepter and symbol of might. Whoever was allowed to hold his pipe for a moment, whomever he entrusted with the office of knocking it out and keeping it in working order, he was the envied favorite. There were other honorary posts for which we pupils competed eagerly. There was the office of "windbag," which for a time I proudly filled. The windbag had to dust off the teacher's desk every day and he had to do this with two rabbit's feet which lay on top of the desk. When this job was taken away from me one day and given to another student, I felt severely punished.

On a winter day, if we were sitting in the overheated, smoke-filled schoolroom and the sun was shining on the frost-covered windows, our rector might suddenly say: "Boys, it stinks hideously in here and outside the sun is shining. Have a race around the house. And before you do, open up the windows!" Or, at those times when we candidates for the provincial examination were much overloaded with extra work, he would invite us unexpectedly to come up to his apartment, and there we would find in a strange room a huge table and on it a quantity of cardboard boxes filled with toy soldiers which we would then arrange in armies and battle array, and when the conflict was joined, the rector would solemnly puff clouds of smoke from his pipe between the battalions.

Beautiful things are transitory and fine times never last long. If I think of those Göppingen days, of the single short period in my school years when I was a good scholar, when I honored and loved my teacher and was heart and soul absorbed in study, then I always have to think too of the summer vacation in the year 1890, which I spent at my parents' home in Calw. For that vacation we were not assigned any school work. However, Rector Bauer had called our attention to the "rules of life" of Isocrates, which were included in our Greek chrestomathy, and he told us that formerly some of his best students had learned these rules of life by heart. It was left to each one of us to take this hint or not.

Of that summer vacation, a few walks with my father linger in my memory. Sometimes we spent an afternoon in the woods above Calw; under the old white pines there were barberries and raspberries aplenty, and in the clearings loosestrife bloomed, and summer butterflies, the red admiral and the tortoise-shell, fluttered about. There was a strong smell of pine resin and mushrooms, and occasionally we came face to face with deer. My father and I would wander through the forest or race here and there in the heather at the forest's edge. And once in a while he would ask me how far I had got with Isocrates. For I sat for a while every day with the book, memorizing those "rules of life." And even today the first sentence of Isocrates is the single bit of Greek prose I know by heart. That sentence from Isocrates and a few verses of Homer are the sole remnant of my whole Greek education. Also, I never attained a mastery of all the "rules of life." Several dozen sentences which I did learn by heart, and for a time carried around with me and could produce at will, have crumbled away and been lost in the course of the years, like everything a man possesses and believes is really his own.

Today I no longer know any Greek, and most of my Latin has long since disappeared—I would have forgotten it completely were it not for one of my Göppingen classmates who is still alive and still my friend. From time to time he writes me a letter in Latin and when I read it, working my way through the beautifully constructed classic sentences, then there is a faint smell of the garden of my youth and the pipe smoke of old Rector Bauer.

About Grandfather

(1952)

A poem written in 1833 by Hermann Gundert for his father's fiftieth birthday, shortly after his mother's death

Am I to lament
That evening comes?
That the sun departs,
Weary from the labors of the day,
That dark shadows fall
From the encircling clouds,
That the constellations sparkle down
Upon the stillness of the night?

Now you are striding abroad
Amid the sere firstlings of autumn,
Sparse victims of the night's cold.
But around you on the hill
Mild wine matures,
The ripening fruits in rich profusion
Drink up maternal energies.
There are even blossoms still astir
In childlike content,
And a friendly star,
Nodding its thanks,
Greets the flowers and vine-leaf garlands,
Leaves and fruit,

And the grave human countenance
That rejoices in these things,
And the wagon laden with grain
That groans toward the granary.

These are images
From God's untrammeled world.
But they change in many-colored aspects,
Only one returns to me unaltered:
The human eye that fastens upon them!

Were not you the flower,
Dreaming on the maternal breast?
Are you not still the ripening grape,
Impatient for the vintner
To test its strength, its lightness?

You are the corn ear too, no doubt,
On the dry furrow,
Watching his sister fall before the reaper
And twisting with pain
At sight of the horses
That bear away his neighbor
To unknown storerooms.

But away from the ever-changing brood of earth
You gaze upward to the eternal sky,
And if the evening wind
Blows leaves upon you,
Withered leaves on withered hair,
You look away from winds and clouds,
Peering past the tired boughs
Toward the blossoming light of the stars.

For that day has ended
When youth's fiery might,

Tiptoe upon the mountain's height,
Swore to become a sun
To countless minds.
Now he perceives that evening has come,
Life's sun is hidden
In the deep-furrowed valley of earth,
His only wish is to imitate the stars,
Gazing eternally upon the sun,
In radiant competition
With those heavenly lights.

You stand upon the threshold of your century.
Here is the cradle in which you wept,
There lie the worlds that await you!
And the perfected ones above
Beckon you to happier activity.
And the trusted ones below
Stagger in noble effort.

Stretch your right hand upward,
The hand you bestowed on your eternal beloved,
And she who has endured the battle
Will aid you in the final step!

But the left hand
And your guardian eye
And the memorial fires of love,
Leave these to the younger pilgrims!

My grandfather Hermann Gundert wrote this poem, which is surely as much an attempt to clarify his own emotions as to comfort his widowed father, when he was a nineteen-year-old undergraduate. The attentive reader will quickly recognize that here is a mind influenced by Hegel and the Hindus, but also a mind well acquainted with Hölderlin, struggling for expression. The author of this brilliant poem never again wrote anything similar. It was composed in the most confused and imperiled period of his life, shortly before this youth's "conversion" caused the enthusiastic pantheist to decide upon a life henceforth devoted to missionary work in India.

I used to have an old copy of this poem of my grandfather's in my mother's handwriting, which I have since turned over to the Schiller Museum in Marbach at their request. Through an accident the poem came into my hands again at a time when I was open to its obvious beauties as well as to the undercurrents of its thought, its shy secret, and it made so strong an impression on me at this second meeting that I decided to rescue the little gem. The Gundert heirs to whom I sent a printed copy thanked me politely for it but seemed rather astonished and bewildered, they did not know what to do with this odd gift, and the majority of the others who received it accepted it respectfully but without showing any sign of excitement at the strength of the youthful poetic effusion or of being touched by the secret fire that glowed in the lines. Since then, however, other voices have reached me, and they greatly outbalance this initial small disappointment. The first to whom the poem really appealed and who was stirred by it was Dr. Lützkendorf, the man who twenty years before had written one of the first dissertations about me and my spiritual and religious antecedents. I quote from his letter of February, 1952:

". . . At the time when I wrote my work about you and found the courage to classify your writing according to kind and origin—today I have no idea how I came by that presumptuous daring—this Hermann Gundert seemed to me from the start a strange, exotic figure about whom I would have liked to know more than could be learned piecemeal. His combination of inspired enthusiasm and tough endurance, which in turn was lighted by mysterious 'Bengal' fires, gave me occasion for many conjectures and made him in my eyes the probable source and origin of many peculiarities which you too possessed. I was very happy to meet him again so strangely in this poem written in 1833. —In many respects this encounter has become a reassurance to me that in our times too we must not always form our judgments simply from the noisy voices, the uproar, and the irresponsibility that are everywhere evident. Unforgettable the essence and the profound silent influence that radiated from this young spirit a hundred years ago; they continue to this day. If he had not been your grandfather we would scarcely have heard of him—and yet all this would have existed. —Surely even today other Hermann Gunderts are alive—important men who are content to complete the circuit of their lives and yet who would have the strength to bear and to endure the greatest fame. It is my belief that such powers remain imminent in a nation and that, however much one may be tempted to despair in times like these, in the end one must not do so."

I do not know whether the author of this fine letter knew that Grandfather Gundert, disguised but nevertheless faithfully represented in the meaning he had for me, plays a role in a fragmentary little composition of mine entitled "Childhood of the Magician." It is contained in the book called *Dream Journeys*. In this grandfather, at whose death I was sixteen years old, I not only came to know a sage very knowledgeable in the ways of men despite his great learning, but in addition I encountered an echo, a survival—somewhat obscured by piety and service to God but still very much alive—of that marvelous Swabian world compounded of material stringency and intellectual grandeur which, in the Swabian Latin schools, in the evangelical monastery seminaries, and in the famous Tübingen training college, has persisted for almost two hundred years, constantly enriching and extending its precious tradition. This is not just the world of Swabian parsonages and schools, to which, however, men of great intellect and exemplary spiritual discipline like Bengel, Oetinger, Blumhardt belonged, but it is also the world in which Hölderlin, Hegel, Mörike became great.

In this world, just as in my grandfather's apartment, there was a smell of pipe smoke and coffee, of old books and herbaria; and since this intellectual world, theologically colored but unwilling to exclude any tendency from pietism to radical free thought, year after year took into itself the elite of the Latin schools of the district, there developed, generation after generation, a throng of important, original, eccentric figures, each one of whom, if he was not himself a center and fixed star, belonged nevertheless to the circle of friends and associates of such a star, left behind him essays, correspondence, drawings, and in his turn introduced sons or students into this tradition. This has produced a wealth, a superfluity of more or less intellectually oriented lives amassed in a way that can scarcely be equaled in any other district of Germany.

Thus in Grandfather Gundert and through him I became acquainted with a somewhat provincial intellectual culture which nevertheless reached to the heights, which had its own stamp, its own speech, its own highly original and at times whimsical vocabulary, and which in him never became attenuated or distorted either by the decades he spent in India or by his countless international relations and friendships conducted in many languages, or through his marriage with a French-speaking lady raised in the Calvinist tradition in a French-speaking district of Switzerland, or through his never-interrupted studies in Indology.

For me the liveliest and most precious memory of him concerns the following incident. I was not quite fifteen years old and as a scholar in the monastery seminary at

Maulbronn was on one of the bottom rungs of the ladder that was to lead to training college, to learning, to the ministry or to the Swabian Parnassus, when I went through the severest crisis of my school life and committed a sin, incredible, scarcely to be expiated, that brought disgrace on me and my most honorable family: I had run away, been searched for in the forest for a day and had been reported to the police, had almost caught my death by spending the night in the open fields in freezing weather, and now after my release from the sickroom had come home for vacation, not permanently dismissed and expelled from the seminary but nevertheless with my academic career almost hopelessly compromised. To be treated as a criminal and a foe, especially by one's relatives, would have been perhaps less terrifying to me than the kindliness and the embarrassed anxiety with which people tiptoed around me as though I were stricken by a mysterious and possibly contagious illness. And now one of the first duty calls that I had to make after my return home, and for me the most important and most difficult, was on my honored, beloved, but at the moment very much dreaded grandfather. I could hardly doubt that my parents had great hopes for this visit and that they had begged the venerable sage to examine me heart and soul, and to bring home to me the magnitude and the presumable consequences of my misdeed. My progress on my way to him, into the dear old house and up the stairs to his high sunny study, was the progress of a sinner to the tribunal. In the big anteroom there were hundreds and thousands of books, which even then exercised a powerful attraction on me and very many of which I was to read later on; it was dim and above all quiet, through the single window I saw the bright wall of the rear of the building gleaming in thc sunlight, with the big dark hole of the skylight, above which somewhat askew and twisted hung the little wheel of the hoist used for hauling up firewood. All this including the solemn, gray rows of the folios on the lower shelves of the bookcases, the exact regularity of the spacing between the faded titles on the long rows of bound periodicals, and the soft evanescent shimmer of gold on the leather spines, all this at that presumably fateful hour seemed to have a super-reality and significance that oppressed me. It spoke of a world of order, cleanliness, and relevance from which I had already taken the first fatal step to withdraw and lose myself, that very step for which I would here have to give an accounting.

And so I entered the sanctuary in fear and trembling, smelled the scent of pipe smoke, papers, and ink, saw the sunlight playing on the table covered with books, magazines, manuscripts in many languages, and saw opposite me with his back to the sunlit window, seated on an old sofa in a sun-drenched cloud of pipe smoke, the sage, who slowly looked up from his writing. I greeted him in a low voice and gave him my hand, prepared for a hearing, a judgment, and conviction. He smiled, his mouth protruding from the wide, white beard, he smiled with those lips that were acquainted with so many languages, and he smiled even more with his bright, blue eyes, and the nervous tension inside me relaxed at once and I realized that not judgment and punishment awaited me here but understanding, the wisdom of age, the patience of age together with a hint of sarcasm and roguery. And now he opened his mouth and said, "So it's you, Hermann? I hear that you've just taken a little temperamental journey."

A half century earlier, "temperamental journey" was the phrase used by Tübingen students to describe those strange runaways and adventures prompted by arrogance, rebellion, or despair. And it was not until many years later that I learned that once he too, my grandfather, the model Christian and scholar, had lived for a time in that dangerous climate in which such tricks of temperament are committed. It was at just that ardent and dangerous period of his youth—about which presumably my grandfather was thinking at that instant and which he and his closest friends had lived through in a lightning flash between the arrogance of gifted youth and suicidal despair —at just that period he had written the poem that I brought to light again one hundred and twenty years after its composition.

And apropos of this same poem, a Parisian Germanist wrote me recently: "I just wanted to tell you how precious the poem by Hermann Gundert is to me, a delicate vine around a firm trunk. It is important to me too because this is the way the meaning of family tradition can be recognized; it is burdensome, but it helps one forward if one has the strength to rise above critical entanglements. I was able to study this in the case of Albert Schweitzer; perhaps you know that J.-P. Sartre is his great-nephew, that is, the grandson of Schweitzer's Parisian uncle. This uncle was a Germanist and a student of Hans Sachs, and he himself finally came precisely to resemble Sachs with his white beard and his rough humor. With such an ancestry of teachers and pastors, Sartre can allow himself nihilism without risk; his followers, most of whom have no such protective reserves behind them, often come to grief . . ."

But for me, who long since have acquired a crowd of grandchildren and have almost reached my forebear's age, there is a special kind of joy and satisfaction in knowing that, though to him it would be no more than a laughing matter, he is now remembered and influential beyond the limits of the pietistic missionary world. Though he himself in his later years may have lost all interest in the subject, nevertheless he had once walked in the path of Hölderlin, Hegel, and Mörike, had copied out with a freshly cut goosefeather quill the piano arrangement of *The Magic Flute*, had written poems, and even on one occasion indulged in a temperamental journey.

Life Story Briefly Told
(1925)

In the years immediately after the First World War, I twice attempted to give a kind of brief survey of my life in legendary and semi-humorous form for the benefit of my friends in whose eyes at that time I had become rather problematic. Of these attempts the one I preferred, "Childhood of the Magician," remained a fragment. The other, in which I daringly tried, after the model of Jean Paul, to anticipate the future in a "conjectural biography," was published in 1925 in the Neue Rundschau. *It appears here with only minor corrections. For many years it was my plan to combine the two pieces in some way, but I was unable to find a means of reconciling two works so different in tone and mood.*

I WAS born toward the end of modern times, shortly before the return of the Middle Ages, with the sign of the Archer on the ascendant and Jupiter in favorable aspect. My birth took place at an early hour of the evening on a warm day in July, and it is the temperature of that hour that I have unconsciously loved and sought throughout my life; when it was lacking I have sorely missed it. I could never live in cold countries and all the voluntary journeys of my life have been directed toward the south. I was the child of pious parents, whom I loved tenderly and would have loved even more tenderly if I had not very early been introduced to the Fourth Commandment. Unfortunately, commandments have always had a disastrous effect on me, however right and well meant they may be

—though by nature a lamb and docile as a soap bubble, I have always behaved rebelliously toward commandments of every sort, especially during my youth. All I needed was to hear "thou shalt" and everything in me rose up and I became obdurate. As can be imagined, this peculiarity had a far-reaching and unfortunate effect during my school years. It is true that our teachers taught us, in that amusing subject called world history, that the world has always been governed, guided, and transformed by men who made their own laws and broke with traditional regulations, and we were told that these men should be revered. But this was just as deceitful as all the rest of our instruction, for when one of us, whether with good or bad intent, summoned up courage to protest against some order or even against some silly custom or way of doing things, he was neither revered nor commended as an example but punished instead, made fun of and crushed by the teachers' dastardly use of their superior power.

Fortunately I had learned even before the beginning of my school years what is most important and valuable in life: I possessed keen, subtle, and finely developed senses which I could rely on and from which I derived great enjoyment, and although later I succumbed irreparably to the enticements of metaphysics and even for a time chastized and neglected my senses, nevertheless a background of tenderly nurtured sensualism, especially in respect to sight and hearing, has always stayed with me and plays a lively part in my intellectual world even when the latter seems abstract. Thus I had provided myself, as I have said, with a certain capacity to meet life long before the beginning of my school years. I knew my way around in the city of my fathers, in the barnyards and in the forests, in the truck gardens and in the workshops of the mechanics, I knew trees, birds, and butterflies, I could sing songs and whistle through my teeth and much else besides that is important for living. To this was now added various sorts of school knowledge, which came easy to me and gave me pleasure; in particular I got real enjoyment from the Latin language and I was writing Latin verses almost as soon as German ones. For the art of lying and of diplomacy I have my second year in school to thank, during which a preceptor and his accomplice afforded me mastery of these accomplishments after I had earlier brought down upon myself in my childish openness and trustfulness one disaster after another. These two educators successfully opened my eyes to the fact that a sense of humor and a love of truth were not qualities they were looking for in pupils. They ascribed to me a misdeed, a quite unimportant one which had occurred in class and of which I was wholly innocent, and since they could not force me to confess that I was the culprit, the trivial matter was turned into an inquisition and the two tortured and beat out of me, not the desired confession, to be sure, but instead all belief in the decency of the teaching profession. In time, thank God, I became acquainted with teachers worthy of respect, but the damage had been done, and my relations not only with schoolmasters but with all authority were distorted and embittered. On the whole I was a good student during my first seven or eight years in school, at any rate I regularly stood among the first in my class. It was not until those battles began which no one who is going to become a person is spared that I came more and more into conflict with the school. Two decades were to pass before I understood those battles; at the time they were simply going on all around me, contrary to my will, and were a great misery.

The thing was this: from my thirteenth year on, it was clear to me that I wanted to be either a poet or nothing at all. To this realization, however, was gradually added a further, painful insight. One could become a teacher, minister, doctor, mechanic, merchant, post-office employee, or a musician, painter, architect; there was a path to every profession in the world, there were prerequisites, a school, a course of instruction for the beginner. Only for the poet there was nothing of the sort! It was permissible and even considered an honor to be a poet; that is, to be successful and famous as a poet—unfortunately by that time one was usually dead. But to become a poet was impossible, and to want to become one was ridiculous and shameful, as I very soon found out. I had quickly learned what there was to be learned from the situation: a poet was simply something you were allowed to be but not to become. Further: native poetic talent and interest in poetry were suspect in teachers' eyes; you were either distrusted for it or ridiculed, often indeed subjected to deadly insults. With the poet it was exactly the same as with the hero, and with all strong, handsome, high-spirited, non-commonplace figures and enterprises: in the past they were magnificent, every school book was filled with their praises; in the present, in real life, people hated them, and presumably teachers were especially selected and trained to prevent as far as possible the rise of magnificent, free human beings and the accomplishment of great and splendid deeds.

Thus I saw between me and my distant goal nothing but abysses yawning; everything was uncertain, everything devoid of value, only one thing remained constant: that I intended to become a poet, whether that turned out to be easy or hard, ridiculous or creditable. The external consequences of this resolve—or rather of this fatality—were as follows.

When I was thirteen years old and this conflict had just begun, my conduct in my parents' house as well as in school left so much to be desired that I was banished to a Latin school in another city. A year later I became a pupil in a theological seminary, learned to write the Hebrew alphabet, and was already on the point of grasping what a *dagesh forte implicitum* is, when suddenly from inside me storms arose that led to flight from the monastery school, punishment by strict imprisonment, and dismissal from the seminary.

Then for a while I struggled to advance my studies at a *gymnasium*; however, the lock-up and expulsion were the end there too. After that, for three days I was a merchant's apprentice, ran away again and for several days and nights, to the great distress of my parents, disappeared. For a period of six months I was my father's assistant, for a year and a half I was an employee in a mechanical workshop and tower-clock factory.

In short, for more than four years everything that was attempted with me went wrong; no school would keep me, in no course of instruction did I last for long. Every attempt to make a useful human being out of me ended in failure, several times in shame and scandal, in flight or expulsion, and yet everywhere they admitted that I had ability and even a reasonable amount of determination! Also I was nothing if not industrious—the high virtue of idleness I have always regarded with awe, but I have never mastered it. In my sixteenth year, after my school career had ended in failure, I consciously and energetically began my own education, and it was my good fortune and delight that in my father's house was my grandfather's huge library, a whole hall full of old books, which contained among other things all of eighteenth-century German literature and philosophy. Between my sixteenth and twentieth years I not only covered a quantity of paper with my first attempts at poetry but I also read half of the world's literature and applied myself to the history of art, languages, and philosophy with a persistence that would have abundantly sufficed for any normal college career.

Then I became a bookseller in order finally to earn my own bread. I had always been on better terms with books than with the vises and cogwheels with which I had tortured myself as a mechanic. At first, swimming in modern, indeed the most modern, literature and in fact being overwhelmed by it was an almost intoxicating joy. But after a while I noticed that in matters of the spirit, a life simply in the present, in the modern and most modern, is unbearable and meaningless, that the life of the spirit is made possible only by constant reference to what is past, to history, to the ancient and primeval. And so after that first joy was exhausted it became a necessity for me to return from my submersion in novelties to what is old; this I accomplished by moving from the bookshop to an antique shop. However, I only stuck to this profession for as long as I needed it to sustain life. At the age of twenty-six, as a result of my first literary success, I gave it up too.

Thus, amid so many storms and sacrifices, my goal had now been reached: however impossible it may have appeared, I had become a poet and had, it would seem, won the long, stubborn battle with the world. The bitterness of my years of schooling and preparation, during which I had often been very close to ruin, was now forgotten or laughed at—even my relations and friends, who had previously been in despair about me, now smiled encouragingly. I had triumphed, and now if I did the silliest or most trivial thing it was thought charming, just as I was greatly charmed by myself. Now for the first time I realized in what dreadful isolation, asceticism, and danger I had lived year after year; the warm breeze of recognition did me good and I began to be a contented man.

Outwardly my life now ran on for a good while in calm and agreeable fashion. I had a wife, children, a house and garden. I wrote my books, I was considered an amiable poet, and I lived at peace with the world. In the year 1905 I helped to found a periodical which was principally directed against the personal government of Wilhelm II, without myself taking this political aim very seriously. I took interesting trips in Switzerland, Germany, Austria, Italy, India. Everything seemed to be in order.

Then came the summer of 1914, and suddenly everything looked different, inwardly and outwardly. It became evident that our former well-being had rested on insecure foundations, and accordingly there now began a period of misery, the great education. The so-called time of testing had come, and I cannot say that it found me better prepared, worthier, or superior to anyone else. What distinguished me from others at that time was only that I lacked the great compensation so many others possessed: enthusiasm. For that reason I came to myself again and into conflict with my environment, I was once more put to school, had to unlearn my satisfaction with myself and with the world, and in this experience I stepped for the first time over the threshold of initiation into life.

I have never forgotten a little encounter during the first year of the war. I had gone to visit a large military hospital in the hope of finding a way of fitting myself in some meaningful fashion into the altered world—something that still seemed possible to me at that time. In that hospital for the wounded, I met an elderly spinster who had formerly lived on a private income in comfortable circumstances and was now serving as a nurse in the wards. She told me with touching enthusiasm how happy and proud she was to have been allowed to witness this great time. I found that understandable, for in this lady's case it had taken the war to transform her indolent and purely egotistical old maid's existence into an active and useful life. But as she expressed her happiness to me in a corridor full of bandaged and shell-crippled soldiers, between wards that were full of amputees and dying men, my heart turned over. Well though I understood Auntie's enthusiasm, I could not share it, I could not commend it. If for every ten wounded men such another enthusiastic nurse came along, then these ladies' happiness cost too much.

No, I could not share the joy over the great time, and so it came about that from the beginning I suffered miserably from the war, and for a period of years strove in desperation to protect myself against a misfortune that had seemed to fall upon me out of a clear blue sky, while everybody around me acted as though they were full of happy enthusiasm over this same misery. And when I read newspaper articles by prominent writers in which they disclosed the blessings of the war, and the clarion call of the professors, and all the war poems issuing from the studies of famous poets, then I became more wretched still.

One day in 1915 a public confession of this wretchedness escaped me, together with an expression of regret that even so-called spiritual people could find nothing better to do than preach hatred, spread lies, and praise the great misfortune to the skies. The result of this rather hesitantly expressed lament was that in the press of my native land I was denounced as a traitor—a new experience for me since despite many contacts with the press I had never before been spat at by the majority. The article containing this denunciation was printed by twenty papers in my country, and of all the friends I thought I had among newspaper men only two dared rise to my defense. Old friends informed me that they had been nurturing a viper in their bosoms and that those bosoms in future would throb only for Kaiser and for Reich and not for a degenerate like me. Abusive letters from strangers came in stacks, and the book dealers gave me to understand that an author with such reprehensible views had ceased to exist so far as they were concerned. On a number of these letters I came to recognize a decoration which I saw then for the first time: a little round stamp with the inscription *God punish England.*

One might think that I would have had a hearty laugh at this misunderstanding. But I could do nothing of the sort. This experience, unimportant in itself, brought me as reward the second great transformation of my life.

The first transformation, you recall, took place at the instant when I recognized my determination to become a poet. The hitherto model pupil Hesse became from then on a bad pupil, he was punished, expelled, he did nothing right, he caused himself and his parents one worry after another—all simply because he saw no possibility of reconciliation between the world as it happens to be or seems to be and the voice of his own heart. Once more I saw myself in conflict with a world with which I had until then been living in complete content. Once more everything went awry for me, once more I was alone and miserable, once more everything I said and thought was deliberately misinterpreted by others. Once more, between reality and what seemed to me good, desirable, and sensible, I saw a hopeless abyss yawning.

This time, however, I was not spared a self-examination. Before long I found myself obliged to seek the cause of my sufferings not outside but inside myself. For this much at least I could clearly see: to accuse the whole world of delusion and brutality was something no human being and no god had a right to do, I least of all. And so there must be all sorts of disorder in me if I was in such sharp conflict with the whole course of the world. And behold, there was in fact a great disorder. It was no pleasure to come to grips with that disorder in myself and try to transform it into order. One thing became clear at once: the benign content in which I had lived with the world had not only been bought at too high a price; it had been just as corrupt as the outer peace of the world. I had believed that through the long, hard battles of youth I had earned my place in the world and that I was now a poet. Meanwhile, success and prosperity had had their usual effect on me, I had become complacent and comfortable, and when I looked carefully the poet was hardly to be distinguished from a writer of cheap fiction. Things had gone too well with me. Now, though, abundant provision was made for heavy going, which is always a good and salutary training, and so I learned more and more to let the business of the world go its way, and I could concern myself with my own share in the confusion and guilt of the whole. To detect this concern in my writings is something I must leave to the reader. And yet I always retained the secret hope that in time my people too, not as a whole but through many alert and responsible individuals, would successfully pass through a similar testing, and in place of laments and curses at the wicked war and the wicked enemy and the wicked revolution, in a thousand hearts the question would arise: How have I myself become a party to this guilt? And how can I regain my innocence? For one can always regain one's innocence if he acknowledges his suffering and his guilt and suffers to the end instead of trying to lay the blame on others.

As this new transformation began to express itself in my writings and in my life, many of my friends shook their heads. Many, too, abandoned me. That was a part of the altered pattern of my life, just like the loss of my house, my family, and other goods and comforts. It was a time when I daily said goodbye and was daily astounded that I was now able to bear this too and still go on living and still find something to love in this strange existence that seemed, really, to bring me only pain, disillusionment, and loss.

However, to make up for this, I had even during the war years something like a good star or guardian angel. While I felt myself very much alone with my suffering and, until the beginning of the transformation, hourly felt my fate as accursed and execrated it, my very suffering and my obsession with suffering served me as shield and buckler against the outside world. I spent the war years, in fact, in such horrible circumstances of politics, espionage, bribery, and corruption as even at that time were rarely to be found concentrated in one place, namely in Bern, amid German, neutral, and hostile diplomacy, in a city that had been flooded overnight by a tidal wave of diplomats, secret agents, spies, journalists, speculators, and profiteers. I lived amid diplomats and soldiers, had contacts with people from many enemy countries, the air around me was a single net of espionage and counter-espionage, of intrigue, denunciations, and political and personal speculation—and of all this in all those years I noticed nothing at all! I was shadowed, listened to, spied upon, I was an object of suspicion now to the enemy, now to the neutrals, now to my own countrymen, and I noticed none of it. Only long afterward did I learn this and that about it, and I could not understand how I had been able to live enveloped in this atmosphere, untouched and unharmed. But that is what happened.

With the end of the war there coincided the completion of my transformation and the climax of suffering in my trial. This suffering no longer had anything to do with the war or the fate of the world; even the defeat of Germany, which we abroad had foreseen with certainty for two years, was at that time no longer terrifying. I was wholly immersed in myself and in my own fate, though at times with the feeling that the lot of mankind was involved as well. I found reflected in myself all the world's lust for war and murder, all its irresponsibility, all its gross self-indulgence, all its cowardice; I had to lose first my self-respect and then my self-contempt; I had no less a task than to carry through to the end my scrutiny of chaos, with the now soaring, now sinking hope of rediscovering beyond chaos nature and innocence. Every human being who has been awakened and really has achieved consciousness has on one or more occasions walked this narrow path through the wilderness—to try to talk to others about it would be a fruitless effort.

When friends were disloyal to me, I sometimes felt sadness but never disgust; I felt this rather as a reassurance on my way. Those former friends were surely right when they said that once I had been so sympathetic as a man and a poet, whereas my present problematic attitude was simply unbearable. In questions of taste and of character I had long since passed beyond them; there was no one among them to whom my vocabulary would have been comprehensible. These friends were perhaps right when they reproached me with having lost beauty and harmony in my writing. Such words simply made me laugh—what is beauty or harmony to one who is condemned to death, who is running for his life between collapsing walls? Perhaps, too, my lifelong belief notwithstanding, I was not a poet, and the whole aesthetic impulse had simply been a mistake? Why not? Even that was no longer of any importance. Most of what I had been confronted with in the course of the journey through the hell of myself had been false and worthless, and perhaps this was also the case with the illusion of my vocation or gift. How unimportant that was, after all! And that which once, full of pride and childish joy, I had regarded as my task was no longer there either. I saw my task, or rather my way of salvation, no longer in the realm of lyric poetry or philosophy or any one of the occupations of specialists but rather simply in letting what little there was in me that was vital and strong live its life, simply in unqualified loyalty now to what I felt to be still alive within myself. That was Life, that was God. —Afterward, when such times of high, mortally dangerous exaltation are passed, all this looks strangely different, because the former contents of consciousness and their names are now without meaning, and what was holy the day before yesterday can sound almost comic.

When the war finally came to an end for me too, in the spring of 1919, I withdrew into a remote corner of Switzerland and became a hermit. Because all my life I had been much occupied with Indian and Chinese wisdom (this was an inheritance from my parents and grandparents), and also because I gave my new experiences expression in part in the picture language of the East, I was often called a "Buddhist." At this I could only laugh, for at bottom I knew of no religion from which I was further removed. And yet there was something accurate, a grain of truth hidden in this, which I first recognized somewhat later. If it were in any way thinkable that a person should choose a religion for himself, then I should certainly out of inner longing have joined a conservative religion: Confucianism, Brahmanism, or the Roman Church. I should have done this, however, out of longing for my polar opposite, not from innate affinity, for it was not by accident alone that I was born the son of pious Protestants; I am a Protestant by temperament and nature as well (to which my deep antipathy to the present Protestant denominations is no contradiction whatever). For the true Protestant is in opposition to his own church just as he is to every other, since his nature constrains him to affirm becoming above being. And in this sense Buddha, too, was certainly a Protestant.

My belief in my vocation as poet and in the value of my literary labors had thus been uprooted since the transformation. Writing no longer gave me any real joy. But a human being must have some joy; even in the midst of my distress I asserted that claim. I could renounce Justice, Reason, Meaning in life and in the world; I had seen that the world could get along splendidly without these abstractions—but I could not get along without some bit of joy, and the demand for that bit of joy was now one of those little flames inside me in which I still believed, and from which I planned to create the world anew for myself.

Often I sought my joy, my dream, my forgetfulness in a bottle of wine, and very often it was of help; praised be it therefor. But it was not enough. And then, behold, one day I discovered an entirely new joy. Suddenly, at the age of forty, I began to paint. Not that I considered myself a painter or intended to become one. But painting is marvelous; it makes one happier and more patient. Afterward one does not have black fingers as with writing but red and blue ones. At this painting, too, many of my friends have taken offense. I don't have much luck that way—whenever I undertake something very necessary, auspicious and beautiful, people become cross. They would like one to stay as he is; they don't want one's face to change. But my face will not conform! It insists on changing often; that's a necessity.

Another reproach thrown at me seems to me fully justified. People say that I have no sense of reality. The poems I write as well as the little pictures I paint do not correspond with reality. When I write I frequently forget the demands that cultivated readers make of a proper book, and more important still, I really do lack respect for reality. I consider reality to be the last thing one need concern oneself about, for it is, tediously enough, always present, while more beautiful and necessary things demand our attention and care. Reality is what one must not under any circumstances be satisfied with, what one must not under any circumstances worship and revere, for it is accidental, the offal of life. And it is in no wise to be changed, this shabby, consistently disappointing and barren reality, except by our denying it and proving in the process that we are stronger than it is.

In my writings people often miss the customary respect for reality, and when I paint, the trees have faces and the houses laugh or dance or weep, but whether the tree is a pear or chestnut, that for the most part cannot be determined. I must accept this reproach. I admit that my own life frequently appears to me exactly like a legend, I often see and feel the outer world connected and in harmony with my inner world in a way that I can only call magical.

A few more absurd occurrences befell me. For example, I once made a harmless observation about the famous poet Schiller, whereupon all the South German bowling clubs denounced me as a desecrator of the sacred relics of the fatherland. Now, however, for a number of years I have succeeded in not saying anything to desecrate relics or make people get red with rage. I consider this an improvement.

Now since so-called reality plays no very important role for me, since the past often occupies me as if it were the present, and the present seems to me infinitely far away, for these reasons I cannot separate the future from the past as sharply as is usually done. I live a great deal in the future and so I need not end my biography with the present day but can let it go quietly on.

I shall give a brief account of how my life completes its curve. In the years up to 1930 I wrote a few more books, only then to turn my back on that profession forever. The question whether or not I was really to be counted among the poets was investigated in two dissertations by diligent young people, but not answered. It transpired, in fact, as the result of a careful examination of modern literature that the aura which distinguishes the poet has become in modern times so very attenuated that the distinction between poets and men of letters can no longer be made. From this objective state of affairs, however, the two Ph.D. candidates drew opposite conclusions. One of them, the more sympathetic, was of the opinion that poesy in such ridiculous attenuation was poetry no longer, and since plain literature is not worth keeping alive, one might as well let what is still called poetry quietly pass away. The other, however, was an unqualified admirer of poesy, even in its flimsiest form, and therefore he believed it was better to admit a hundred non-poets as insurance rather than wrong a single poet who might perhaps still have a drop of the genuine blood of Parnassus in his veins.

I was principally occupied with painting and with Chinese magic spells, but in the following years became more and more absorbed in music. It was the ambition of my later life to write a sort of opera in which human life in its so-called reality would be viewed with scant seriousness, ridiculed, in fact; in its eternal value, however, it would shine forth as image and momentary vesture of the Godhead. The magical conception of life had always been close to my heart, I had never been a "modern man," and had always considered Von Hoffmann's "Pot of Gold" and even *Heinrich von Ofterdingen* more valuable textbooks than any natural history or history of the world. (In point of fact, whenever I read any of the latter I always looked upon them as delightful fables.) But now I had entered upon that period of life in which it no longer makes sense to continue elaborating and differentiating a personality that is already complete and more than adequately differentiated, in which instead the task becomes that of allowing the estimable I to disappear once more into the universe and, in the face of mutability, to take one's place in the eternal and timeless order. To express these thoughts or attitudes toward life seemed to me possible only by means of fairy tales, and I looked upon the opera as the highest form of fairy tale, presumably because I could no longer really believe in the magic of the word in our ill-used and dying speech, whereas magic continued to seem to me a living tree on whose branches apples of paradise might grow even today. In my opera I wanted to do what I had never quite succeeded in doing in my poetry: to establish a high and delightful meaning for human life. I wanted to praise the innocence and inexhaustibility of nature and to present her course up to that point where, through inevitable suffering, she is forced to turn toward spirit, her distant polar opposite, and the oscillation of life between these two poles of nature and of spirit would be revealed as blithe, playful, and complete as the arch of a rainbow.

However, I was never, alas, successful in completing that opera. My experience with it was the same as with my poetry. I had had to give the latter up after I had seen that everything that seemed to me important to say had already been said a thousand times more clearly in "Pot of Gold" and in *Heinrich von Ofterdingen* than I was able to say it. And that is the way it now went with my opera. Just when I had completed my years of preparatory musical studies and had made several drafts of the text and was once more trying to visualize as penetratingly as possible the real meaning and content of my work, just then I had a sudden realization that in my opera I was attempting exactly the same thing that had been so magnificently accomplished long before in *The Magic Flute*.

I therefore laid this work aside and now devoted myself entirely to practical magic. If my dream of being an artist had been an illusion, if I was incapable of a "Pot of Gold" or a *Magic Flute*, at least I was a born magician. By the Eastern path of Lao-tse and the I Ching, I had long ago advanced far enough to know with certainty about the accidental nature and mutability of so-called reality. Now through magic I manipulated this reality according to my wishes and I must say I took much joy in doing so. I have to confess, however, that I did not always confine myself to the noble garden known as white magic, but from time to time was drawn over to the black side by that lively little flame within me.

At the age of more than seventy, just after two universities had singled me out for honorary degrees, I was brought to trial for the seduction by magic of a young girl. In jail I begged for permission to pass the time by painting. This was granted. Friends brought me paints and artist's materials, and I painted a little landscape on the wall of my cell. Thus I had once more returned to art, and all the shipwrecks I had suffered as an artist could not deter me for a moment from draining once more that noblest of cups, from building up once again like a child at play a lovely little play world, and from sating my heart with it, from once more throwing away all wisdom and abstraction and turning to the primitive lust of creation. Thus I was painting once more, I was mixing colors and dipping brushes in them, drinking in again with enchantment all that endless magic: the bright, happy sound of cinnabar, the full, clear note of yellow, the deep, moving tone of blue, and the music of their mixture out to the furthest, palest gray. Happy as a child, I carried on this game of creation and so painted the landscape on the wall of my cell. This landscape contained almost everything that had given me pleasure in life: rivers and mountains, sea and clouds, peasants at harvest time, and a crowd of other beautiful things in which I had taken joy. But in the middle of the picture there ran a very small railroad train. It was going straight toward the mountain and its head was already buried in it like a worm in an apple, the locomotive had already entered a little tunnel out of whose dark mouth sooty smoke was pouring.

Never before had my play enchanted me as it did this time. In my return to art I forgot not only that I was a prisoner, an accused man with little prospect of ending my life anywhere save in a penitentiary—I even frequently forgot my magical exercises and seemed to myself magician enough when I created with my thin brush a tiny tree, a small bright cloud.

Meanwhile, so-called reality, with which I now had in fact completely fallen out, was at great pains to make fun of my dream and to shatter it again and again. Almost every day I was led under guard into extremely uncongenial chambers where amid many papers unsympathetic men sat and questioned me, refused to believe me, barked at me, threatened me now like a three-year-old child and now like a hardened criminal. One doesn't need to be accused in order to become acquainted with this remarkable and truly hellish business of courts, papers, and ordinances. Of all the hells that men have so strangely had to create for themselves, this has always seemed to me the most hellish. All you need to do is to plan to move or to marry, to request a passport or a certificate of citizenship, and you find yourself at once in the midst of this hell, you have to spend bitter hours in the airless space of this paper world, you are questioned by bored yet hurried, disgruntled men, snapped at, you are met by disbelief for the simplest, truest statement, you are treated now like a schoolchild, now like a criminal. Well, everyone knows this. I should long since have been smothered and desiccated in this paper hell if it had not been that my paints constantly comforted and revived me and my picture, my beautiful little landscape, gave me renewed air and life.

It was in front of this picture in my cell that I was standing one day when the guards came hurrying up once more with their tedious summons and tried to tear me away from my happy activity. At that moment I felt weariness and something like revulsion against all this bustle, this whole brutal and spiritless reality. It seemed to me high time to put an end to my torment. If I was not allowed to play my innocent artist's game undisturbed, then I must have recourse to those sterner arts to which I had devoted so many years of my life. Without magic this world was unbearable.

I called to mind the Chinese formula, stood for a minute with suspended breath, and freed myself from the illusion of reality. I then affably requested the guards to be patient for a moment longer since I had to step into my picture and look after something in the train. They laughed in their usual way, for they considered me mentally unbalanced.

Then I made myself small and stepped into my picture, got aboard the little train, and rode in the little train into the little black tunnel. For a while sooty smoke continued to be visible, pouring out of the round hole, then the smoke dispersed and disappeared and with it the entire picture and I with the picture.

The guards remained behind in great embarrassment.

Remembrance of India
(1916)

In connection with the paintings of Hans Sturzenegger

WHENEVER I see the pictures and drawings that Hans Sturzenegger brought back from India, the days of our journey to the East together sweep over me in memory in a flood of powerful, deeply etched images. These works of his evoke the eventful months of a trip which, for the painter as well as for me, was significant and during which, in the prolonged and close association on shipboard and ashore, we came to know each other thoroughly. Presumably, indeed very likely, the journey had the same effect on him as on me; I not only got to know a strange, exotic land, but in experiencing what was foreign, I found that especially within myself I had discoveries to make and tests to withstand.

It was in the hot summer of 1911 that we traveled together through Switzerland and the scorched regions of upper Italy to Genoa, and from there by sea without interruption to the Straits Settlements. On a damp, hot, glorious evening in Penang, for the first time the surging life of an Asiatic city burst upon us; for the first time we saw the Indian Ocean glittering between innumerable coral islands, and we stared with astonishment at the many-colored spectacle of street life in the Hindu city, the Chinese city, the Malayan city. A wild, colorful human swarm in the ever-crowded alleys, at night a sea of candles, motionless cocoanut palms reflected in the sea, shy naked children, dark fishermen rowing antediluvian boats! From these first impressions of the already somewhat Europeanized harbor cities to the silent, pathless, tropical forest in southeastern Sumatra, the pictures increased in number and in power until each of us had found his India, his Asia, and bore it within him. Even these images were altered later on, their value and significance changed. But what has remained is the experience of a dream visit to distant forebears, a return to the legendary childhood of humanity, and a deep reverence for the spirit of the East, a spirit that has visited me again and again since that time in Hindu or Chinese guise and has been a comforter and a prophet. For never can we, the elderly sons of the West, return to primeval humanity and the paradisial innocence of primitive peoples; but surely homecoming and fruitful renewal beckon to us from that "spirit of the East" which leads from Lao-tse to Jesus, which was born of ancient Chinese art and today still speaks in every gesture of the true Asiatic.

During our journey, however, we seldom thought of such matters and spoke of them even less. The sensuous impressions of each hour demanded our whole attention. I sought out Chinese temples and theaters, butterflies, huge trees, and other beautiful rarities, while my traveling companion tasted to the full the initial difficulties of a painter in an exotic city. I can still see him seated high up in a rented rickshaw, towering alone above the crowded masses in a Chinese street in Singapore, sketching in the dust and heat until the crowd, grown intrusive, forced him to leave.

How many marvelous, unseizable pictures, what magnificently rich multiplicity in this phenomenal world all around us! I have always been filled with astonishment and envy at how much Hans Sturzenegger was able to bring back with him in his sketches. But I can find well stored in my memory hundreds of such pictures that were impossible to record or even to make note of at the moment.

Perhaps an afternoon in Jahore, in the great gambling hell of Indochina, where in narrow, dim rooms at rude tables hundreds of Chinese coolies stood in close-pressed coils and clusters of bodies, awaiting the result of their wagers—breathless, silent, pale, all their life concentrated in their greedy, watchful eyes.

Or an evening on shipboard, quietly standing at the rail, the vast blue night full of stars, flashes of phosphorus in the pale wake.

An evening in a Malayan theater: enormously gifted actors, agile as monkeys, working with fabulous skill, hopelessly and eagerly, to produce a caricature of a European play—without, alas, any ironic intent.

And how intense and mysterious it was to approach a Malayan village on a riverboat through the primeval forest! From afar the little, inhabited stretch of shore can be seen; in place of the unvarying green wall of the jungle, cocoanut palms rise, and below them fat, juicy plantains. Then the rush roofs of the huts appear, a small rice field, a primitive landing place. Naked black children full of curiosity stand by the shore, but hardly have we caught sight of them, hardly has the boat swerved toward shore when the figures melt soundlessly away and in an instant have disappeared; as we disembark we can see here and there at a safe distance, behind palm trunks, the glitter of intent, black eyes.

We saw cities standing on piles in the waters of great rivers that were silently traversed by thousands of boats, floating businesses, small floating stores with rugs, fruit, Mohammedan prayer books, and fish.

We saw islands, islands of rock, of earth, of coral, of mud, islands as big as mushrooms and islands as big as Switzerland. We saw them lying far off and deep blue in the summer sunset, or blazing at midday with indescribable colors, or gray and ghostly disappearing under the heavy veil of a mighty thunderstorm. And what fantastic monstrosities of thunderstorms, of thunder and lightning, of mad cloudbursts assailed us!

We were waited on by Chinese, by Malayans, by Singhalese, by men with gleaming black queues and men whose hair was heaped high and secured with metal combs above splendidly solemn faces.

And the animals! What animals we saw! Neither wild elephants (we saw only tame ones) nor tigers, but what a multitude of beautiful, strange, unforgettable shapes! We saw monkeys big and small, single and in families, and at times even in great teeming expeditions. We saw the wild monkeys set out on their touchingly instinctive, fantastically noisy journeys, whole families and clans under way, high in the branches of the twilight forest. And we saw tame domestic monkeys on a leash run up the trunks of cocoanut palms at their master's order, to fetch the nuts. And the crocodiles in the river, the sharks playing astern of the ship, the primitive iguana, the pale, rosy water buffalo, the great red squirrel of Sumatra. Perhaps most beautiful of all were the birds, the white herons on the river, the many eagles, the huge, screeching rhinoceros birds, the miniature birds like many-colored gems. But perhaps even more exquisite were the beetles, the dragonflies, the butterflies, the gray silk moths as big as a man's hand, the golden beetles, the lizards, and also the occasional snake. And what terrifying encounters with flowers; pale white giant calyxes in the poisonous dampness of the dark forest and masses of cinnabar-red blooms on the high trees, greenish-white palm blossoms in panicles taller than a man!

But always finer than even all this was what we saw of human beings—the dreamy gait of the Hindu, the soft, sadly lovely gaze of the gentle Singhalese, like the glance of a deer, the dazzling white of the eyeballs in the bronze-black faces of Tamil coolies, the smile of a distinguished Chinese. The mumbling of a beggar in a strange, gargling language, the fact of being understood without words by men of ten different races and languages, sympathy with the oppressed, scorn for the vanity of the oppressor, and everywhere the special happy feeling that these are all human beings, our equals, brothers, comrades in fate! Lightly disguised, each in his own strangeness, manner, and race, they moved past us: the Indian Mohammedan, proud and self-aware; the Chinese with relaxed step, dignified and cheerful; shy and maidenly the small slim people of Ceylon; nimble and eager to serve, the pretty Malayans; small and clever and active the Japanese. They all had something in common, however different they were in color and stature—they were all Asiatics, just as we foreigners, no matter whether we came from Berlin or Stockholm, Zurich or Paris or Manchester, all in some mysterious but quite unmistakable fashion belonged together and were Europeans.

This in itself was beautiful and often surprising to observe, how there was something in common that united all Europeans, just as there was among all Asiatics, even when they did not understand one another and despised one another. But even more beautiful and to my mind infinitely more important was the now and again repeated recognition, in all its freshness and sensuousness, that not only East and West, not only Europe and Asia are unities, but that there is a unity and an association over and beyond that—humanity. Everyone knows this and yet it becomes infinitely new and precious if, instead of reading it in a book, one experiences it eye to eye with wholly alien peoples.

But this little, age-old platitude—that over and beyond

the boundaries of nations and the quarters of the globe there is humanity—this for me was the last and greatest reward of the journey, and it has become constantly more precious to me since the Great War.

It is only from this point of view, from the recognition of brotherhood and inner equality, that what is strange and dissimilar, the colorfulness of nations and of peoples, attains its profoundest charm and enchantment. How often have I, like a thousand other travelers, regarded the people and cities in foreign countries simply as curiosities, have merely glanced at them as though into a menagerie where all is interesting but has no essential connection with us! It was only when I abandoned this viewpoint and was able to see Malayans, Hindus, Chinese, and Japanese as human beings and close relatives, it was only then that the experience commenced that gave that journey worth and meaning.

I seldom talked about all this with Hans Sturzenegger. But whenever I look at his Indian works, then in those long, dark, slitted eyes, it is no object of curiosity I see but instead, peering back at me, kindred, comprehensible, lovable humanity. We cannot talk with these people, or not much, but their souls are like ours, completely like our own, and they cherish dreams and desires throughout their lives that differ from ours less than the leaves on a single tree differ from one another.

Pidurutalagala
(1911)

To bid India a proper and dignified farewell in peace and quiet, on one of the last days before I left I climbed alone in the coolness of a rainy morning to the highest summit in Ceylon, Pidurutalagala. Measured in English feet, its height sounds very respectable; in reality it is only a little over 2,500 meters and the ascent is a walk.

The cool green mountain valley of Nuwara Eliya was silvery in the light morning rain, typically Anglo-Indian with its corrugated tin roofs and its extravagantly extensive tennis courts and golf links, the Singhalese were delousing themselves in front of their huts or sitting shivering, wrapped in woolen shawls, the landscape, resembling the Black Forest, lay lifeless and shrouded. Except for a few birds I saw no signs of life until, in a garden hedge, I came upon a fat, poison-green chameleon whose malevolent movements in snatching insects I observed for some time.

The path began to climb upward through a little ravine, the straggling roofs disappeared, a swift brook roared below me. Narrow and steep, the way led steadily upward for a good hour, through dry underbrush and tormenting swarms of gnats; only rarely did a turn in the road afford a view and this always presented the same pretty, rather boring valley together with the sea and the hotel roofs. The rain gradually stopped, the cool wind subsided, and now and again the sun came out for minutes at a time.

I had climbed the shoulder of the mountain, the path

now led across flat country, springy moor, and several pretty mountain rills. Here the rhododendrons grow more luxuriantly than at home, trees three times a man's height, and there is a furry, silvery plant with white blossoms, very reminiscent of the edelweiss; I found many of our familiar forest flowers but all were strangely enlarged and heightened and alpine in character. The trees here, moreover, pay no heed to timber lines but grow sturdily, with heavy foliage, right up to the greatest heights.

I was approaching the last ascent of the mountain, the path suddenly began to climb again, soon I found myself once more surrounded by forest, a strange, dead, enchanted forest where trunks and branches, intertwined like serpents, stared blindly at me through long, thick, whitish beards of moss; a damp, bitter smell of foliage and fog hung between.

This was all very fine, but it was not really what I had secretly pictured to myself and I was already beginning to fear that today a new Indian disillusionment would be added to many earlier ones. Then the forest came to an end; I stepped, warm and somewhat breathless, out onto a gray heath, like some landscape in Ossian, and saw the bare summit capped by a small stone pyramid close before me. A high, cold wind was blowing against me, I pulled my coat tight and slowly climbed the last hundred paces.

What I saw up there was perhaps not typically Indian, but it was the grandest and purest impression I took away from all Ceylon. The wind had just swept clean the whole long valley of Nuwara Eliya, I saw, deep blue and immense, the entire high mountain system of Ceylon piled up in mighty walls, and in its midst the beautiful, ancient, and holy pyramid of Adam's Peak. Beside it at an infinite depth and distance lay flat blue sea, in between a thousand mountains, broad valleys, narrow ravines, rivers and waterfalls, in countless folds, the whole mountainous island on which ancient legends placed paradise.

Far below me mighty processions of cloud moved and thundered over individual vallcys, behind me swirling clouds of mist rose from blue-black depths; over everything swept, raw and cold, the roaring mountain wind. And objects near and far stood transfigured in the moist air, deeply saturated with a stormy fusion of colors as though this land were truly paradise and the first man were descending from its blue, cloud-ringed mountains, tall and vigorous, into the valleys.

This primeval landscape spoke to me more strongly than anything I had seen elsewhere in India. The palms and birds of paradise, the rice fields and the temples of the rich coastal cities, the valleys in the tropical lowlands steaming with fruitfulness, all this and the primeval forest itself were beautiful and enchanting, but they were always strange and extraordinary to mc, ncvcr quitc closc or quite my own. Only up here in the cold air and the seething clouds of the raw heights did it become fully clear to me how completely our being and our northern culture are rooted in raw, impoverished lands. We come full of longing to the South and the East, impelled by dark and thankful intimations of home, and we find here paradise, the manifold and rich profusion of all natural gifts, we find the simple, unpretentious, childlike people of paradise. But we ourselves are different, we are strangers here and without citizenship. We have long since lost paradise, and the new one we hope to have and to build will not be found on the equator or on warm Eastern seas, it lies within us and in our own northlandic culture.

A Guest at the Spa
(1924)

PROLOGUE

MOTTO: *Indolence is the beginning of all psychology.*

NIETZSCHE

It is said of the Swabians that they only reach the years of discretion at forty, and the Swabians themselves, never strong in self-confidence, sometimes see this as a kind of disgrace. It is, however, the reverse, it is a great honor, for the discretion intended in the maxim (it is nothing but what young people call "the wisdom of age," knowledge about the great antinomies, about the secret of the cycle and of bipolarity) must be very rare even among Swabians, however gifted they may be, in persons of forty. On the other hand, once one is past the middle forties, whether he is gifted or not, then that wisdom or mentality of the aging appears quite of itself, especially if incipient bodily aging helps it along by various warnings and disabilities. Among the commonest of these afflictions are gout, rheumatism, and sciatica, and it is just these sufferings that bring us patients here to the baths in Baden. And so the milieu is altogether favorable to the kind of mentality into which I have now slipped, and one drifts quite automatically, it seems to me, guided by the *genius loci*, into a certain skeptical piety, a simplistic wisdom, a very subtle art of simplification, a highly intelligent anti-intellectualism, which like the warmth of the baths and the smell of sulphur water form a specific part of the Baden cure. Or, to put it more briefly, we guests at the spa, we arthritics, are quite especially bent on making life's rough edges smooth, on letting two and two equal five, on not cherishing large illusions but, by way of compensation, on having and preserving a hundred comforting small illusions. We patients in Baden, unless I am mistaken, have a special need of knowledge about the antinomies, and the stiffer our joints become, the more pressing is our need of a flexible, two-sided, bipolar way of thinking. Our sufferings are real sufferings, but they are not of that heroic and picturesque kind that entitles the sufferer to consider them world-shaking without sacrificing our respect.

If I speak as though I were elevating my personal time of life and the sciatic's way of thought into a type, a general norm, if I behave as though I were talking here not in my name alone but in the name of a whole class of people and an age group, then in doing so I am well aware, at least at moments, that this is a serious error and that not a single psychologist, unless he were my soul brother and twin, would consider my mental reaction to my surroundings and to fate to be normal and typical. On the contrary, after a little tapping, he would quickly recognize me as a moderately gifted lone wolf belonging to the family of schizophrenics but not requiring commitment. However, I calmly make use of the prescriptive right of all men, even of psychologists, and I project not only into people but also into things and the arrangements of my surroundings, yes, into the whole world, my way of thought, my temperament, my joys and sorrows. To regard my thoughts and feelings as "right," as justified, this is a pleasure that I will not permit to be taken away, although the world around me strives hourly to convince me of the opposite; yes, I think nothing of having the majority against me, I prefer to consider that they are wrong rather than that I am. It is the same with my judgment of the great German poets whom I do not honor, love, and make use of any the less because the great majority of living Germans do the opposite and prefer rockets to the stars. Rockets are beautiful, rockets are enchanting, long life to rockets! But the stars! An eye and a mind filled with their quiet lights, filled with the vast resonance of their universal music—oh friends, that after all is something quite different!

And while I, belated minor poet, undertake to sketch out a stay at the spa, I bear in mind the many dozens of visits to spas and expeditions to Baden that have been recorded by good writers and bad, and I think with enchantment and reverence of the star among all the rockets, of the gold piece amid the paper money, of the bird of paradise among all the sparrows, in short of Dr. Katzenberger's visit to the baths, nevertheless I do not allow these thoughts to keep me from sending my rocket in pursuit of the star, my sparrow after the bird of paradise. Fly then, sparrow! Rise, little paper dragon!

A GUEST AT THE SPA

Barely had my train arrived in Baden and I with some difficulty descended the steps of the car when the spell of Baden was upon me. Standing on the damp cement of the station platform and peering about for the hotel porter, I saw getting off the same train three or four colleagues, sciatics, clearly indicated as such by the nervous tightening of their buttocks, the insecure step and rather helpless and tearful facial expressions which accompanied their cautious movements. Each of them, to be sure, had his specialty, his own kind of suffering, and therefore his own way of walking, hesitating, tottering, limping, and each also his own special facial expressions, and yet what they had in common predominated, I recognized them all at the first glance as sciatics, as brothers, as colleagues. Anyone who has ever become acquainted with the actions of the *nervus ischiadicus*, not from a textbook but from personal experience, called by the doctors "subjective sensation," will understand this at once. Immediately I stopped and observed these marked characters. And behold, all three of them were making uglier faces than I, propping themselves more heavily on their canes, lifting their hands more jerkily, setting their feet down on the ground more hesitantly and unwillingly than I, all were sicker, more wretched, in greater pain, more pitiable than I, and this did me a world of good and remained during the period of my stay in Baden a constantly recurring, inexhaustible comfort: that all around me people limped, people crawled, people sighed, people rode in wheelchairs, all of them much sicker than I, with far less reason for good humor and hope than I had! There and then I had discovered, in the very first minute, one of the great secrets and spells of all spas and I savored my discovery with true delight: companionship in suffering, "*socios habere malorum.*"

And as I now left the station and cheerfully entrusted myself to a street that flowed gently downhill toward the baths, every step I took confirmed and increased this precious experience: everywhere patients were creeping, sitting weary and somewhat askew on green benches, limping past in chattering groups. A woman was being pushed along in a wheelchair, smiling wearily, a half-wilted flower in her sickly hand, her nurse behind her bursting with health and energy. An old gentleman was coming out of one of the stores where the rheumatics buy their picture postcards, ashtrays, and paperweights (of which they require a great many, I could never understand why) —and this old gentleman who was coming out of the store required for each step of the stairs a whole minute and looked at the street that lay before him the way a weary and uncertain man looks at some heavy task imposed upon him. A man still young, with a gray-green army cap on his bristly head, was working his way along powerfully but laboriously with the aid of two canes. Oh yes indeed, these canes you met everywhere, these damnably serious sick people's canes which ended in broad rubber ferrules that stuck to the asphalt like leeches! To be sure, I too carried a cane, a handsome Malacca bamboo, whose assistance was very welcome, but if necessary I could walk without it, and no one had ever seen me with one of those sorry rubber-shod sticks! No, it was so clear, it must strike anyone how smartly and gracefully I paraded down this agreeable street, how little and playfully I used the Malacca cane, this article of pure adornment, this decoration; how extremely mild and harmless in my case was the characteristic mark of the sciatic, the nervous retraction of the thigh, indicated or rather merely hinted at, lightly sketched; in general how erect and proper my bearing as I walked along this street, how young and healthy I was compared with all these older, poorer, sicker brothers and sisters whose ailments were so clearly, so undisguisedly, so pitilessly displayed! I breathed in appreciation, I gulped affirmation at every stride, I already felt myself almost well, in any case infinitely less sick than all these poor people. Yes, if these half-lame, limping folk still hoped for a cure, these people with rubber-shod canes, if Baden could even now help them, then my small incipient trouble would disappear here like snow before the south wind, then the doctor must surely find in me a fine specimen, a highly rewarding phenomenon, a small miracle of curability.

Full of sympathy and good will, I looked with kindliness at these stimulating figures. Now an old woman came billowing out of a candy store, she had obviously long ago given up attempting to hide her infirmity, she denied herself no smallest reflex movement, she took full advantage of every conceivable mitigation, every available play of auxiliary muscles, and so she wrestled, balanced, and swam along like a sea lion crossing the street, only slower. My heart bade her welcome and I cheered her on, I praised the sea lion, I praised Baden and my own fortunate state. I saw myself surrounded near and far by fellow strugglers, competitors to whom I was vastly superior. How lucky that I had come here in time, still in the first stage of a mild sciatica, still with the first faint symptoms of incipient arthritis! Turning around and leaning on my cane, I looked after the sea lion for a while with that familiar feeling of satisfaction which proves that language cannot yet express psychological processes, for the linguistic opposites, malice and sympathy, are here most profoundly united. My God, the poor woman! It could really get as bad as that.

It is true that even in this enthusiastic moment of heightened well-being, even in the fine euphoria of a good hour, that annoying voice within me was not entirely silent, the voice I am so reluctant to hear and that I need so much, the voice of reason, and in its cool, disagreeable tone it reminded me softly and regretfully that the source of my comfort was simply a mistake, a faulty procedure: I was thankfully comparing myself, the limping literary man with his Malacca cane, with every lame, badly crippled, and twisted figure, but neglecting to take into account the endless gamut of symptoms extending in the direction opposite to my state, not recognizing all those figures who were younger, straighter, healthier, and more vigorous than I was. Or rather, I noticed them but I refused to draw a comparison; in fact, during the first two days I was utterly convinced that all those contented-looking people I saw strolling about without canes, without noticeable lameness or limp, were not brothers and colleagues, not patients and competitors but normal, healthy residents of the city. That there might also be sciatics who could get along without a cane and walk without convulsive movements, that the sufferings of many arthritics no one, not even a psychologist, could recognize on the street, that I with my slightly crooked walk and my Malacca cane was by no means in the harmless beginning stage of metabolic disease, that if I aroused envy in the truly halt and lame I also got derisive sympathy from numerous colleagues for whom I served as the comforting sea lion; in short, that I with my sharp-eyed observation of degrees of suffering was not carrying on an objective investigation but rather an optimistic self-deception—this realization came to me in my usual tardy way only after a number of days.

Well, I enjoyed this happiness of the first day to the full, I indulged in orgies of naïve self-affirmation, and it did me good. Attracted by the figures of my fellow guests at the spa, my sicklier brothers bobbing up everywhere, flattered by the appearance of each cripple, aroused to cheerful sympathy and self-satisfied interest by each wheelchair I encountered, I strolled down the street, this street so conveniently, so flatteringly laid out, on which the arriving guests were rolled down from the station and which led in soft undulations and agreeably uniform slopes to the ancient baths, and there below, like a river sinking into the sand, lost itself in the entrances to the spa hotels. Full of good resolutions and cheerful expectations, I approached the Heiligenhof, where I planned to stay. It was simply a matter of enduring it here for three or four weeks, bathing daily, walking as much as possible, keeping excitement and worry as far away as possible. It would perhaps on occasion be monotonous, there would be moments of boredom because the opposite of the intensive life was prescribed here, and for me, the old solitary, the life of the herd and of the hotel is profoundly obnoxious, comes extremely hard, and there would be some discomforts to accept, some reluctance to overcome. But without doubt this to me new and completely unfamiliar life would bring amusing and interesting experiences as well, in spite of its possibly rather bourgeois, rather insipid character—after years of a peaceful, wild, rusticated, and lonesome existence devoted to study, wasn't I really in the greatest need of associating with people again for a while? And the principal thing: beyond the difficulties, beyond these weeks of the cure now beginning, lay the day when I would leave this hotel and vigorously ascend this same street, the day on which, rejuvenated and healed, I would bid farewell to the baths and with elastic play of knee and hip dance my way up the pretty street to the station.

Too bad, though, that at the very moment when I entered the Heiligenhof a gentle rain began to fall.

"You're not bringing us good weather," said the young lady at the desk by way of friendly greeting.

"No," I said, at a loss. What did this mean? Could it really be, I wondered, that it was I who had called up this rain, who had created it and brought it with me? That the common-sense way of looking at things contradicted this could not exonerate me, the theologian and mystic. Yes, just as fate and character were names for a single concept, just as I had in a certain sense chosen and created my name and position, my age, my face, my sciatica, and must not make anyone but myself responsible, just so very likely did it stand with the rain. I was ready to assume responsibility.

After I had said so to the young lady and filled out a registration form, I entered into those negotiations about my room which the normal person does not experience, of whose horror the simple, contented person has no inkling, whose total misery is known only to a hermit and writer accustomed to loneliness and deep quiet, to a sufferer from sleeplessness who finds himself stranded in a strange hotel.

For a normal person, selecting a hotel room is a trivial,

commonplace, by no means emotionally charged action that can be carried out in two minutes. But for our sort, for us neurotics, insomniacs, and psychopaths, this banal action is fantastically overloaded with memories, emotions, and phobias to the point of being a martyrdom. The genial hotel manager, the sympathetic receptionist who at our hesitant but insistent request point out and recommend their "quiet room" have no idea of the storm of associations, fears, ironies, and self-mockery this fatal phrase arouses in us. Oh, how precise—oh, how dreadfully exact—how horribly profound is our knowledge of these "quiet rooms," these stations of our most painful sufferings, our most grievous defeats, our most secret humiliation! How false and deceptive, how demonic the look of these friendly furnishings, these well-intentioned rugs and cheerful wallpapers! What a deadly annihilating grin there is on that bolted door communicating with the adjoining room, a door that unhappily is to be found in most rooms, generally aware of its own evil role and therefore shamefacedly hiding behind a wall hanging! With what a painful and resigned expression we look at the whitewashed ceiling of the room, which always at the moment of inspection is smirking silently and emptily, only later, morning and evening, to resound with the steps of those living above—oh, and not only steps, they are familiar and therefore not the worst foe! No, above that innocent white surface in the desperate hour, just as through that thin door and wall, come unimaginable rattlings and vibrations, boots are thrown down, canes fall to the floor, there are mighty rhythmic shudderings (pointing to hygienic exercises), chairs are upset, book or glass falls from the night table, trunks and furniture are moved. Also human voices, dialogues, monologues, coughing, laughing, snoring! And further, worse than all this, the unknown, inexplicable rustlings, those strange, ghostly sounds we cannot interpret, whose provenance and presumable duration we cannot guess, those tapping and whirling spirits, all that cracking, ticking, whispering, blowing, sucking, rustling, sighing, crackling, pecking, seething—God knows what a multitudinous invisible orchestra can be hidden in the few cubic meters of a hotel room!

And so the selection of a bedroom for our sort is an extremely delicate, important, and at the same time rather hopeless undertaking with twenty, with a hundred possibilities to be taken into consideration. In one room it is the wall cabinet that is the source of acoustic surprises, in another the steampipes, in a third a neighbor who plays the ocarina. And since from all experience there is not a single room in the world in which longed-for peace and undisturbed sleep can be guaranteed, since the apparently quietest room conceals surprises (have I not stayed in a remote servant's room on the fifth floor in order to be sure that no disturber of the peace was above me or next to me, only to discover over my head a creaking attic alive with rats?)—oughtn't one finally to give up all choice, simply leap head first at fate and let chance prevail? Instead of tormenting and worrying oneself, only to be sad and disillusioned after a few hours because of the inevitable, isn't it smarter to leave it to blind chance and take the first room offered? Certainly that is smarter. But we do not do it, or only rarely, for if being smart and avoiding excitement should dictate all our undertakings, how would life look then? Don't we know that our fate is inborn and inescapable, and don't we nevertheless cling passionately to the illusion of choice, of free will? Couldn't everyone when he chooses a doctor for his ills, a profession and place of residence, when he picks out a beloved bride, just as well and perhaps with better success leave it to pure chance—and doesn't he choose just the same, doesn't he devote a great deal of passion, effort, and care to all these things? Perhaps he does it naïvely, believing with childlike enthusiasm in his own power, convinced that fate can be influenced; or perhaps he does it skeptically, deeply convinced of the futility of his efforts but equally certain that action and effort, choice and self-torment are finer, livelier, more seemly or at least more amusing than congealing in resigned passivity. Just so do I behave in my foolish search for a room despite my deep conviction of the uselessness, the silly meaninglessness of my action, just so over and over again do I carry on long negotiations about the room to be chosen, conscientiously informing myself about neighbors, about doors and double doors, about this and that. It is a game I play, a sport I indulge myself in, when in dealing with these small and commonplace questions I give myself over to the game's illusionary, fictitious rules that things of this sort are in general accessible to and worthy of rational management. In doing so, I behave just as cleverly or just as stupidly as a child buying candy or a gambler placing his bet according to a mathematical system. In all such situations we know very well that we are confronted by pure chance, and yet out of a deep psychic need we behave as though there could be no such thing as chance, as though each and every thing in the world were subject to our sane judgment and control.

And so I thoroughly discuss with the obliging young lady the five or six vacant rooms. One of them I learn has a violin player next door who practices for two hours every day—well, that at least is something definite, now I strive in the further choice for the greatest possible distance from that room and floor. In any case, in the matter of the conditions and possibilities of hotel acoustics I have a sensibility, a capacity to foresee, that would be invaluable to many an architect. In short, I did what was necessary, what was reasonable, I behaved cautiously and conscientiously, the way a neurotic must behave when selecting a bedroom, with the usual result, which might be expressed somewhat like this: "Of course, it does no good and naturally I am going to encounter in this room the same disturbances and disillusionments as in every other, but nevertheless I have now done my duty, I have taken pains, the rest I leave in God's hands." And at the same time the other softer voice deep inside me said as usual: "Wouldn't it be better to leave the whole thing to God and stop this play-acting?" I heard the voice as always, and yet I did not hear it, and because I was in such good humor just then the procedure went off agreeably, I contentedly saw my wicker trunk disappear into No. 65 and went on my way, for this was the time of my appointment with thc doctor.

And behold, here too things went well. In retrospect I can admit that I was a little frightened at the prospect of this visit, not because I feared some crushing diagnosis but because, to my way of thinking, doctors belong to the spiritual hierarchy; I attribute a high rank to the doctor and I take to heart any disillusionment from him which I could easily accept from a railroad conductor or bank clerk or even from a lawyer. I expect in a doctor, I do not know exactly why, some remnant of that humanism to which a knowledge of Latin and Greek and a certain philosophical preparation belong and which is no longer required in most other callings today. In this respect I, who am usually full of enthusiasm for the new and revolutionary, am completely conservative, I demand from the more highly educated classes a certain idealism, a certain readiness to understand and to explain quite independent of material advantage—in short, a bit of humanism, although I know that this humanism in reality no longer exists and that even its representation will soon be found only in waxworks.

After a short wait I was shown into a very attractive, tastefully decorated room that at once inspired my confidence. After the usual splashing of water in the next room, the doctor entered; an intelligent face promised understanding, and we greeted each other with a hearty handshake, as befits well-mannered boxers before the match. We began the battle cautiously, trying each other out, guardedly testing our first blows. We were still on neutral ground, our debate concerned metabolism, nourishment, age, earlier sicknesses, and exuded harmlessness. Only at certain words did our glances cross, bared for battle. The doctor had at his command a number of expressions from the secret language of medicine which I could only vaguely decipher, but which aided him substantially in the elegance of his explanations and appreciably strengthened his position in relation to me. Nevertheless, after a few minutes it was clear to me that with this doctor there was no need to fear that horrid disillusionment which is so painful for people like me, particularly with their doctors: that behind a winning façade of intelligence and education one comes upon a rigid dogmatism, the first utterance of which postulates that the point of view, way of thought, and vocabulary of the patient are purely subjective phenomena whereas those of the doctor have strictly objective validity. No, here I was dealing with a doctor with whom it would be worthwhile to fight for understanding, who was not only intelligent in the literal sense but wise to an as yet undetermined degree—that is, possessed of a lively feeling for the relativity of all intellectual values. Among educated and mature people it happens constantly that one recognizes the mentality and language, the dogmatism and mythology of the other as subjective, as mere approximations, mere fleeting similes. But that each should make this discovery in respect to himself and apply it to himself and that each should grant to himself as well as to his opponent the right to his own inner-directed and inevitable manner, way of thought and speech, that is to say, that two people should exchange ideas with one another and in doing so remain constantly aware of the fragility of their tools, the ambiguity of all words, the impossibility of truly precise expression as well as the necessity of intensive surrender of the self, a cordial reciprocal alertness and intellectual chivalry—this excellent situation, something that it really ought to be possible to take for granted between thinking beings, actually occurs so dreadfully seldom that we inwardly rejoice at any approximation to it, any even partial realization of it. Now in the presence of this specialist in metabolic diseases, something like the possibility of such understanding and exchange suddenly blazed up.

The examination, subject to the results of blood tests and X-rays, brought comforting conclusions. Heart normal, breathing splendid, blood pressure quite satisfactory; on the other hand, there were unmistakable signs of sciatica, a few arthritic deposits, and a rather deplorable state of the whole musculature. There was a short pause in our conversation while the doctor washed his hands again.

As expected, this was the turning point, neutral territory was abandoned, my partner took the offensive by asking with cautious intonation and apparent casualness: "Don't you think that your pains might be partly psychic in origin?" So there we were, what I had expected, what I had known in advance, had happened. The objective findings did not quite justify my claims to suffering, there was a suspicious plus in sensibility here, my subjective reactions to the arthritic pains did not correspond to the anticipated normal ones, and so I was recognized as a neurotic. Well, up then and give battle!

With equal caution and casualness I explained that I did not believe in the partial psychic causation of pains and illness, that in my personal biology and mythology the "psychic" was not a kind of auxiliary factor added to the physical but the primary power, and that I therefore regarded every condition of life, every feeling of joy and sorrow as well as every sickness, every misfortune and death as psychogenic, as born out of the soul. If I develop arthritic bumps on my finger joints, it is my soul, it is the revered principle of life, the It in me, that is expressing itself in plastic material. If the soul is suffering, it can say so in very different ways, and what in one person takes the form of uric acid in preparation for the disintegration of the I, can perform this same service in another through alcoholism, in a third it can congeal into an ounce of lead that suddenly crashes into the skull. At the same time I admitted that in most cases the possibilities of help from a doctor must be confined to hunting down the material or secondary changes and combatting them with equally material means.

Even now I continued to count on the possibility of being left in the lurch by the doctor. To be sure, he would not say straight out: "My good sir, what you say is nonsense," but he would perhaps agree with a shade too considerate a smile, say something banal about the influence of temperament, especially on the artistic soul, would perhaps in addition to this temporizing also produce the deadly word "imponderables." This word is a touchstone, a delicate scale for measuring spiritual quantities, which the average scientist calls "imponderable." That is, he always uses this convenient word when it is a question of measuring and describing the manifestations of life for which not only are the present material measuring devices too coarse, but the determination and ability of the speaker too small. In fact the natural scientist generally knows very little; among other things he does not know that for just these fleeting, changeable values which he calls imponderables there are, outside natural science, ancient, highly developed methods of measurement and description, that the entire accomplishment of both Thomas Aquinas and Mozart was in weighing, each in his own language, with extreme precision the so-called imponderables. Could I expect from a spa doctor, Phoenix though he might be in his own domain, this subtle knowledge? I did expect it, nevertheless, and behold, I was not disappointed,

I was understood. This man recognized that in me he was being confronted not by an alien dogmatism but rather by a game, an art, a music, in which there was no longer a contest or a question of being right but only a sympathetic resonance or its absence. And he did not fail, I was understood and recognized, recognized not as being right, of course, something I have never wished to be, but as a seeker, as a thinker, as a polar opposite, as a colleague from another far-removed but equally competent faculty.

And now my spirits, already lifted by the results of the tests for blood pressure and breathing, reached a higher point. Let the rainy weather, the sciatica, and the cure turn out as they might, I was not abandoned to the barbarians, I was in the presence of a human being, a colleague, a man of flexible and discriminating mind! Not that I counted on talking with him often and at length, threshing out problems with him. No, this was not necessary, though it remained a pleasant possibility; it was enough that this man, to whom for a time I had granted power over myself and in whom I had to have confidence, in my opinion held the diploma of human maturity. For today let the doctor continue to regard me as an intellectually active but unfortunately somewhat neurotic patient; conceivably the hour would come when he would pry open the upper story of my edifice where my own belief, my most private philosophy, would enter into play and competition with his. Perhaps, too, my theory of the neurotic based on Nietzsche and Hamsun would be advanced a step in the process. But no matter, this was not very important. The neurotic character seen not as sickness but, painful though it was, as a highly positive process of sublimation—this was a pretty thought. However, it was more important to live it than to formulate it.

Contented and armed with numerous prescriptions for the cure, I said goodbye to the doctor. The list in my notebook gave directions that were to be begun very early next morning and promised all sorts of health-restoring and entertaining things: baths, medicinal potions, diathermy, quartz lamp, theurapeutic gymnastics. And so there couldn't be much room left for boredom.

That my first day at the spa reached its climax in a beautiful and cheery evening was due to my host. Dinner, to my astonishment, proved a noble, festive meal of delicacies untasted by me for years, such as gnocchi with foie gras, Irish stew, strawberry ice. And later I sat over a bottle of red wine in lively conversation with the landlord, in a beautiful ancient room at a heavy, antique walnut table, and had the joy of discovering a responsive echo in a stranger, a man of different heritage, different calling, different ambition and style of life, of being able to share his concerns and joys and finding many of my views shared by him. We voiced no lofty pretensions to each other, but we quickly found points of contact and met each other with that openness that quickly turns to sympathy.

While taking a short walk that night before going to bed, I saw stars reflected in the rain puddles, I saw a pair of extremely beautiful old trees in the night wind on the shore of the deep murmuring river. They would be beautiful tomorrow too, of course, but at this moment they had that magic, that non-recurrent beauty that comes from our own soul, and which according to the Greeks only blazes up in us when Eros has looked our way.

THE DAY'S ROUTINE

In undertaking to describe the usual course of a day at the spa, I will in fairness choose an average day, a day of no extremes, a kind of half-cloudy, half-mild, normal day without special outward events and without unusual symptoms or spells from within. For here, of course, and not for nervous literary men only but for the whole crowd of sciatics according to their condition and the stage of the cure—here there are days full of pain and depression and soft, gentle days full of well-being and blossoming hope, days on which we skip and others on which we painfully drag ourselves around or hopelessly remain in bed.

But however great the care I may take in reconstructing a well-tempered, average day, a normal, plain plus-and-minus day, I must make one painful confession, for every day, even a day at the spa, alas, begins with the morning: I have no use whatever for morning, praised in so many wonderful poems. Presumably there is a connection with my greatest distress and vice, bad sleeping, as well as with every aspect of my being, my philosophy, my temperament and character. All this is a disgrace and it comes hard to me to admit it, but what sense can there be in writing if the will to truth is not behind it? The morning, that celebrated time of freshness, of new beginnings, of happy youthful impulse, for me is deadly, it is vexatious and distressing; the morning and I, we do not love each other. At the same time I am not without some understanding, some empathy for that beaming morning joy that resounds so bright and clear in so many poems by Eichendorff and Mörike; in poems, in paintings, and in memory, I, too, find the morning poetic, and from my childhood I retain a half-faded memory of real morning joy, although for very many years now I have not felt happy on a single morning. And also, in the most resounding tribute to fresh morning joy I know, the verses of Eichendorff set to music by Wolf, "Morning That Is My Joy," I hear a faint dissonance, for marvelous though it sounds and completely though Eichendorff's morning mood convinces me, I cannot quite believe in Hugo Wolf's morning joy, and I think he has indulged himself in a melancholy, poetic yearning, rather than an actually experienced glorification of morning. Everything that makes my life heavy and difficult, that makes it a dangerous, hateful problem, proclaims itself too loudly in the morning, stands before me giantlike. Everything that makes my life sweet and beautiful and unusual, all grace, all enchantment, all music, is far away in the morning, hardly visible, can barely be heard even as saga or legend. Out of the all-too-shallow grave of my all-too-often-interrupted sleep I rouse myself in the morning, not winged with feelings of resurrection, but weighty, weary, timorous, without shield or armor against the assault of the world around me, a world that imposes all its vibrations on my sensitive morning nerves as though through a powerful amplifier, howls its voices at me through a megaphone. Only from midday on does life become once more bearable and good, and on lucky days, in the late afternoon and evening—wonderful, gleaming, floating, inwardly transfused with the soft light of God, full of order and harmony, full of enchantment and music, making golden restitution for the thousands and thousands of bad hours.

In another place I plan to take the opportunity of saying why this suffering from insomnia and this morning misery seems to me not just a sickness but also a sin, why I am ashamed of it and yet feel that it must be this way, that I dare not lie away these things or forget them, nor dare I "cure" them by material means, for I need them as incentive and constantly renewed spur to my real life and its task.

In one respect a day at the baths in Baden has an advantage for me over the usual days of my life: each day during the cure begins with an important, central morning duty, a task that is easy, yes, agreeable to perform. I mean the bath. When I wake up in the morning, no matter what the hour, this first and most essential duty awaits me, not something vexatious, not dressing or exercising or shaving or reading the mail, but the bath, a soft, warm, frictionless occasion. With a slight feeling of dizziness I sit up in bed, get my rusty limbs in motion again by a few cautious movements, stand up, put on my dressing gown, and walk slowly along the half-darkened, silent corridor to the elevator, which takes me down through all the floors to the cellar, where the bathing cubicles are. Down here it is pleasant. A wonderful soft warmth constantly pervades the very old, softly echoing stone cellars, for everywhere hot water runs from the springs; a mysterious, cozy feeling of being in a cave always comes over me, such as I used to have as a small boy when I created a cave out of a table, two chairs, and a couple of bedspreads or carpets. In the cubicle reserved for me there is a deep masonry tank sunk in the floor and full of hot water just run from the springs. I climb slowly down two little stone steps, reverse the hourglass, and sink up to my chin in the hot, acrid water smelling faintly of sulphur. High above me in the barrel vault of my massively constructed cell, which strangely reminds me of a cloister, daylight falls through translucent windowpanes; up there, a story above me, behind the milk glass, lies the world, distant, milky, no sound from it reaching me. And around me plays the wonderful warmth of the mysterious water which for thousands of years has been flowing up out of the unknown kitchens of the earth and is falling continuously in a thin stream into my bath. According to directions, I should move my limbs as much as possible in the water, performing gymnastic and swimming movements. Dutifully I do so, for a few minutes, but then I lie motionless, close my eyes, fall half asleep, and presently am watching the quiet trickling of the sand in the hourglass.

A withered leaf, blown in through the window, a small leaf from a tree whose name I cannot recall, lies on the edge of my tank, I look at it, read the text of its ribs and veins, smell the peculiar intimation of mortality at which we shudder and without which there would be nothing beautiful. Marvelous, how beauty and death, joy and mortality, promote and depend on each other! I feel distinctly, like something sensuous around and within me, the borderline between nature and spirit. Just as flowers are transitory and beautiful but gold is lasting and boring, so all movements of the natural life are transitory and beautiful, but the spirit is immortal and boring. At this moment I reject it, by no means do I see the spirit as eternal life but as eternal death, as what is congealed, fruitless, shapeless, and can only regain shape and life by surrendering its immortality. Gold must become a flower, spirit must become body and must become psyche in order to live. No, in this mild morning hour between the hourglass and the wilted leaf I want nothing to do with spirit, which at other times I revere so greatly; I want to be transitory, I want to be a child and a flower.

And I am reminded that I am transitory when after half an hour's lying in the warm flood the moment comes to get up. I ring for the attendant, who appears and lays out a warm bath towel for me. And now I stand up in the water and the feeling of transitoriness flows through me, weakening all my limbs, for these baths are very tiring, and when I attempt to stand up after a bath of thirty or forty minutes my knees and arms will obey only slowly and laboriously. Creeping out of the tank, I throw the towel over my shoulders and try to rub myself vigorously, try to make a few energetic movements to encourage myself but cannot manage it and sink down on the chair, feeling two hundred years old, and take a long time in compelling myself to stand up, put on nightshirt and dressing gown again, and depart.

Weak-kneed and slow, I make my way through the quiet cellars, listening to the splash of water here and there behind cubicle doors, to the sulphur spring which bubbles and boils under glass between yellowish-coated rocks. A puzzling story is told of this spring. On its stone edge for the use of the guests there always stand two water glasses, or rather that's just it: they do not stand there; each guest when he comes thirstily to the spring is faced with the fact that both glasses have disappeared again. Then he shakes his head, insofar as a patient after his bath is capable of such an action, calls for service, and presently the houseman or the waiter or the chambermaid or a bath attendant or the elevator boy appears, and they all shake their heads too and cannot understand what has become of these mysterious glasses again. Each time a new glass is hastily brought, the guest fills it, empties it, puts it on the stone, and departs—and if he comes back in two hours to have another swallow, again there is no glass. For the employees this puzzling business of the glasses is vexatious and means added work. Each of them has his own explanation for the glasses fraud, no one of which is really convincing. The elevator boy says naïvely that the glasses are frequently taken by the guests to their rooms. As though they would not, in that case, be found each day by the chambermaids! In short, the mystery has not been explained, and in my own experience it has already happened eight or ten times that I have had to have a new glass brought. Since our hotel has perhaps eighty guests and since these patients, serious, elderly folk with arthritis and rheumatism, presumably do not steal glasses, I assume it is either a pathological collector or some nonhuman being, a demon of the fountain or a dragon, who takes these glasses away, perhaps to punish men for exploiting the spring; and perhaps some day a lucky soul, losing his way in the vaulted cellars, will come upon the entrance to the hidden shaft where a whole mountain of goblets is heaped up, for according to my conservative reckoning at least two thousand glasses must be stored there in a single year.

At this spring I now fill my glass and drink the warm acrid water with satisfaction. Usually I sit down while doing this and then have trouble summoning the resolve to get up again. I drag myself to the elevator, my head filled with agreeable notions of duty fulfilled and repose earned, for what with bathing and drinking I have actually carried out the most important orders of the day. On the other hand, it is still early, seven or seven-thirty at latest, there are many hours still until noon, and I would give anything if I knew a magic spell that would transform morning hours into evening hours.

For the moment, to be sure, the regulations of the cure come to my aid; they prescribe that after the bath I should get into bed again. My drowsiness after the bath fits perfectly with this, but by now life in the hotel has long since begun, floors resound under the hasty steps of chambermaids and waiters carrying breakfasts, doors slam. As a result, sleep is out of the question except for minutes, for earplugs have not yet been invented that will really protect the overwakeful, sensitive ear of the insomniac.

Nevertheless, it is agreeable to lie down again, to close one's eyes once more, not to think of all the stupid actions demanded of us every morning: stupid dressing, stupid shaving, stupid tying of one's tie, saying good morning, reading the mail, making up one's mind to some sort of activity, resuming the whole mechanical routine of life.

Meanwhile, I lie in bed, hear my neighbors laugh, curse, gargle, hear the bell in the corridor ring and the servants run, and soon see that there is no point in postponing the inevitable any longer. Up then, my boy, and eat! I get up, I wash, I shave, I carry out those complicated activities which are necessary to get into one's clothes and shoes, I choke myself with the shirt collar, I stuff my watch into my waistcoat pocket, I adorn myself with glasses, all with the sensations of a convict who for decades has followed the prescribed routine and knows that it will last his whole lifetime, it will never come to an end.

At nine o'clock I appear in the dining room, a pale silent guest, seat myself at my little round table, silently greet the pretty girl who brings me coffee, butter half my breakfast roll, stuff the other half into my pocket, cut open the envelopes lying at my plate, stuff breakfast down my throat and the letters into my pocket, see a bored patient waiting in the corridor who wishes to strike up a conversation with me and is already smiling invitingly from afar and even beginning to speak, in French at that; I brush determinedly and quickly past him, murmuring "*Pardon,*" and hurry out into the street.

Here and in the spa garden or in the woods I now succeed in completely killing the morning in wished-for isolation. Sometimes I succeed in working; that is, seated on a bench in the park, my back toward the sun and people, I set down some of the thoughts that still linger in my mind from the night hours. For the most part I walk, and I am happy about the half a roll in my pocket, for it is my greatest morning pleasure (that expression is, of course, too strong) to crumble up this bread and feed it to the many finches and titmice. In doing this I make it a matter of principle not to reflect that in Germany a few miles from here, even on the tables of the rich, there is no such white bread and that thousands have no bread at all. I prohibit this too-obvious thought from entering my consciousness, and I often find this prohibition quite exhausting.

In sun or rain, working or walking, somehow and somewhere I have finally used up the forenoon, and the high point of the day arrives, the midday meal. I can give assurance that I am no gourmand, but even for me who am acquainted with the joys of the spirit and of asceticism, this hour is solemn and important. But this is a point that demands further consideration.

As I have already hinted in the prologue, it is part of the temperament and way of thought of the no-longer-young rheumatic and arthritic that he is aware of the impossibility of understanding the world along straight lines, that he has a feeling and respect for the antinomies, for the necessity of opposites and contradictions. Many of these contradictions, leaving aside their deep philosophic foundations, find expression with amazing clarity in the life of the Baden spa. Many examples could be found. I only mention, to choose something quite banal, the many benches that are placed everywhere in Baden: they invite all the easily wearied patients on not wholly reliable legs to sit down and rest, and a patient all too eagerly accepts the friendly hint. But he has hardly been seated a minute when he struggles to his feet again in alarm, for the philanthropic manufacturer of these many benches, a profound philosopher and ironist, has made the seats of iron, and the sciatic sitting upon them finds the most sensitive part of his ailing frame exposed to an annihilating current of cold, which instinct compels him to flee at once. Thus the bench reminds him how much he needs rest and a minute later warns him with equal emphasis that life's core and fountain are movement and that rusty joints do not need rest so much as exercise.

Many such examples could be found. But more monumentally than anywhere else, the Baden spirit, which constantly moves in antithesis, finds its expression in the midday and evening hours in the dining hall. There sit dozens of sick people, each of whom has brought his arthritis or sciatica with him, each of whom has come to Baden on that account alone, to get rid, if possible, of his ailments through the cure. Now, any simple rectilinear, youthful, puritanic, practical wisdom would, based on the clear and simple teaching of chemistry and physiology, strongly recommend to these sufferers in addition to the hot baths a simple, Spartan, meatless, alcohol-free, unappetizing diet, if possible even a regimen of fasting. But people in Baden do not think in such a straightforward, unambiguous, youthful way; instead, for hundreds of years Baden has been as much renowned for its rich and delicious cuisine as for its baths, and in fact in the whole country there are few towns or inns where people eat so well and so abundantly as in those in Baden that cater to patients suffering from metabolic illnesses. There the most delicate ham is washed down with Dézaley, the most succulent schnitzels with Bordeaux; between soup and roast, blue trout swim delicately, and the abundant meat courses are followed by marvelous cakes, puddings, and creams.

Earlier authors have attempted in various ways to explain this ancient Baden peculiarity. To recognize and approve of the high state of the cuisine there is easy; each of the thousand patients does so twice a day; to explain it is harder since the causes are of a very complex nature. I shall mention some of the most important ones presently, but first I would like to reject emphatically those coarse, rationalistic explanations one meets so often. For example, one frequently hears from vulgar thinkers that the tradition of good food at Baden, which is really contrary to the best interests of the patients, has grown up over the years and results from competition among the various spa hotels, and that it is in the interest of each innkeeper not to fall behind his competitors, at least. This cheap and superficial argument will not stand up under examination if only because it avoids the heart of the problem and tries to bypass the question of the actual origin of the good Baden cuisine by referring it to tradition and the past. And least of all will we be satisfied with the absurd thought that a desire for profit on the part of the innkeepers is responsible for the good food! As though any hotel owner would be interested in greatly increasing his payments to butcher, baker, and confectioner, especially here in Baden where every owner of a spa hotel possesses a magnet for guests, the great attraction that has not failed for centuries, there in his own cellar in the form of the hot mineral springs!

No, we must dig considerably deeper to form a hypothesis about this phenomenon. The secret lies neither in the customs and traditions of the past nor in the calculations of the innkeepers, it lies deep in the structure of the universe as one of the eternal antinomies that have to be accepted. If the food in Baden were traditionally frugal and sparse, the innkeepers could save two thirds of their expenses and still have their hotels full, for the guests are not drawn by the food but are driven here by the twitching of their *nervus ischiadicus*. But let us assume for the sake of argument that people in Baden lived rationally, fighting uric acid and sclerosis not just with baths but with abstinence and fasting, what would be the probable result? The patients at the spa would presumably get well and in a short time throughout the whole country there would be no more sciatica, which, however, like all forms of nature has its right to existence and continuance. The baths would become superfluous, the hotels would necessarily fall into disrepair. And if one should consider this last loss unimportant or reparable, nevertheless the absence of arthritis and sciatica in the system of the universe, the squandered flowing of those precious fountains, would spell no improvement of the world but the reverse.

Next to this somewhat theological explanation, let us consider the psychological one. Which of us guests at the spa, in addition to the baths and massages, the worry and the boredom, would be willing to stand fasting and mortification as well? No, we prefer to become just half well and in compensation to have things a bit more comfortable and pleasant; we are not youngsters making unqualified demands on ourselves and others but older people deeply enmeshed in the limitations of life, accustomed to being not overparticular. And let us seriously consider the question: Would it be proper and desirable for each one of us to be made well, to be made completely and wholly well through an ideal cure, and never to need to die? If we consider this question conscientiously, the answer will be: No. No, we do not want to be entirely well, we do not want to live forever.

To be sure, each one of us, if asked about himself alone, might perhaps answer yes instead. If I, the writer Hesse, a patient at the spa, were asked whether I agreed that the writer Hesse should be spared sickness and death, whether I considered his eternal continuance good, desirable, and necessary, I would, vain as writers are, perhaps answer the question first by saying yes. But as soon as this same question was put to me in regard to others, the patient Müller, the sciatic Legrand, and the Dutchman in No. 64, I would very quickly decide upon no. No, it is in fact not necessary that we elderly, no longer very beautiful people should live on endlessly, even without arthritis. It would even be deadly, it would be very boring, very ugly. No, we will gladly die, later on. But for today we prefer, after the fatiguing baths, after the laboriously murdered forenoon, to indulge in a bit of comfort, to nibble on a chicken wing, remove the skin from a good fish, down a glass of red wine. That's the way we are, cowardly and weak and self-indulgent, old, egoistic people. That is our psychology and since our soul, that of rheumatic and elderly people, is also the soul of Baden, we see the Baden tradition of dining justified from that point of view as well.

Now is that enough proof, enough justification for our high living? Are other reasons required? There are hundreds more. Let a single, very simple additional one be mentioned: the mineral baths "deplete" one; that is, they make you hungry. And since I am not simply a guest at the spa and a gourmand but at other times seek the opposite pole and know the joys of fasting, it does not weigh on my conscience to join in this gluttony for the space of three weeks, even in the face of a starving world and at the expense of my metabolism.

I have gone far afield. Let us return to the day's routine.

I am sitting there at the luncheon table, I watch the fish, the roast, the fruit follow one another, in the intervals I stare long and thoughtfully at the legs of the waitresses, all in black stockings, I stare thoughtfully but not so long at the legs of the headwaiter. They (the legs of the headwaiter) are a precious sight and a great comfort to all of us patients. This waiter, you must know, a very agreeable gentleman by the way, once suffered from extremely severe and painful rheumatism so that he was no longer able to walk, and through a course at Baden was completely cured. All of us know this, to many of us he has told it himself. That is why we often stare so thoughtfully at the headwaiter's legs. The legs of the young waitresses, however, in black stockings, are slim and agile of themselves without benefit of any cure, and this seems to us worthy of even deeper reflection.

Since I live completely alone, mealtimes are the only occasions for me to become somewhat better acquainted with my fellow guests. Their names, to be sure, I do not know and I have exchanged only a few words with them, but I see them sitting and eating and I learn a good deal. The Dutchman, my next-door neighbor, whose voice coming through the wall every evening and morning robs me of sleep for hours, here at table converses in such low tones that I would never recognize his voice if it did not come from No. 64! Oh, gentle youth!

Some figures in our midday theater entertain me daily by the sharpness of their outlines and the definiteness of their roles. There is a giantess from Holland here, more than six feet tall and extremely heavy, majestic in appearance, worthy to play the part of Princess of the spa. Her posture is regal but her movements leave something to be desired; she makes an oddly coquettish and disquieting, almost terrifying appearance when she enters the hall supported on a delicate, thin, ornamental cane which one expects to see break at any moment. But perhaps it is made of iron.

Then there is a dreadfully serious gentleman here, I wager he is at least a member of the national assembly, moral, manly, and patriotic through and through, his lower eyelids somewhat red and drooping like those of the loyal St. Bernard, the back of his neck broad and stiff, unflinching under any blow, his forehead full of wrinkles, his wallet full of well-earned and carefully counted bank notes, his breast full of unexceptionable, high but intolerant ideals. Once during a dreadful night I dreamed that this man was my father and I was standing in front of him having to answer, first, for lack of patriotism; second, for a gambling loss of fifty francs; third, for having seduced a girl. On the day after this deadly dream I was most anxious to encounter the physical presence of the gentleman before whom I had shuddered so in my dream. A sight of him would cure me, for reality is, of course, so much more harmless than the images of our nightmares, the man would perhaps smile at me or nod to me or crack a joke with the waitress, or at least through his bodily appearance correct the caricature of my dream. But when midday came and I saw that stern gentleman again in the dining room, he did not nod or smile at me, he sat glowering in front of his bottle of red wine, and every fold in his forehead and the back of his neck expressed inexorable morality and determination, and I was dreadfully afraid of him, and in the evening I prayed that I might not have to dream about him again.

On the other hand, how noble, how lovable, how full of charm is Herr Kesselring, a man in the prime of life, his occupation unknown to me, a hidalgo no doubt, or something of the sort. His light blond, silky hair lies in waves around his clear forehead, delicately alluring is the merry dimple in his cheek, his bright blue child's eye bespeaks enthusiasm and enchantment, his lyric hand glides delicately over his elegantly colored waistcoat. No falsity can lodge in this bosom, no base impulse stain the nobility of these poetic features. Rosy from top to toe as a girl by Renoir, Kesselring in his younger years may well have taken part in the roguish games of Cupid, the noble fellow. But how this sweet lad shocked and disillusioned me when in a twilight hour in the smoking room he showed me a small pocket collection of pornographic pictures, words fail me to say.

But the most interesting and handsomest guest I have ever seen in this hall is not present today, I saw him only once when he sat opposite me at my little round table all evening long with his merry brown eyes and slender, clever hands, a lonesome flower of youth and luster among all the patients. Dear companion, come back so that we can eat this good food together, savor the good wine, and brighten the hall with our tales and our laughter!

We guests check up on one another as is customary at any summer resort, only fashion and elegance play a minor rolc hcrc. All the more avidly do we keep track of the health of our fellow patients, for in them we see ourselves reflected, and if the aged gentleman in No. 6 has a good day and is able to walk by himself from his door to the table, it cheers us all, and all of us shake our heads regretfully if we hear that Frau Flury cannot leave her bed today.

Then after we have eaten well and looked at one another for an hour, we reluctantly give up this pleasure and leave the hall of our satisfaction. For me the easier part of the day now begins. In good weather I go into the hotel garden, where I have a deck chair placed in a hidden spot, my notebook and pencil and a volume of Jean Paul beside it. At three or four o'clock I usually have "my treatment," which means that I must appear at the doctor's and be attended to by his assistants in accordance with the most modern methods. I sit under a quartz lamp, longing to make the utmost use of the solar powers of this magic lantern and to bring the most ailing parts of my body as close as possible to the touchhole. A few times I have burned myself in doing so. Further on, the doctor's indefatigable associate for diathermy fastens little pads, electrical contacts, to my wrists and turns the current on while at the same time she belabors my neck and back with two similar pads, and I have nothing to do but cry out if it burns too much. During this treatment there is also the possibility—an added attraction—that the doctor will come in and we will have a conversation; if this hope is unfulfilled nineteen out of twenty days, it nevertheless is something to consider.

I decide on a short walk, and as I pass the gate of the spa garden I see from the numbers of people that up in the casino there must be another of the many concerts going on; they occur regularly, and I have not yet heard a single one. And so I go in and find in the casino a very large audience assembled, and it is the first time I have come upon the patients here *in corpore*, so to speak. Hundreds of my colleagues, male and female, are sitting there in chairs, some with tea or coffee in front of them, others provided with books or knitting needles, listening to a small company of musicians who in the far reaches of the hall are playing vigorously. For some time I stand in the doorway looking and listening, for there is no empty chair. I see the musicians at work playing complicated pieces, mostly by unknown composers, and it is not the quality of their playing that fails to rouse any sympathy for their performance in me. The musicians, as a matter of fact, do their part very well—and for that very reason I wish they would play decent music instead of all these clever pieces, extracts, and arrangements. And yet I don't really wish this either. I would not be a bit happier if, instead of this entertaining bit from *Carmen* or *Die Fleder-*

maus, a Schubert quartet or a duo by Handel were being played. For God's sake, that would be even worse. I once had to endure that in similar circumstances when the first violinist of a café orchestra was playing Bach's *Chaconne* in a sparsely filled hall, and while he played, my ear noted the following simultaneous sounds: two gentlemen paying the waitress their check and the small coins being counted out on the table; an energetic lady noisily reclaiming her umbrella at the cloakroom; an enchanting youngster about four years old entertaining a tableful with his shrill chirping; bottles and glasses, cups and spoons in continuous use; and an old lady with poor eyesight pushing a plate of pastries off the edge of the table and badly frightening herself. Each one of these incidents by itself was a valid occurrence worthy of my sympathy and attention, but the simultaneous assault and solicitation of so many auditory impressions were more than I felt psychically up to. And the music was to blame for this. Bach's *Chaconne*—it was this alone that was disturbing—no, all respect to the musicians in the casino! But for me this concert lacked the principal thing: meaning. That two hundred people are bored and do not know how to get through the afternoon is no adequate reason in my eyes for good musicians to play arrangements from well-known operas. What was lacking in this concert was simply the heart, the soul: the necessity, the living need, the tension of souls waiting for release through art. I could, however, be mistaken about this. At any rate, I soon see that even this rather stolid audience is not a homogeneous crowd but consists of many individual souls and one of these souls is reacting to the musicians with the greatest sensibility. In the front of the hall, very close to the podium, sits a passionate friend of music, a gentleman with a black beard and golden pince-nez who is leaning far back in his chair, eyes closed, drunkenly swaying his handsome head in time to the music, and when a piece comes to an end he starts up, suddenly opens his eyes and bursts into the first salvo of applause. Not content with clapping, he gets up and steps to the podium, manages to get the attention of the bandmaster, and overwhelms him with enthusiastic praise amid the continuing applause of the crowd.

Tired of standing and less carried away by the music than the bearded enthusiast is, I am considering leaving during the second intermission, when I hear a puzzling sound from the next room. I question a sciatic beside me and learn that that is the gambling hall. Delightedly I hurry over. Right. There stand the palms and the round plush seats in the corners of the room, and at a big green table roulette is being played. I make my way toward the table, which is surrounded by a crowd of curious onlookers between whose shoulders I am able to observe part of the proceedings. My eye is caught first of all by the master of the table, a clean-shaven gentleman in a frock coat, of no discernible age, with brown hair and a quiet philosophical mien, who possesses astonishing skill in whisking coins like lightning from any square on the table to any other, with one hand and the aid of a strangely elastic stick or rake. He manipulates the flexible coin rake like a very skillful trout fisherman handling his rod, and also he can pitch the coins in an arc through the air so that they land exactly on the right square. And during all this activity—its rhythm controlled by the cries of his young assistant, who looks after the ball—the quiet, clean-shaven, rosy face under the brown, somewhat lifeless hair remains consistently calm and expressionless. For a long time I watch him sitting there immobile on his oddly constructed little chair with an inclined seat, I watch how only the darting eyes move in his expressionless face, how he pitches the coins out playfully with his left hand and playfully with his right hand gathers them in with the rake and whisks them into the corners. In front of him stand piles of big and small silver coins, even Stinnes cannot have more. Again and again his assistant tosses in the ball that rolls into a numbered hole, urges the crowd to play, announces that the bets have been made, warns "*Rien ne va plus*," and the solemn master of the table goes on playing and working. I had seen this often years before, in the faraway legendary time before the war, in the years of my travels and wanderings, in many cities of the world I had seen those palms and upholstered seats, those green tables and balls, and then I had thought of the handsome, flushed gamblers' faces of Turgenev and Dostoevsky and I had turned away. Here, one thing struck me as I stood looking on—the whole game was being carried on solely for the entertainment of the gentleman in the frock coat. He threw down his coins, pushed them from 5 to 7, from even to odd, paid out what was won, raked in what was lost, but it was all his money. Not one of the onlookers made a bet. All were patients at the spa, mostly from rural districts, who followed with delight and great admiration, just as I did, the gyrations of the philosopher and listened to the cries of his assistant, in French and icy cold. When I, seized by pity, put down two francs on the corner of the table nearest me, fifty startled eyes were turned upon me and so upset me that I could hardly wait for my francs to disappear under the rake so that I could rapidly depart.

Today I also spend some minutes in front of the store windows on Badestrasse. In a number of shops there, the guests at the spa can buy those articles that seem to be indispensable to them, postcards, bronze lions and lizards, ashtrays with portraits of famous men (so that the buyer can, for example, amuse himself daily by crushing out his burning cigar in Richard Wagner's eye), and many other objects about which I venture no opinion since despite long observation I have been unable to fathom their nature and purpose; many of them seem suited to the cult needs of primitive tribes, but this may be a mistake, and all of them together make me sad, for they show me all too clearly that, despite the best will to be sociable, I nevertheless live outside the middle-class real world, know nothing about it, and despite all my years of writing effort, will never really be able to understand it any more than I can make myself understandable to it. When I look into these show windows displaying not things of everyday need but so-called gifts, luxury items, and jokes, then the foreignness of this world horrifies me; among a hundred objects there are twenty or thirty whose intention, meaning, and use I can only vaguely discern, and there is no single one I can imagine worth having. There are some that make me wonder for a long time: Do you put it in your hat? Or in your pocket? Or in a glass of beer? Or does it belong to some kind of card game? There are pictures and inscriptions, mottoes and quotations that come from worlds of the imagination completely unknown and inaccessible to me, and again there are revered and well-known symbols used in a way that I can neither understand nor excuse. The carved figure of Buddha or some Chinese divinity, for example, on the handle of a lady's parasol is and remains for me puzzling, alien, and distressing, yes, uncanny; it can hardly be a conscious and intentional sacrilege—but what notion, need, or state of soul moves suppliers to make and buyers to purchase these idiotic objects, this is what I would be eager to know and what I cannot in any way discover. Or take a fashionable coffeehouse where people gather around five o'clock! I can fully understand that wealthy people might find pleasure in drinking tea, coffee, and chocolate with whipped cream accompanied by expensive, delicate pastries. But why free men in possession of their faculties should allow their enjoyment of these things to be disturbed by an intrusive, insinuating, oversweet music, by unspeakably uninviting, narrow, and uncomfortable seats in narrow, overfilled rooms crowded with superfluous ornaments and decorations, or why they should experience these things not as disturbances, discomforts, and contradictions but rather as something to be liked and sought after—this I shall never fathom, and I have got used to ascribing my failing to my, as remarked, slightly schizophrenic mentality. But again and again it worries me. And the same wealthy and elegant people who sit in these cafés hindered from talking by sticky-sweet music, from thinking, almost from breathing, surrounded by thick clotted luxury, by marble, silver, rugs, mirrors, these same people listen in the evening with apparent delight to a lecture about the noble simplicity of the Japanese way of life and have on their tables at home the legends of monks and the sermons of Buddha beautifully printed and bound. I certainly do not wish to be a zealot or a moralist, I am even easily tempted by many daring and dangerous sins, and I am pleased when people are happy, for it is pleasanter to live with happy people—but are these people really happy? Is all the marble, whipped cream, and music really worth anything? Don't these same people, with plates full of fine, delectable cuisine, set in front of them by liveried servants, don't they read in their newspapers reports of famine, rebellion, shootings, executions? Beyond the huge plate-glass windows of these coffeehouses is there not a world full of bleeding poverty and despair, full of madness and suicide, fear and horror? Well, yes, I know all this has to be, that all is in some way right, and God wills it so. But it is something I know only in the way one knows the multiplication table. It is not a convincing sort of knowledge. In truth, I find all this not right at all or according to God's will, but mad and horrible.

Troubled in my mind, I turn toward the stores where picture postcards are displayed. Here I know my way about very well, I venture to say that I have studied the picture postcards of Baden in a fairly exhaustive fashion, all in an attempt to gain a better knowledge of the average patient at the spa, to judge his psyche from this symptom of his needs. There is quite a collection of pretty pictures of scenes of old Baden, also of old paintings and etchings of bathing scenes from which one can see that in earlier times in Baden bathing was approached less seriously, less circumspectly, and perhaps less hygienically than today, but by way of compensation life and bathing were decidedly more enjoyable. And all these old scenes with their towers and gables, their fashions, give one a slight feeling of homesickness, although naturally one would not want to have lived in those times. These pictures of cities, of street scenes, of the baths, whether from the sixteenth or eighteenth century, silently and softly radiate the quiet sorrow that is intrinsic to all such pictures, for everything in them is beautiful, over everything peace seems to reign between nature and men, houses and trees seem not to be at war with one another. Beauty and uniformity enfold everything, from the alder coppice to the gowns of the shepherdesses, from the crenelated gates to the bridges and fountains and even to the slender hound pissing against an Empire column. You find things that are funny, stupid, vain in many of these little pictures but you find nothing ugly, nothing strident; the houses stand next to one another like fieldstones or like birds perched in a row on a railing, while in present-day cities almost every house screeches at the others, competes with them, tries to shove them away.

And I remember how once my beloved, at a beautiful banquet where everyone was wearing costumes of Mozart's time, suddenly had tears in her eyes, and when I questioned her in dismay she said: "Why must everything be so ugly nowadays?" I comforted her by saying that our life was by no means worse, that it was freer, richer, and larger than in those days, that under the pretty perukes there were lice and behind the splendor of the mirrored halls and the chandeliers there were hungry and oppressed people, and that it was all to the good that we had preserved from those times only what was most beautiful—the memory of their cheery Sunday side.

But it is not every day that one is so sensible.

To return to the postcards: in this part of the country there is a special category of picture postals that are not lacking in originality. In popular parlance the region is called Turnip Land, and various series of pictures show folk scenes of every sort, scenes from school, from army life, family excursions, fistfights, and all the people in these pictures are represented as turnips. You see turnip lovers, turnip duels, turnip congresses. These cards enjoy, no doubt deservedly, great popularity, and yet even they do not cheer me up. Along with the historical views and the turnip pictures, a third large category must be mentioned, that of erotic scenes. In this field, one would think something could be accomplished, some quality, some sap, some bloom could be introduced into the dingy world of shop windows by pictures of this kind. But I had to give up on them after the first few days. I was astounded to see that love life in this picture world was treated much too summarily. All the hundreds of pictures in this category distinguished themselves by a lamentable innocence and bashfulness. Here, too, I was way off the track of what would appear to be the popular taste, for if someone had given me the assignment of collecting representations of love life, I would certainly have assembled completely different pictures. In those displayed here, there was neither the pathos of pure eroticism nor the poetry of the half-hidden game, but the prevailing atmosphere of sweet, bashful betrothal; the many pairs of lovers were carefully and modishly dressed, the bridegrooms frequently in morning coats and high hats, bouquets of flowers in their hands, sometimes in addition the moon was shining, and under the picture there was a verse to explain the situation. For example:

O beauteous creature, by the light of the moon,
In thine eyes I see mirrored my longed-for boon.

I was much disillusioned; obviously the manufacturer of these postcards was aware of only the conventional and uninteresting aspect of love. Nevertheless, I noted some of the verses as examples of popular poetry in our time. This, for example:

Hand in hand with my dearest one,
That's my ideal of soul's holy union.

Lacking in genius though the verse may appear to us, it was classical in comparison with the picture it accompanied. A young girl, whose head had obviously been borrowed from a wax model in a hairdresser's shop, was sitting on a bench under a tree, and a young gentleman in fine attire was standing in front of her, busily putting on or taking off his gloves.

And so today I stood again for a while in front of these pictures and since I felt desolation and boredom and a strong, burning desire to get this whole world of doubtless laudable concerts, gamblers, conventional lovers, and turnip pictures behind me, I shut my eyes and in my heart beseeched God for rescue, for I felt that I was not far from an attack of that deep disillusionment and dull disgust with life which, to my sorrow, always overwhelm me just when I am attempting in all good faith and seriousness to eschew my solitary, hermit ways and share the joys and sorrows of the majority.

And God helped me. Hardly had I shut my eyes and turned my heart away from the world of spas and turnips, full of inner longing for a word, a sound from those other spheres, better known to me and more holy, when the rescuing inspiration came. In our hotel there was a remote corner not known to all the guests where our host, who had many such amiable ideas, had put two young martens in a wire cage of humane dimensions. Suddenly I felt a longing to see the martens, surrendered to it blindly, and hurried back to the hotel to look for the animals' cage. No sooner had I reached them than everything was all right, I had found exactly the thing I needed at that critical moment. The two beautiful, noble creatures, trustful and curious as children, were easily coaxed out of their den, raced about intoxicated by their strength and nimbleness, making wild leaps through the wide cage and then stopping close to me at the wire, breathing heavily through their rosy snouts and snuffling warmly and moistly at my hand. I needed nothing more. To look into those clear animal eyes, to see those splendid, furred masterpieces, those thoughts of God, to feel their warm living breath, to smell their sharp, wild, predatory-animal scent—that sufficed to convince me of the unimpaired existence of all planets and fixed stars, all palm forests and tropical rivers. The martens were my guarantee of this, something for which the sight of any cloud, of any blade of green grass, should have been sufficient evidence; but I had had need of just this stronger proof.

The martens were more potent than the picture postcards, than the concerts, than the gambling hall. As long as there were still martens, still the scent of the primeval world, still instinct and nature, so long was the world still possible for a poet, still beautiful and full of promise. With a deep breath I felt the nightmare disappear, laughed at myself, fetched a piece of sugar for the martens and, freed once more, wandered out into the evening. The sun was already nearing the line of forest-covered mountains, blue sky lightly covered by thin golden cloud shone bright and childlike over the valley of my errors; smiling, I felt my good hours approaching, thought of my beloved, toyed with emerging verses, felt music, sensed happiness and adoration flowing through the world, reverently cast from me all the burdens of the day, swung myself—bird, butterfly, fish, cloud—across into the happy, transitory, childlike world of forms.

I will make no report here about that evening, on which I returned home late, tired and happy. My whole sciatic's philosophy might fall to pieces if I did. Happy, weary, and singing, I came back and, behold, even sleep did not flee me that night, even sleep, that timorous bird, confidently approached and bore me away on blue wings into paradise.

THE DUTCHMAN

For a long time I have been trying to force myself to write this chapter. Now I must do it.

Two weeks ago when, with such care and prudence, I picked out my hotel room, No. 65, I had on the whole made not a bad choice. The wallpaper is bright and agreeable, the bed stands in an alcove, and the room in general pleases me because of its unusual and original proportions, its good light, and its view out over the river and vineyards. Since it is on the top floor of the building, there is no one above me, and noises from the street are hardly audible. I had chosen well. I had also been reassured when I asked who was in the adjacent rooms. On one side lived an old lady, from whom I have heard nothing at all. But on the other side in No. 64 lived the Dutchman! In the course of twelve days, in the course of twelve bitter nights, this gentleman has become extremely important, much too important, he has become for me a legendary figure, an idol, a demon and a ghost whom I have overcome only in the past few days.

No one to whom I might point him out would believe me. This gentleman from Holland who has interfered with my work, who has kept me from sleeping nights, is neither a madman gone berserk nor an enthusiastic musician, he does not come in drunk at unexpected hours, or beat his wife or quarrel with her, he doesn't whistle or sing, in fact he doesn't even snore, or at least not loud enough for me to hear. He is a solid, law-abiding, no longer young man, he lives as regularly as a clock and has no conspicuous bad habits—how is it possible that this ideal citizen should make me suffer so?

But it is possible, it is, alas, a fact. The two chief points, the reasons for my misery, are these: between rooms Nos. 64 and 65 there is a door; it is, to be sure, a closed door, it is also locked, and barricaded with a table, but it is by no means a thick door. This is a misfortune, it cannot be done away with. The second is worse: the Dutchman has a wife. She too cannot be got out of the world or out of No. 64 by any lawful means. And then too, there is the unusual misfortune that my neighbor, like myself, belongs to the comparatively small number of hotel guests who spend the greater part of their days in their rooms.

Now if I had a wife with me, or if I were a singing teacher or had a piano or violin, a bugle, a cannon, or a kettledrum, I could take up the battle against the Dutchman with some hope of success. But the situation is this: during the twenty-four hours of the day the Dutch couple hear from me no sound, they are treated by me the way kings and the gravely ill are treated, they are continuously granted the unimaginable favor of complete and absolute silence. And how do they repay this favor? They give me a daily reprieve of six hours by sleeping each night from twelve to six o'clock in the morning. I have those hours to devote to work, to sleep, to prayer or meditation. Over the remaining eighteen hours of the day I have no control whatever, they do not belong to me, in a certain sense these daily eighteen hours do not exist in my room but only in No. 64. For eighteen hours of the day in No. 64 there is talking and laughter, toilets are made, visitors received. There is no shooting off of firearms or playing of music, nor do fistfights take place, this I must admit. Neither is there any reflection, any reading, any meditation, any silence. Continuously the river of their conversation flows on, often there are four or five people in there, and in the evenings the couple chat together until eleven-thirty. Then comes the clattering of glass and china, the brushing of teeth, the moving of a few chairs, and the melody of gargling. Then the beds creak, then it is quiet (let this be once more acknowledged) until about six in the morning, at which time one of the pair, I do not know whether he or she, gets up and makes thc floor shake. He goes to the bathroom, returns shortly thereafter; meanwhile, the hour for my bath has come, and from the time I get back, the flood of conversation, the rustlings, laughter, moving of furniture, and so forth go on uninterrupted until shortly before midnight.

Now if I were a reasonable, normal human being like others, I could easily adjust myself to this situation. Since two are stronger than one, I would give up, would spend the day somewhere other than in my room, in the reading room or the smoking room, in the corridors, in the casino, in the restaurants, as most of the guests do. And at night I would simply sleep. Instead, I am obsessed by the laborious, silly, and irritating passion of spending many daytime hours alone at my desk, struggling to think, struggling to write, often only to destroy afterward what I have written; and at night I have, of course, a great and burning desire for sleep, but falling to sleep is for me a complicated, twilight process which takes hours, and even then my sleep is very light, very thin and delicate, a breath is enough to tear it to pieces. And if at ten, at eleven o'clock, I am dead tired and very close to slumber, I nevertheless cannot fall asleep as long as next door the Dutch couple carry on their social life. And while I wait, exhausted and yearning for midnight to come, for the man from The Hague to grant me permission to fall asleep at last, the waiting, the listening, and thinking of tomorrow's work have got me so wide awake and excited that the greater part of the hours of quiet granted to me pass before I can finally go to sleep.

Need I say explicitly that I know how unjustified I am in demanding of the Dutchman that he let me sleep more? Need I say that I am very well aware that he is not responsible for my bad sleeping or my intellectual inclinations? I write these notes on Baden, however, not to accuse others or to exculpate myself but to record experiences, even though they are the strangely distorted experiences of a psychopath. That other more complex question about the justification of the psychopath, that dreadful, shocking question as to whether under certain conditions of time and culture it is not more dignified, more proper to be a psychopath than to adapt oneself to circumstances of the time at the sacrifice of all ideals—this nasty question, the question for all discriminating minds since Nietzsche, I shall leave untouched in these pages; in any case, it is the theme of almost all my writings.

And so in the circumstances recounted above, the Dutchman became a problem for me. I cannot entirely explain to myself why in thought and word I am always concerned with just the Dutchman in the singular. There are, after all, a couple—two of them. But whether out of instinctive gallantry I feel more tolerance toward the woman than toward the man, or whether the man's voice and rather heavy footfall are really the things that particularly distress me, it is in any case not "she," it is "he," the Dutchman, who makes me suffer. In part, this instinctive omission of the woman from my feelings of hatred and my mythologizing of the man into a foe, an adversary, rests on very deep elementary impulses: the Dutchman, the man of lusty good health, of prosperous appearance, of dignified deportment and fat wallet, is for me the outsider, an enemy by reason of his very type.

He is a gentleman of about forty-three, average height, powerful, somewhat squat build, giving an impression of health and normality. Face and body are round and chubby, though not conspicuously so. The great, imposing head with its rather heavy eyelids seems to press down massively on the body since it rests on a short, barely visible neck. Although he moves sedately and has admirable manners, his heartiness and bodily weight unfortunately make his movements and footsteps more emphatic and audible than is desirable in a neighbor. His voice is deep and even, not varying much in tone or volume, the whole personality impartially considered makes a serious, reliable, reassuring, almost sympathetic impression. On the disturbing side, however, is the fact that he is subject to minor colds (this is true of all the guests at the spa) which make him cough and sneeze violently; and in these sounds a certain vigor and exuberance find expression.

And so this gentleman from The Hague has the misfortune to be my neighbor, by day the enemy, the menace, and often the destroyer of my intellectual labor, during part of the night the enemy and destroyer of my sleep. To be sure, I did not find his existence a punishment and a burden on every single day. There were a number of warm sunny days which allowed me to take my work outdoors; in a remote little grove in the hotel garden, my portfolio on my knees, I filled pages with my writing, thought my thoughts, pursued my dreams, or contentedly read my Jean Paul. But on the cool rainy days, and there were a great many of them, I saw myself all day long face to face with my enemy beyond the wall; while I hung over my desk concentrating in silence on my work, the Dutchman rushed up and down, spat in the basin, threw himself into his chair, conversed with his wife, laughed over jokes with her, entertained company. For me these were often very troubled hours. However, I was enormously helped by my work itself. I am no hero of labor and deserve no prize for diligence, but once I have allowed myself to be caught up in a vision or a sequence of ideas, if after due resistance I have involved myself in the attempt to give these thoughts a form, then I am dogged in keeping at it and aware of nothing that might otherwise seem important to me. There were hours when all Holland could have been celebrating a church festival in No. 64 and I would hardly have noticed it, for I was enchanted and swept away by the lonely, fantastic, absorbing game of solitaire, I raced breathlessly after my thoughts with frantic pen, constructed sentences, chose among a flood of associations, angled persistently for the suitable word. The reader may laugh, but for us writers, writing is every time a mad, exciting business, a voyage in a tiny craft on the high seas, a solitary flight through the universe. While one seeks to choose the single word among three that present themselves, at the same time struggling to hold the feeling and tone of the whole sentence he is constructing—while forging the sentence into the selected structure and tightening the bolts of the edifice, he strives at the same time to keep in mind the tone and proportion of the whole book; that is an exciting activity. I know from personal experience only a single other activity that has a similar tension and concentration; that is, painting. There it is the same: to blend each individual color with its neighboring color properly and carefully is pleasant and easy, one can learn to do it and then practice it at any time. Over and beyond that, however, to have really before one's mind the as yet unpainted and invisible parts of the whole picture and to take them into account, to experience the whole fine network of intersecting vibrations, that is astonishingly difficult and seldom succeeds.

It is in the nature of literary work to make such a heavy demand on concentration that a writer in the grip of an intense creative impulse can quite well overcome outside hindrances and disturbances. The author who seems to be able to work only in a comfortable chair, in the best light, with his own accustomed writing materials, special paper, and so forth, is suspect in my eyes. Of course, we do look instinctively for all alleviations and conveniences, but when they are not to be had, you go ahead without them. And so I often succeeded in writing a protective distance or isolating wall between me and No. 64, which shielded me for a productive hour. However, the moment I began to grow weary, something which the cumulative lack of sleep contributed to greatly, the disturbances next door were there again.

The situation was much worse with sleep than with work. I am not going to explain here my purely psychologically based theory of insomnia. I will only say that the temporary immunity against Holland, my concentrating away of No. 64, now and again succeeded while I worked, with the help of the winged powers, but my attempts to sleep did not share this good fortune.

No, the insomniac, if he has been a victim of his suffering for a considerable period, like most other people in a situation of advanced nervous exhaustion, directs feelings of rejection, of hatred, yes, of the wish to destroy, against himself as well as against his immediate surroundings. Since for me the immediate surroundings consisted exclusively of Holland, during these sleepless nights there slowly accumulated feelings of rejection, bitterness, hatred against Holland, feelings that could not be dissipated during the day since the tension and the disturbance went on steadily. If I was lying in bed, sleepless because of the Dutchman, if, feverish from exhaustion and unsatisfied yearnings for rest, I heard the Dutchman next door striding with his heavy, firm, solid strides, making his firm, vigorous movements, speaking in his powerful voice, then I felt for him a quite vehement hatred.

Nevertheless, even in the midst of these episodes, I remained to some degree aware of the stupidity of my hatred, could always now and again smile for a few moments at my hatred and thereby dull its point. But the situation became deadly when the impersonal hatred directed only against the disturbances to my sleep, against my own nervousness, against the thin door, became in the course of the day more and more impossible to neutralize and differentiate, when it gradually grew more and more foolish, one-sided, and personal. Finally, it no longer helped for me to tell myself that the Dutchman was personally innocent. I simply hated *him*, not only when late at night his heavy steps, his talk and laughter were perhaps actually inconsiderate, no, I now really and truly hated him with that genuine, naïve, stupid hatred with which an unsuccessful little Christian storekeeper hates the Jews or a Communist hates the capitalists, with the stupid, animal, unreasoning, essentially cowardly or envious kind of hatred I always so much deplore in others, which poisons politics, business, and public life, and of which I had considered myself incapable. I no longer hated simply the Dutchman's cough, his voice, but himself, his actual person, and if during the day he encountered me somewhere, contented and unsuspecting, for me the meeting was with an out-and-out enemy and malefactor, and it took all my philosophy to keep me from giving vent to my feelings. His smooth, happy face, his heavy eyelids, his thick happy lips, his belly beneath the stylish waistcoat, his walk and deportment, all these together were obnoxious and hateful to me, and most of all I hated the innumerable indications of his strength, health, and indestructibility, his laughter, his good humor, the energy of his movements, the superior indifference of his glance, all such evidences of his biological and social superiority. Naturally, it was easy to be healthy and cheerful and to play the part of self-satisfied gentleman if day and night one preyed upon the sleep, the strength, of others, if one constantly gulped down and relished the quiet behavior, the self-control of his neighbors, day and night according to his whim making the air in the house quiver with the tones and vibrations of his voice. May the devil take this gentleman from Holland! Dimly I recalled, too, the flying Dutchman—had not he too been a damnable demon and spirit of torment? Especially, however, I remembered that other Dutchman whom the poet Multatuli once described, that fat gourmand and moneygrubber whose wealth and cheery bonhomie were derived from the exploitation of Malayans. Brave Multatuli!

Friends of mine who are intimately acquainted with my way of thinking and feeling, with my beliefs and the life of my imagination, will be able to understand how I suffered in this undignified situation, how seriously this compulsive hatred for an innocent man, unsanctioned by my heart, troubled and tormented me—and indeed, not because of the innocence of my "enemy" and the injustice I was doing him but principally because of the unreasonableness of my behavior, the profound fundamental contradiction between my actual feelings and everything that I knew, believed, and revered. To be specific, I believe in nothing in the world so deeply, no conception is so holy to me, as unity, the conviction that everything in the world forms a divine whole, that the "I" takes itself too seriously. I had suffered much pain in my life, had done much that was stupid and unpleasant, but again and again I had managed to free myself, to forget my "I" and yield to the feeling of oneness, to recognize that the division between inner and outer, between "I" and the world, is an illusion and to enter willingly with closed eyes into the unity. It had never been easy for me, no one could have less talent for the holy than I; nevertheless, again and again I had encountered that miracle to which the Christian theologians have given the beautiful name of "grace," that divine experience of reconciliation, of ceasing to rebel, of willing agreement, which is indeed nothing other than the Christian surrender of the "I" and the Hindu realization of unity. And now here I was once more so completely outside that unity, a separate suffering, hating, hostile I. To be sure, there were others in the same case, I was not alone, the entire lives of millions of people were a battle, a warlike self-assertion of the I against the world around them, to whom the idea of unity, of love, of harmony, was unknown and would have seemed alien, silly, and weak; yes, all the practical average religion of modern man consisted in the glorification of the I and its battles. But to feel comfortable in this exaltation of the I and its battles was possible only for the naïve, strong, unbroken creatures of nature; to the wise, to those who had gained vision through pain, to minds that had grown discriminating through suffering, it was forbidden to find happiness in this battle, for them happiness was conceivable only through surrender of the I, through experience of the unity. Oh, to be sure, those simple-minded people who loved themselves and hated their enemies, those patriots who never needed to doubt themselves because, for all the misery and mischief in their country, they were never to blame, but naturally it was the French or the Russians or the Jews—no matter who, only always someone else—they were the "enemy"! Perhaps these people, nine tenths of all the people alive, were actually happy in their barbaric, primitive religion, perhaps they really lived enviably happy and easy lives in their armor of stupidity and extremely shrewd aversion to thought—although to me this was highly doubtful, for where was there a common measuring rod for their happiness and for mine, for their sufferings and for mine?

It was a long, an agonizingly long night in which I thought these thoughts. I lay in bed hot and exhausted, a victim to the Dutchman next door, who coughed and spat, rushed up and down; with my eyes strained from long reading (what else was I to do?) I felt that now, definitely, there must be an end to this situation, to this torment and outrage. Hardly had this clarity, this conviction or decision, flashed through my mind, bright and cold as morning sunshine, hardly had I taken a stand clear and firm before my soul—"This must immediately be endured to the end and brought to a conclusion"—than at once the usual vulgar fantasies well known to every sufferer from nerves in moments of especial pain bobbed up in my head. Only two ways, so it seemed, could lead out of this miserable situation, I had to choose between them: either to kill myself or to have it out with the Dutchman, seize him by the throat and conquer him. (Just then he was coughing again with impressive energy.) Both ideas were beautiful and soothing, if somewhat childish. There was attraction in the notion of doing away with oneself by one of the usual, oft-considered methods, accompanied by the characteristic suicide's feeling: "It will serve you right if I now cut my throat." Attractive, too, was the other idea: instead of attacking myself, to seize the Dutchman, choke him or shoot him dead and survive as victor over his brutal, undiscerning vitality.

These naïve fantasies of doing away either with myself or my enemy were, however, soon played out. One could give oneself up to them for a while, seek refuge in wishful imaginings which quickly wilted and lost their magic; after a short wandering through these mazes, the wish lost its power and I had to admit that my desires were simply momentary exaltations, that I did not really want my extinction or that of the Dutchman. His removal would be quite sufficient. Now I tried to picture that removal. I turned on the light, got my travel guide out of the night-table drawer and took the pains to put together a flawless travel plan by which the Dutchman could leave early next morning and reach his home as quickly as possible. This occupation gave me some pleasure; I saw him getting up in the dismal cold of the early morning, heard him for the last time making his toilet in No. 64, pulling on his boots, slamming the door, shivering as he was driven to the station; I saw him get on the train, quarreling that morning at eight o'clock with the customs men at Basel, and the farther my wishful thinking took him the better I felt. But by the time he reached Paris my powers of imagination were flagging, and the whole picture fell to pieces long before my man reached the Netherlands frontier.

But these were mere pastimes. The enemy, the enemy in myself, was not to be overcome in so simple, so inexpensive a fashion. It was not a matter of taking vengeance of some sort on the Dutchman, it was simply a question of achieving a positive attitude toward him that was worthy of myself. The task was perfectly clear: I had to tear down my meaningless hatred, I had to love the Dutchman. Then let him spit and rumble, I would be superior to him, I would be proof against him. If I succeeded in loving him, then all his health, all his vitality, would no longer be of any help to him, then he would be mine, his image would no longer be in opposition to the idea of unity. To work, then, the goal was worth it; it was up to me to make good use of my sleepless night!

Simple though the task was, it was equally difficult, and I literally spent almost all that night solving it. I had to transform the Dutchman, remodel him from an object of my hatred, rework him from a source of my suffering and recast him into an object of my love, interest, sympathy, and brotherhood. If I did not succeed, if I could not produce the degree of heat necessary for this remelting, then I was lost, and the Dutchman would remain stuck in my throat to strangle me in future days and nights. I had simply to fulfill that wondrous saying, "Love your enemies." For a long time I had been accustomed to take this strangely compelling maxim from the New Testament not morally, not as an order—"Thou shalt"—but as a friendly suggestion from one who was truly wise, who was advising us, "Just try following this maxim literally, you will be amazed how much good it will do you." I knew that the advice contained not only the highest moral demand but also the most penetrating psychological doctrine of happiness, and that the whole theory of love in the New Testament, in addition to all its other meanings, also consisted in a most carefully thought-out psychological technique. In this case it was obvious, the youngest and most naïve psychoanalyst could only have confirmed it, that between me and my salvation there stood only the unfulfilled demand to love my enemy.

Well, I succeeded. The Dutchman did not remain stuck in my throat, and he *was* recast. It was not easy, it cost me sweat and labor, it cost two or three night hours of the most strenuous exertion. But then it was done.

I began by summoning the dreaded figure before my mind in the sharpest detail possible, until not a hand, not a finger on a hand, not a shoe, not an eyebrow, not a crease in the cheek was missing, until I saw him complete before me, until I inwardly possessed him entire, could make him walk, sit, laugh, and go to sleep. I pictured him brushing his teeth in the morning, falling asleep on the pillow at night, I saw his eyelids growing weary, saw his neck relax and his head gently droop. It probably took an hour for me to get that far. But at that point much had been won. For the poet to love something means to catch it up in his imagination, to warm it and foster it there, to play with it, to saturate it with his own soul, to animate it with his own breath. This is what I did with my enemy until he belonged to me and had entered into me. Without his too-short neck I probably would not have succeeded, but his neck came to my rescue. I could undress or dress the Dutchman, clothe him in knickerbockers or morning coat, seat him in a rowboat or at the luncheon table, I could make him a soldier, a king, a beggar, a slave, an old man or a child, and in each one of these varied guises he had a short neck and slightly protuberant eyes. These characteristics were his weak points, they were where I must get hold of him. It was a long time before I succeeded in making the Dutchman grow younger, until I could see him before me as a young husband, as a bridegroom, as an undergraduate, as a schoolboy. When I had finally transformed him backward into a small lad, that neck of his for the first time elicited my sympathy. By the gentle path of sympathy he won my heart when I saw this strong active boy causing his parents concern because of this slight indication of a tendency to asthma. By the gentle path of sympathy I proceeded to move forward in his life, and it took little art to envision the future years and stages. When I had got as far as seeing the whole man, older by ten years, suffering his first stroke, suddenly everything about him became touching, the thick lips, the heavy eyelids, the generally uninflected voice, everything enlisted my sympathy, and even before he had suffered death in my intense imagining, his mortality, his weaknesses, the necessity of his death, had come so close to me in brotherly feeling that I had long since lost all resistance to him. Then I was happy. I firmly closed his eyes and shut my own, for it was already morning and I was suspended like a ghost among the pillows, completely exhausted by my long night of poetical creation.

During the following day and night I had ample confirmation of the fact that I had conquered the Dutchman. The fellow could laugh or cough, he could sound as hearty as he liked, he could stride about noisily or push the chairs around or make jokes, but he no longer disturbed my equanimity. During the day I could work passably well, during the night I could rest passably well.

My triumph was great, but I did not enjoy it for long. On the second morning after my night of victory, the Dutchman suddenly left, thus becoming once more the victor. He left me strangely disillusioned, since I no longer had any use for my hard-won love and irreproachability. His departure, once so deeply yearned for, now almost caused me pain.

His place in No. 64 was taken by a little gray lady with a rubber-shod cane whom I seldom got to see or hear. She was an ideal neighbor, neither disturbing me nor arousing my anger and enmity. But only now, retrospectively, can I acknowledge this. For a number of days my new neighbor was a constant source of disillusionment. I would much rather have had my Dutchman back again, he whom I was now finally able to love.

DESPONDENCY

When I think back now to the optimism of my first days in Baden, to my childish hopefulness and joy at that time, to my naïve trust in this cure and to the even more frivolous, complacent self-deception and boyish vanity by which I considered myself a comparatively young and healthy, a promising and only slightly ailing patient; if I recall the whole rash, playful mood of those first days, my faith, like that of some primitive Negro, in the baths, in the mildness and curability of my sciatica, in the warm springs, in the spa doctor, in diathermy and the quartz lamp: then I have trouble resisting the impulse to stand in front of the mirror and stick my tongue out at myself. My God, how those fancies evaporated, how those hopes vanished! What is left of that erect, resilient, benignly smiling newcomer who, playing with his Malacca cane and enchanted with himself, went tripping down Badestrasse? A real monkey is how I see him now. Yes, and what is left of that optimistic, brightly varnished, adaptable worldling's philosophy with which I toyed and adorned myself, just as I did with my Malacca cane!

To be sure, the cane is still unchanged. Just yesterday

when the bath attendant offered to put one of those damned rubber ferrules on the end of my handsome cane, I rejected his offer indignantly. But who knows whether I may not accept tomorrow if the offer is repeated?

I have horrible pains, not only when I am walking but also when I am sitting, so that since day before yesterday I have spent almost all my time lying down. In the morning when I get out of my bath, the two little stone steps make me work hard; wheezing and sweating, I drag myself up by the railing, have hardly enough strength left to wrap the bath towel around me, and then for a while I collapse in the chair. Putting on my bedroom slippers and dressing gown is a detestably heavy task, the walk to the sulphur springs and later from the springs to the elevator, from the elevator to my bedroom is a horribly difficult, endless, painful journey. On these morning expeditions I make use of every conceivable aid, I support myself on the bathing attendant, the doorposts, on every railing, I feel my way along the walls, I move my limbs and back without any aesthetic concern, in that heavy, sad, half-swimming fashion which once (oh, how inexpressibly long ago!) I observed with sympathetic humor in the case of that old lady whom I felt called on to compare to a sea lion. If ever a frivolous joke rebounded in punishment on the scoffer's head, it certainly did this time.

In the morning when I sit on the edge of the bed, dreading the painful task of bending down to tie my shoes, or when after the bath, dead tired and half asleep, I rest on the chair in the bathing cubicle, then memory tells me that only a short time ago, only a few weeks, there were mornings when, barely out of bed, I would undertake vigorous and precise breathing exercises, stretching my chest, drawing in my belly as though with a belt, controlling my retained breath, allowing it to escape rhythmically as though out of an oboe. It must be true, but already I have trouble believing it, that with rigid legs, knees locked, I once could stand quivering on my toes, that I was able to do deep, slow knee-bends and all the other excellent gymnastics.

To be sure, at the beginning of the cure, I had been told I would have these reactions, that the baths were very fatiguing and that with many patients the pains increased at the outset of the cure. Well, yes, I had nodded my head in understanding. But that the weariness should be so distressing, the increase in pain so great and oppressive, I had never suspected. In a week I have become an old man who sits around in the hotel and in the garden, here and there on benches, and always has a hard time getting up again, who does not use the stairs any more and whom the elevator boy has to help in and out of the elevator.

From outside, too, came all kinds of disappointments. In Zurich, a few meters from here, there are a number of close friends of mine, and they know that I am sick and am taking the cure here, two of them went so far as to promise to visit me when I looked them up on my way here. But no one has come, and naturally no one will come; that I was depending on it and rejoicing is one more instance of my ineradicable infantilism. No, of course they will not come, after all I know how much they have to do, all these poor pestered people, and how late it often is when they get to bed after the theater, the restaurant, entertaining guests; it was stupid of me to think of it and simply childish to take it for granted that these people would find pleasure in visiting me, a sick and boring person. But I always assume in advance the most amazing things, cherish the most extravagant expectations; barely do I meet someone and find him sympathetic when I impute the very best to him, yes, demand it of him, and am disillusioned and saddened if it is not forthcoming. This was the case, too, with a rather pretty young lady in the hotel with whom I had chatted several times and who pleased me very much. After she had named to me as her favorite books several bad works of light fiction, I was a bit taken aback for a moment, but immediately said to myself that as a specialist and connoisseur in literary matters I had no right to assume judgment and understanding of this field in others. I swallowed those book titles, rebuked myself, and went on attributing all that is good and noble to the lady. And just yesterday evening, right there in the drawing room, she committed murder! An agreeable, cheerful, even pretty lady, a woman who would certainly not beat a child in my presence or torture an animal, she nevertheless, with serene brow and innocent eyes, seated herself at the piano and with unpracticed but powerful hands overcame and slaughtered a charming eighteenth-century minuet! I was horrified, saddened, and red with shame, but it did not occur to anyone else that something dreadful had happened. I sat alone with my silly feelings. Oh, how I longed for my loneliness, for my cave which I should never have left, where of course there are pain and misery, but no pianos, no literary conversations, no educated fellow men!

And the whole cure, all of Baden, has become so horribly repulsive to me. Of the guests at our hotel, by far the larger number I know are not here for the first time, many are paying the baths their sixth, their tenth visit, and according to the laws of probability I will have the same experience, the same as all sufferers from metabolic ailments: the pains will become more and more deadly from year to year, and the hope of a cure will yield to the more modest hope that through these cures I shall find at least temporary relief each year. The doctor, to be sure, remains firm in his reassurances, but after all, that's his profession; and if we patients seem outwardly all right and give the impression of the most wholesome well-being, that is because of the rich food and the quartz lamp, which tans us most becomingly, so that we look like people who have just returned blooming from the high mountains.

In the process, one goes to pieces morally, too, in this lazy, enervating atmosphere of the baths. The few Spartan habits that I have acquired through the years, breathing and exercising, the preference for a meager diet, have been lost, and this, moreover, at the direct instigation of the doctor; also, the initial enthusiasm for observation and work has almost entirely disappeared. Not that this *Psychologia Balnearia** would be any great loss—on the contrary, from the beginning it was not a work, not a planned attempt at composition, but simply an occupation, a small daily exercise for eye and wrist. But indolence has taken charge here too, I now use very little ink. If it weren't for my victory over the Dutchman, which in itself turned out to be disproportionately hard, I would simply have to conclude that I had become dissolute and slatternly. And in many instances I must really be so. First of all, an inertia, an ill-tempered laziness, has taken possession of me and keeps me from everything that is good and useful, especially from every physical effort, no matter how slight. I can barely bring myself to take the shortest walk, after meals I lie for hours on my bed or on the chaise longue just as I do after the baths and treatments, and what my intellectual state is I will be able to see clearly enough later on, if I ever read over these silly notes with which from time to time I torment myself for an hour out of some remnant of a feeling of duty. I now consist simply and entirely of inertia, boredom, somnolence.

An even more shameful confession is not to be avoided; that I am inclined neither to work nor to think and barely to read, that intellectually and bodily I have lost all freshness and energy would be bad enough, but there is worse to come. I have begun to surrender myself to the superficial and stultifying, the barren and reprehensible side

---

* This was the original title of the present work.—Ed.

of this indolent spa life. For instance, at noon I eat all the good rich dishes, not just to join in playfully and with inner superiority or at least irony, as I did at the beginning —no, I eat, I gobble, although I no longer know what hunger is, these fine, long menus twice a day with the uncontrolled, stupid gluttony of the bored, the fat, loveless bourgeois; in the evening I usually drink wine, and before going to sleep I have formed the habit of having a bottle of beer, something that I have not drunk for well on twenty years. In the beginning I took it as a sleeping medicine because it was recommended to me, but for days now I have been drinking from habit and gluttony. It is unbelievable how quickly one can learn what is bad and stupid, how easy it is to become an idle dog, a piggish fat gourmand!

But my talent for depravity is by no means confined to eating and drinking, to lying quiet and doing nothing. With physical indulgence and inertia, spiritual indulgence goes hand in hand. What I would never have considered possible has happened: I not only avoid in intellectual pursuits all strenuous, difficult, and dangerous paths, but dull and greedy I seek out in intellectual matters exactly those jejune, perverse, idiotically pompous and meaningless pleasures which I have always shunned and detested and on account of which I have from time to time denounced and despised the bourgeois and the city dweller in particular and our time and civilization in general. I have now approached so closely to the average level of the patients that I no longer hate and avoid their diversions but instead search for and take part in some of them. It won't be long now until I begin to read the list of guests (this to me is the most puzzling of all the patients' entertainments), and spend a whole afternoon gossiping with Frau Müller about her rheumatism and about all the kinds of infusions that can be used to combat it, and send my friends postcards of bridal couples or of those daring turnip characters.

The concerts in the casino, which for a long time I carefully avoided, I now frequently attend, and I sit on a chair just like all the others, listen to the popular music flowing by, and have the pleasant feeling that a period of time is audibly and tactilely flowing by with it, time of which we patients have so much to spare. Often the music itself wins me over and enchants me, the purely sensuous charm of a few well-played instruments, but none of the character or content of the piece penetrates to my consciousness. Shallow numbers, whose very type and signature would at other times have roused my disgust, I now listen to without distress all the way to the end. I sit for a quarter of an hour, sometimes for half an hour, weary and in bad posture, amid a crowd of other bored people, I listen like them to time flowing by, like them I wear a bored expression, thoughtlessly like them scratch my head or neck, support my chin on the handle of my cane, or yawn, and only for a brief instant does my soul start up in rebellion like an animal of the steppes suddenly awakening in captivity, but soon it nods again and falls asleep and goes on dreaming, subterraneously, without me, for I have been separated from it ever since I sat down on this concert-hall chair.

And only now, when I have become completely a part of the crowd, an average guest at the spa, a bored, weary Philistine, only now do I feel how ridiculous and frivolous it was when on the first pages of this essay I posed as a normal representative of this world and mentality. I did it ironically, and only now when I actually belong to this normalized everyday world, when I sit soulless in a concert hall and consume popular music the way people consume tea or pilsner, only now do I feel again how intensely, how bitterly, I hate this world. For now I hate and despise and deride myself in this world and not the others any longer. No, to come to an understanding with this world, to belong to it, to have a place in it and to feel comfortable there—I feel this at present with every fiber of my being—that is not for me, that is forbidden, that is a sin against everything good and holy that I know and in which it is my happiness to be a part. And simply for that reason, simply because at this time I am committing this sin, because I have come to terms with this world and accepted it, for this reason I am in such deathly low spirits! And yet I still stick to it, the inertia is stronger than my insight, the fat, lazy belly stronger than my timidly protesting soul.

Sometimes now I let myself be drawn into conversation with my fellow patients. After meals we stand around for a while in the corridor and express completely concordant opinions about the political situation and the stock exchange, about the weather and the spa, also about our philosophy of life and family responsibilities: that young men simply have to have someone in authority over them and that it doesn't hurt anyone to go through the college of hard knocks and other views of this sort, with all of which I agree, my stomach stuffed with good food. Now and again my soul rebels, the words turn to gall in my mouth, and I have to hurry away in search of solitude at all costs (oh, how hard it is to find here), but by and large I too have committed these sins against the spirit, I too am guilty of stupid, purposeless chattering, of lazy, mindless acquiescence.

Another distraction I am beginning to get used to here is the cinema. I have already spent a number of evenings at it, and if I went there in the first instance simply to be alone, not to have to listen to conversation and to escape from the Dutchman's sphere of influence, by the second time I went for pleasure, out of a desire for distraction (I have now accustomed myself to the word "distraction" which formerly had no place in my vocabulary!). I have gone a number of times and, seduced and deadened by the eye's delight in the play of pictures, I have not only unprotestingly accepted the most hair-raising and loveless substitute and pseudo-drama along with ghastly music, I have also endured the physically as well as intellectually evil atmosphere of the place. I am beginning to stand anything, to swallow anything, even the most stupid and ugly. For hours I watched a film about an ancient empress unroll, complete with theater, circus, church, gladiators, lions, saints, and eunuchs, and I sat there and watched while the highest values and symbols; the throne and scepter, vestments and halos, cross and imperial globe, together with all possible and impossible qualities and conditions of the soul, and men and animals by the hundreds were summoned up for laughable reasons and put on show; this potentially splendid display was degraded by interminable, completely idiotic subtitles, and poisoned by false dramatization, and disgraced and cheapened by a heartless and headless public (I too am a part of it). At many moments it was so dreadful I was on the point of running away, but it isn't very easy for a sciatic to run away, I stayed, I watched the trash to its end, and presumably tomorrow or the next day I'll go there again. It would be unfair to deny that I also have seen enchanting things in the cinema, especially a charming French acrobat and humorist who had better inspirations than most poets. What I denounce, what arouses my anger and disgust, is not the cinema, it is I alone, the cinema visitor. Who forces me to go there, to stand the horrible music, to read the ludicrous subtitles, to listen to the whinnying of the crowd, my more innocent brothers? In that long film I saw a dozen or more splendid lions full of life and vitality, and then two minutes later saw them being dragged over the sand, lifeless corpses, and I heard half the audience greeting this sad and grisly sight with roars of laughter! Is there then in the local thermal waters some salt, some acid, some chalk, something that evens people out, that produces an inhibition against everything lofty, noble, precious, and removes the inhibitions against what is low and vulgar? Well, I bow down in shame, and for later on, for the time after my return to my steppe, I have made certain vows.

Have I now come to the end of my list of bad habits and newly acquired vices? No, I am not yet at the end. I've also become acquainted with games of chance, on a number of occasions I have played at the green table with pleasure and excitement and also at a machine to which one feeds silver coins through various little openings, and it swallows them. Unfortunately I can't really play properly because I haven't much money, but what I could spare I have wagered, and twice I have succeeded in playing for something like a full hour and ended up not losing more than one or two francs. Of course, this kind of play has not given me the true gambler's experience, but I too have smelled of this flower and I must admit that it gave me great pleasure. I must also confess that I have not had a bad conscience about it, as I did with the concerts, the conversations with the patients, and with the cinema lions; on the contrary, the flavor of the disreputable and antisocial in this vice appealed most strongly to me and I am sincerely sorry that I cannot make juicier wagers.

My sensations while playing were something like this: first I stood for a little while at the edge of the green table, looking at the numbered fields and listening to the voice of the man at the roulette wheel. The number this man called out, the number chosen by the rolling ball, which a second earlier had been a blind, silly number among many others, now blazed up bright and warm in the man's voice, in the hole occupied by the ball, in the ears and hearts of the hearers. It would be *quatre*, or *cinq*, or *trois*, and not only in my ear and consciousness, not only on the rounded conical pathway of the ball would this number shine forth, but also on the green table. If the number 7 came up, then the stiff black numeral 7 in its own green field took on a festive radiance for seconds, it crowded all the other numbers into non-existence, for all the others were simply possibilities, it alone was fulfillment, possessed reality. The realization of the possible, the waiting for it and being involved with it, was the soul of the game. Now when I had watched and listened for a few minutes and began to be drawn into the game, then came the first beautiful and marvelously exciting moment: 6 was called and it did not surprise me, it fell out so properly, so understandably, and really as though I had specifically expected it, yes, as though I myself had called it, had made and created it. From this second on, my soul was involved in the game, scenting fate, feeling on good terms with chance, and it is, I must admit, a completely joyous feeling, it is the core and magnet of the whole sport. And so I heard 7, then 1, then 8 come up, did not feel surprised or disappointed, believed that I had expected just those numbers, and now contact had been established, I was in touch with the current and could let myself go with it. Now I looked steadily at the green field, read the numbers and was drawn to one of them, heard it softly calling (sometimes there were two at once), saw it gently signaling to me, and put my coins on that number. Now if it did not come up, I was not disappointed or disenchanted, I could wait, my 6 or 9 would come in time. And it came the second or third time, it really came. This moment of winning is marvelous. You have appealed to fate and yielded to it, you believe you are in contact with the great secret, you have a feeling of being in friendly alliance with it—and behold, it is true, it is confirmed, your silent, secret imagining, your little hidden, wishful picture blazes up, a miracle has occurred, the presentiment becomes reality, your number has been chosen by the almighty ball of happiness, the man at the wheel calls it out and the man at the table tosses a handful of silver coins to you in a gleaming arc. That is extraordinarily fine, it is a pure joy and does not depend on the money, for I who write this have not kept a single franc of all that I won, the game gobbled them all up again, and yet those beautiful moments of winning still shine in retrospect, those marvelous, childishly complete and satisfying instants of fulfillment, untroubled and precious, each a full and splendidly decorated Christmas tree, each a miracle, each a feast, even more, a feast of the soul, a confirmation and affirmation and heightening of the innermost, deepest life instinct. Certainly one can experience the same joy, the same marvelous happiness, at higher levels, in nobler and more discriminating forms: the flash of a deep perception about life, the moment of an inner victory, and most of all the creative instant, the instant of finding, the lightninglike inspiration, the triumphant touching of the lucky number in the artist's work, all this is as similar to the experience of winning at gambling as a picture is to its reflection. But how often does even the most fortunate, the most gifted, encounter these high godlike moments? How often for us weary, latter-day men does any satisfaction, any gratifying feeling of happiness, stand comparison in strength and splendor with the joyous happiness of childhood? It is these experiences that the gambler seeks, even if he seems to be intent on money. The bird of paradise, of happiness, become so rare in our smooth, jejune lives, that is what he tries to hunt down, that is what stirs the smoldering yearning in his eyes.

Then back and forth went the luck. At moments I was completely at one with it, sat myself in the rolling ball and won, and a precious feeling of excitement flooded shudderingly through me. Then the high point was past. I had in my trousers pocket a big handful of coins I had won, and I went on betting time after time, and slowly the feeling of certainty gave way, a 1 sprang out and a 4, which were complete surprises to me, were hostile and jeered at me. Now I became restless and fearful, I bet on numbers without having any feeling of presentiment about them, I hesitated for a long time between even and odd, but compulsively went on betting until my playing money was all lost. And not just afterward but simultaneously, at the very time of the game, I realized the depth of the similarity, saw in the game a copy of life, where things go exactly the same way, where inscrutable, unreasoning presentiment gives us control of the strongest magic, releases the greatest powers, where with the flagging of sound instinct, criticism and intellect take over, get by for a while and try to hold their own, then finally what had to happen happens entirely without us and over our heads. The flagging gambler who has passed his high point and yet cannot stop, who is no longer guided by any intuition or deep gift of confidence, is exactly like the man who in important life situations does not know which way to turn, and instead of waiting and closing his eyes does the wrong thing from sheer calculation and effort and over-exertion of the mind. One of the very safest rules of play at the green table is this: When you see a fellow player who grows weary and is having bad luck, who bets first on this number several times and then on that, changing abruptly—then every time bet on the number he has just been fruitlessly besieging and which he has now abandoned in disgust; it will certainly come up.

Playing for money is strangely different from all the other middle-class and spa entertainments. Here at the green table, books are not read, dull conversations are not carried on, nor are socks knitted as at the concerts and in the casino garden, there is neither yawning nor scratching of necks, in fact the rheumatics do not even sit down, they stand, stand for long and painful periods heroically on their own legs, otherwise so carefully spared. Here in the gambling hall jokes are not cracked, there is no conversation about illnesses or Poincaré, there is hardly any laughter, but the crowd, serious and whispering, stands around the playing table, the announcer's voice sounds subdued and solemn, subdued and soft the clinking together of the silver coins on the green table, and this reverence, this discretion and dignity, make the game immeasurably more appealing than other forms of entertainment at which people are so noisy, slovenly, and undisciplined. Here in the gambling hall prevails a holiday mood of solemn festiveness, the guests enter silently and somewhat self-consciously as though coming into a church, they dare only whisper, and look with awe at the gentleman in the cutaway. And the latter's behavior is exemplary, not like that of an ordinary person, but of a holder of office or post of honor.

I cannot examine here the psychological causes of this celebratory mood and beautiful, beneficent solemnity, for I have long since given up the pretense that my *Psychologia Balnearia* concerns any other psyche but my own. Presumably the holy, whisperingly reverent attitude, the solemnity and devoted attention that prevail in the gambling hall, come simply from the fact that the people are not concerned with music, drama, or any other such childishness but with the most serious, best loved, and holiest thing they know, with money. But, as I have said, I do not intend to examine this, it lies outside my province. I merely repeat that, unlike any other popular entertainment, gambling is carried on in an atmosphere that is not devoid of reverence. And whereas in the cinema, for example, the audience makes little attempt to control its verbal or inarticulate expressions of pleasure or disgust, the gambler, even in moments of most violent, legitimate, and justifiable emotion, that is, while winning and losing money, feels obliged to maintain his self-discipline and dignity. I see the same people who at their daily game of cards greet the loss of twenty centimes with outbursts of bad temper, with curses and imprecations, lose a hundred times as much at the roulette table—I dare not say "without moving an eyelash," for the eyelashes quiver violently —but without becoming noisy and disturbing their neighbors with indecorous ejaculations.

Since wise governments are interested in any contribution to the education of the people, and encourage and support all institutions that serve that purpose, I venture here, although I am a complete layman in this field, to call the experts' attention to the fact that no game, entertainment, or diversion educates the participant so well in self-control, calm, and decorum as the game of chance in a public gambling hall.

Sympathetic, yes, beneficial though gambling seems to me, nevertheless I had occasion to reflect upon its shadow side, or rather to experience it myself. When the nation's economists object to gambling so often and with such passionate moralistic pathos, I find their arguments irrelevant. That the gambler is in danger of winning money too easily and therefore learning to despise the sacredness of labor, that on the other hand he is in danger of losing all his money, and third, that after long observation of the rolling of the balls and the coins he could even forget the basic conception of middle-class economic morality, unqualified reverence for money, all this, to be sure, is true, but I cannot take these various dangers very seriously. To me as a psychologist, it would seem that for many people seriously ill with psychic disturbances, the sudden loss of their fortunes and the destruction of their belief in the sacredness of money would be no misfortune but rather the surest, indeed the only possible, means of rescue, just as in contrast to the single cult of work and money that dominates life today, a feeling for the play of the moment, openness to chance, trust in the whims of fortune seem completely desirable and something we all greatly lack.

No, in my opinion the flaw in gambling, and it is this that makes it a vice despite its splendid aspects, is something completely psychological. According to my personal and highly agreeable experience, it is exciting and cheering to spend twenty minutes a day under the tension of roulette and in the highly unreal atmosphere of the gambling hall. For a bored, empty, weary soul, this is a true balm, one of the best I have ever tried. The fault is only (and gambling has this fault in common with the equally agreeable uses of alcohol) that in gambling the whole pleasant excitement comes from outside and is purely mechanical and material, and the great danger is that in trusting to this consistently effective mechanism of excitement one may neglect and finally forfeit one's own exertion, one's spiritual activity. If one sets the soul in motion through the purely mechanical means of the roulette wheel instead of by thinking, dreaming, fantasying, or meditating, it is about the same as making use of bath and masseur for one's body but giving up one's own exertions in sport and gymnastics. The mechanism of excitement in the cinema as well, which substitutes a purely material feeding of the eye for one's own visual artistic contribution, the discovery, selection, and retention of what is interesting and beautiful—this is based on the same fraud.

No, just as one needs exercise in addition to the masseur, so the soul most decidedly needs instead of, or in addition to, gambling and all the other attractive excitements, its own achievements. Therefore, a hundred times better than games of chance is every active exertion of the kind: strict, clear exercise in thinking and memorizing, in visualizing with closed eyes things seen, in reconstructing in the evenings the happenings of the day, free association and fantasy. I add this for the benefit of friends of the public good and perhaps as a corrective to my layman's suggestion above—for in this field, that of pure psychological experience and education, I am not a layman but rather an old, almost too experienced expert.

Now I have wandered far from my theme again; it seems that these notes are fated to fail in working through any single problem to a conclusion, but to string together accidental and associative notions that press upon me. Perhaps, however, I can assume that this is just a part of the psychology of a guest at the spa.

I abandoned my theme, my so unexciting theme, in favor of a little panegyric to games of chance, and I have been inclined to spin out the panegyric because it is hard to return to my subject. But I must do so. Let us get back to Hesse, the guest at the spa, let us look once more at this now contented, aging gentleman with the listless, weary posture and the halting gait. He does not please us, this man, we cannot love him, we cannot with an honest heart wish him an endless or even a long continuation of his neither exemplary nor interesting life. We would have no objection if he should simply leave the stage, where for a long time he has not cut an agreeable figure. If, for example, some morning in the bath he should succumb to weariness, slide under the water, and stay there, we would not find it a cause for regret.

If, however, we express such disinterest in this guest at the spa, we refer simply to his present state, his physical condition of the moment. We must not lose sight of the ever-present possibility that his condition may change, that it may be recalculated with a new denominator. This miracle, often experienced before, is possible at any moment. If we shake our heads as we look at the patient Hesse and find him fit for destruction, then let it not be forgotten that we can believe in destruction not in the sense of annihilation but only as transformation, for the foundation and soil of all our opinions, as well as our psychology, is belief in God, in the unity—and the unity can, through grace and understanding, be restored again even in the most desperate cases. There is no invalid who could not with a single step, though the step be through death, become well again and enter into life. There is no sinner who could not with a single step, though that step be through execution, become innocent and divine. And there are no careworn, lost, and apparently degraded people whom a sign of grace could not in an instant renew and turn into happy children. May this my belief, this my knowledge, never be forgotten in the writing as well as in the reading of these pages. And their author would not, in fact, know where to find the courage, the justification, the audacity for his criticisms and whims, his pessimisms and psychologies, if in his soul knowledge of the unity did not stand as an indestructible counterweight. On the contrary, the farther out I venture on the one side and the more I expose myself, the more relentlessly I criticize, the more willingly I yield to whims, the brighter shines the light of reconciliation on the opposite side. Were it not for this endless, constantly fluctuating adjustment, where should I find the courage to say a single word, make a judgment, feel and express love or hate, or live for a single hour?

IMPROVEMENT

Soon my cure will be over. And, thank God, it is going better, it is going well. For a whole week I was completely lost and submerged, there was nothing to me but sickness, weariness, boredom, and self-disgust. I came very close to having a rubber ferrule made for my cane. I came very close to starting to read the list of guests. Instead of listening to the popular music for a quarter or half an hour, I was on the point of consuming the whole one- or two-hour concerts; instead of drinking one bottle of beer in the evening, I was on the point of drinking two. I came near to gambling away my whole supply of cash in the casino. In addition, I've allowed myself to become somewhat involved with my neighbors in the hotel dining room, nice, agreeable people whom I respect and from whom I could have learned a great deal if I had not made my old mistake of trying to do this through conversation. Conversation with people with whom one has no genuine relationship is almost always so barren and disappointing. Also there is the fact that strangers talking to me unfortunately see the specialist in me and think they have to get around to discussing literature and art, and then naturally nonsense is talked, and one comes to see the most charming people from the one side on which they are indistinguishable from eleven out of twelve other people.

On top of this the pains, and the bad weather during which I caught a new cold every day (now I understand my Dutchman's perpetual colds), and the dreadful cure-weariness—those were a string of days I can't brag about. But, as such things go, one day the string was simply at an end. There came a day when I was so completely worn out with suffering that I remained in bed and could not be persuaded even to take my daily bath. I was on strike, I simply lay there, but only for one day; on the next, things were going better. That day of the turning point is memorable to me because the change and the reversal came quite suddenly and surprisingly. A man can get out of any situation, even the most repellent, only if he first wills it, and so I too never doubted even during the most barren and depressing times of this cure, in the midst of all my despondency, that I would creep up again out of this slough. The process of creeping up, the slow, laborious conquest of the outer world, the gradual seeking and finding of the most reasonable attitude—that, as I knew, was an always possible road, it was the very possible, very commendable road of reason. From earlier experiences, however, I knew that there was another way which could not be sought but could only be found, that of luck, of grace, of miracle. That this miracle was just now close to me, that I might be freed from the shameful state of these miserable days, not by the laborious and dusty highway of reason or of conscious effort but on wings, along the flower-bordered path of grace, this was something I had not dared to hope.

On the day when I roused myself once more from stupefaction and decided to go on with the cure and with life, I was, of course, somewhat rested but by no means in a good mood. My legs ached, my back hurt, the back of my neck was stiff, standing up was difficult, the way to the elevator and to the bath was hard and so was the way back. When noon finally came and I was creeping to the dining room, peevish and without appetite, I suddenly became aware of myself, I was suddenly no longer simply the guest at the spa who with heavy limbs and joyless face was creeping down the hotel staircase, but I was at the same time a witness of myself. On some one of the many steps, it suddenly happened, I saw this guest without appetite creeping down the stairway, saw him put his hand helplessly on the banister, saw him entering the dining room past the welcoming headwaiter. Often before I had been in this state of awareness, and I immediately hailed it as a lucky sign, that in the middle of this fruitless and vexatious period it was suddenly here again.

I sat down in the high bright dining room at my lonesome little round table, and at the same time I saw how I was sitting down, how I was straightening the chair under me and biting my lip a little because it hurt to sit down, then how I mechanically picked up the vase of flowers and moved it a little closer, how I slowly and indecisively took my napkin out of the ring. Here and there other guests came in, seated themselves at their little tables like the dwarfs in *Snow-White,* plucked their napkins out of the rings. The guest Hesse, however, was the principal object of my observing I. The guest Hesse with disciplined but profoundly bored expression was pouring a little water into his glass, was breaking off a bit of bread, all simply as pastime, for he did not intend to drink the water or eat the bread; he was spooning his soup, glancing with lackluster eye at the other tables in the big hall, glancing up at the walls painted with landscapes, watching the headwaiter hurrying through the room, and looking at the pretty waitresses in their short black dresses and white aprons. A few of the guests in groups or in pairs were sitting at somewhat larger tables; most of them, however, were alone in front of their solitary plates with disciplined but deeply bored expressions, slowly pouring some water or wine into their glasses, plucking at the bread, looking over with lackluster gaze at the tables of the others, looking up at the walls painted with landscapes, watching the hurrying headwaiter and the pretty waitresses in short black dresses and white aprons. On the walls, friendly, silent, and a little embarrassed, waited the pretty landscapes, and down from the ceiling of the hall, friendly and unembarrassed, the inspiration of some forgotten decorator, looked four painted elephants' heads, which had often given me pleasure in earlier days, for I am a friend and devotee of the Hindu gods and I saw in those heads the fine, intelligent elephant god, Ganesa, whom I greatly reverence. And oftên while I was looking up at the elephants from my little table, I had pondered just why it was that in my childhood I had been told that the advantage of Christendom consisted principally in the fact that it knew no gods or godlike images and that I, the older and wiser I become, see the greatest disadvantage to this religion in that it has, except for the marvelous Catholic Mary, no gods or godlike images. I would give a great deal, for example, if the apostles, instead of being somewhat boring and fearsome preachers, were gods with all kinds of splendid powers and nature symbols, and I see only a very feeble though still welcome substitute for this in the animals of the Evangelists.

Now the one who was keeping watch on me and the guests and all the rest, on Hesse eating in boredom, on his fellow guests eating in boredom, was not the guest and sciatic Hesse but rather the old somewhat antisocial hermit and lone wolf Hesse, the old wanderer and poet, the friend of butterflies and lizards, of old books and religions, that Hesse who faced the world with determination and strength and who became deeply disturbed if he had to have a certificate of residence filled out by the authorities, or even had to fill out a form for the census takers. This old Hesse, this "I" that recently had become somewhat alien and lost, was back again now and observing us. It observed the appetiteless guest Hesse dismembering a fine fish with a halfhearted play of his fork and without hunger putting bite after bite ill-humoredly into his mouth. It observed how, without any need, without any sense, he moved water glass and saltcellar back and forth, now stretched out his feet under his chair and now drew them back, how the other guests did the same thing, how the bored people were waited on with extreme care by the headwaiter and the pretty young girls, although no one was hungry, and how outside in a different world, behind the high solemn bay windows of the hall, the clouds drifted by in the sky. All this the secret observer saw, and suddenly the whole arrangement seemed to him enormously odd, droll and comic, and even uncanny, this waxwork cabinet of anxious, rigid human figures who were not really alive, this bored Hesse eating without appetite, these other bored persons. It was unbearably laughable, unbearably idiotic, this play of meaningless solemnity, this whole heaped-up mass of food, china, and glass, of silver, wine, bread, service, all for a few long-since satiated guests whose boredom and melancholy neither the food nor the drink nor the sight of the drifting clouds could heal.

The spa guest Hesse was just lifting his glass, simply out of boredom he was raising it to his lips without really drinking, he was adding to all the other unplanned and automatic pseudo-actions of the mealtime a new one, when the union of the two I's took place, the eating I and the observing I, and all at once I had to put the glass down, for I was shaken from inside by the sudden explosion of an immense desire to laugh, a quite childlike merriment, a sudden insight into the infinite absurdity of this whole situation. For an instant I saw mirrored in this image of the hall full of sick, cheerless, spoiled, and lethargic people (assuming their souls looked the same as mine) our whole civilized life, a life without strong impulse, running compulsively along fixed tracks, joyless, without connection with God or with the clouds in the sky. For the space of a moment I thought of the thousand dining rooms that looked exactly the same, of the hundred thousand coffeehouses with spotted marble tables and sweet, overspiced music dripping with lust, of the hotels and offices, of all the architecture, music, all the customs within which our race lives, and it all seemed to me equivalent in significance and value to the bored toying of my lazy hand with the fish fork, to the unsatisfied, barren hithering and thithering of my loveless eyes through the hall. All of this together, however, dining room and world, patients and humanity, seemed to me for the space of an instant by no means horrible and tragic but simply enormously funny. All you needed to do was laugh and the spell was broken, the mechanism destroyed, then God and the birds and the clouds swept through our desolate hall, and we were no longer disconsolate guests at the spa table but happy guests of God at the many-colored tables of the world.

In that second I set down my glass as quickly as I could,

shaken and overwhelmed from inside by a great laughter. I made a supreme effort to control it, not to let it explode. Oh, that's something we experienced so often as children, sitting at table, or in school or church, filled right up to the nose and eyes with a huge, well-justified need to laugh and yet not daring to laugh and having to deal with the situation somehow on account of the teacher, on account of one's parents, on account of rules and regulations. Unwillingly we harkened to and obeyed those teachers, those parents, and were very much surprised, and still are today, that behind their regulations, their religious and moral teachings, is supposed to stand the authority of that Jesus who is the very one who blessed the children. Is he supposed really to have meant only model children?

This time, too, I succeed in controlling myself. I remain quiet and simply endure the pressure in my throat and the itching in my nose and seek earnestly for some small vent or outlet, a permissible and possible way for what will otherwise choke me. Would it be feasible to give the headwaiter a small pinch in the leg as he comes by or to sprinkle the waitresses with a little water from my glass? No, that wouldn't do, everything was forbidden, it was the old story just as it had been thirty years ago.

While I was thinking this, with the laughter stuck in the upper part of my throat, I was staring straight across to the neighboring table and into the face of a woman I did not know, an ill-looking lady with gray hair, her invalid's cane leaning against the wall beside her; she was busy playing with her napkin ring, there being just then one of those pauses in the meal, and we were all making use of our usual means of filling up the time. One man was diligently reading an old newspaper; you could clearly see that he knew it by heart and yet he ate up again and again the news of the illness of the president and the report of the activities of an educational commission in Canada. An old woman was mixing two little powders in her glass, medicines she would take after the meal. She looked a little like one of those dreadful old ladies in fairy tales who mix magic potions to hurt other, prettier folk. An elegant and weary-looking gentleman, as though out of a novel by Turgenev or Thomas Mann, distinguished and melancholy, was inspecting one of the landscapes painted on the wall. I still liked best of all our giantess, who was posed in impeccable posture and good spirits, as almost always, in front of her empty plate and looked neither angry nor bored. On the other hand, that strictly moral gentleman with the furrows and the powerful neck was sitting on his chair with the weight of a whole court of assizes and was making a face as though he had just condemned his only son to death, whereas in fact he had just eaten a plate of asparagus. Herr Kesselring, the rosy-faced page, today still looked pretty and rosy and yet a little aged and dusty, he seemed not to be having a good day, and the dimple in his childlike cheek seemed as improbable and superfluous as the little package of piquant pictures in his breast pocket. How strange and droll it all was! Why did we sit here like this and wait and grin? Why did we sit and wait for more food when all of us had long since ceased to be hungry? Why was Kesselring brushing his poet's hair with a tiny pocket brush? Why did he carry those stupid pictures in his pocket, why was that pocket lined with silk? Everything was so spurious and improbable. It was all such a strong temptation to laughter.

And so I sat staring at the old lady's face. Then all at once she dropped her napkin ring and looked at me, and while we stared at each other for an instant the laughter rose to my face and I could not help myself, I grinned at the woman in the most friendly fashion, and all the accumulated laughter within me forced my mouth open and ran out of my eyes. Now what she thought about that I do not know, but she reacted splendidly. At first she quickly lowered her eyes and hastily picked up her toy again, but her face had become restless, and while I observed it with the greatest attention, it became more and more distorted and went through the strangest grimaces. She was laughing! Grimacing and swallowing, she fought against the compulsion to laugh with which I had infected her! And so there we sat, we two who were known to our fellow hotel guests as staid, elderly folk, like two schoolchildren at our desks, looking in front of us, peeping at each other, and our faces moved and twitched in an attempt to contain our laughter. Two or three others in the hall noticed us and began to smile, amused and somewhat scornful; and as though a pane in one of the windows had broken and the blue and white sky had flooded in, for minutes a happy and titillating mood, a grin, ran through the hall, as though everyone now had also noticed how unspeakably silly and laughable we were, sitting there in all the dignity and weary melancholy of the spa.

Since that instant things have gone well with me again, I am no longer simply a guest at the spa, a specialist in being sick and being cured, but rather the sickness and the cure are now of secondary importance. I still have pain, to be sure, that is not to be denied. But then, for God's sake, let it hurt; I abandon the sickness to its own devices, I am not here to pamper it all day long.

After the meal a hotel guest addressed me, a very unsympathetic, opinionated gentleman who had frequently offered me newspapers and thrust his company upon me; only a short while ago in a long, extremely boring conversation about the school system and education, I had unscrupulously and most humbly agreed with all his treasured principles and views. Now this character emerged again from his usual ambush in the corridor and placed himself in my way.

"Good day," he said. "You look very pleased today!"

"Certainly I'm pleased. During lunch I saw clouds moving across the sky, and since up to now it was my opinion that these clouds were made of paper and were part of the dining-room decoration, I was very happy at the discovery that there were real air and clouds. They drifted away before my eyes, they weren't numbered and they had no price tags on them. You can imagine how happy I was at that. Reality still exists, in the middle of Baden! It's marvelous!"

Oh, how far from pleasant was the face the gentleman made at these words!

"Well, well," he said, drawing it out so that it took a full minute. "So you thought that reality no longer existed! Well, just what do you mean by reality, may I ask?"

"Oh," I said, "that is a complicated philosophical question. But actually I can answer it very easily. By reality, dear sir, I understand pretty much the same thing that is otherwise called 'nature.' In any case, I do not mean by reality what constantly surrounds us here in Baden, not stories of the cure and of sick people, not romances of rheumatism and arthritis, not promenades and casino concerts, menus and programs, not bathing attendants and guests at the spa."

"Why, the guests have no reality for you then? And so, for example, I, the man who is talking to you, am not a reality?"

"I'm sorry, I certainly don't want to offend you, but, in fact, for me you are without reality. As you present yourself to me, you are without those convincing characteristics that make what we perceive and experience, make what happens, real. You exist, sir, that I cannot deny. But you exist on a level that in my eyes lacks time-space reality. You exist, I might say, on the level of paper, of money and credit, of morality, of laws, of intellect, of respectability, you are a space-and-time companion of virtue, of the categorical imperative, and of reason, and perhaps you are related to the Thing-in-Itself or to capitalism. But you have not the reality I find convincing in the case of every stone and tree, every toad, every bird. I can give you my unlimited respect and approval, sir, I can doubt you or consider you valid, but it is impossible for me to experience you, it is wholly impossible to love you. You share this fate with your relations and worthy next of kin, with virtue, with reason, with the categorical im-imperative, with all humanity's ideals. You are magnificent. We are proud of you, but real you are not."

The gentleman opened his eyes very wide. "Now if by chance you should feel the flat of my hand on your facc, would that convince you of my reality?"

"If you should try that experiment, it would be the worse for you, for I am stronger than you are and at the moment I am marvelously free from all moralistic inhibitions; but aside from that, you would not achieve your purpose by this proof you so kindly offer. I would, to be sure, enter into your experiment with that marvelously coordinated apparatus of self-preservation, but your attack would not convince me of your reality, of your existence, of a purpose and a soul in you; if I bridge the space between two electric poles with my arm or my leg, I expose myself immediately to a shock, but I would not mistake the electrical current for a person, for a being of my own kind."

"You have the artist's temperament and that, of course, gives you a certain license. It seems that you hate and attack the intellect, conceptual thought. But, poet, how does this accord with so many of your own pronouncements? I have read sentences, articles, books by you in which you preach exactly the opposite and give your support to reason and intellect instead of to unreasoning and accidental nature, where you argue for ideas and recognize the intellectual as the highest principle. How about all that now, eh?"

"So—do I do that? Yes, it may well be. I have the misfortune, you see, constantly to contradict myself. Reality always does that, only the intellect and virtue do not and you do not, my little-honored sir. For example, after a vigorous walk in summertime I can be completely obsessed by the desire for a cup of water, and declare that water is the most wonderful thing in the world. A quarter of an hour later there is nothing in the world less interesting to me than water. That's just the way I feel about eating, sleeping, thinking. My relation to the so-called 'intellect,' for example, is exactly the same as it is toward eating or drinking. Sometimes there is nothing in the world that attracts me so much and seems so indispensable as the intellect, as the possibility of abstraction, of logic, of ideas. Then again when I am satiated with it and need and long for the opposite, all intellect disgusts me like spoiled food. I know from experience that this attitude is considered whimsical and lacking in character, indeed impermissible, but I have never been able to understand why. For just as I must constantly alternate between eating and fasting, sleeping and waking, I must also swing back and forth between naturalism and intellectualism, between experience and Platonism, between order and revolution, between Catholicism and the spirit of the Reformation. That a person all his life long should be able consistently to honor intellect and despise nature, always be a revolutionary and never a conservative, or the other way about, that seems to me, of course, very virtuous, dependable, and steadfast, but it equally seems to me deadly, repulsive, and crazy, as though one wanted always to eat or always simply to sleep. And yet all factions political and intellectual, religious and scientific, are based on the presupposition that such crazy behavior is possible, is natural! You too, sir, find it improper that at one hour I should be violently in love with the intellect and attribute the impossible to it but at another time should hate the intellect and spit upon it, seeking instead the innocence and profusion of nature! Why not? Why do you find what is natural without character, what is healthy and self-evident impermissible? If you can explain that to me, then I will gladly confess verbally and in writing that I am beaten on all points. I would grant you as much reality as I possibly could, I would loan you a complete halo of reality. —But, you see, you simply can't explain it! You stand there, and under your waistcoat undoubtedly there is a meal you have eaten, but no heart, and in your cleverly counterfeited skull there is no doubt intellect, but no nature. I have never seen anything so laughably unreal as you, you rheumatic, you spa guest! Paper gleams through your buttonholes, intellect runs out of your seams, inside there is nothing but newsprint and customs forms, Kant and Marx, Plato and tax tables. If I blow, you're gone! If I think of my beloved or even of a small yellow primrose, that is enough to squeeze you completely out of reality! You are no object, you are no human being, you are an idea, a barren abstraction."

And in fact, having got somewhat excited but still in the best of moods, when I stretched out my arm with my fist clenched in order to demonstrate to this fellow his unreality, my fist went straight through him and he was gone. Only then did I notice, as I came to a stop, that I had left the hotel without my hat and had made my way to the lonely riverbank; I stood alone under the beautiful trees, and the water gurgled and murmured. And once more I was passionately devoted to the pole opposite to the intellect, was inwardly and drunkenly in love with the stupid, lawless world of chance, with the interplay of splashes of sun and shade on the bright rosy ground, with the many melodies of the flowing water. Ah, I knew those melodies! I remembered a riverbank in India I had once sat on as companion to an old ferryman, his name I no longer remember, a thousand years ago; I was intoxicated with ideas of oneness, not less intoxicated by the play of multiplicity and accident. I thought of my beloved, of the part of her ear that peeps out from under her hair, and I was heartily ready to deny and destroy all the altars I had ever built to reason and ideas, and to build a new altar in honor of that half-visible, mysterious ear. That the world is a unity and yet full of diversity, that beauty is possible only in the transitory, that grace can be experienced only by the sinner, for these and a hundred other profound and eternal truths, that beautiful ear could serve just as well as symbol and holy sign as any Isis, Vishnu, or lotus flower.

How the river murmured below me in its stony bed, how the light at midday sang up and down on the spotted boles of the plane trees! How fine it was to be alive! Blown away and forgotten was that mad desire to laugh in the dining room, tears stood in my eyes, admonitions came to me from the murmuring of the holy river, my heart was full of peace and thankfulness. Now for the first time I could see as I walked up and down under the trees the abyss of peevishness, error, pain, and foolishness in which I had recently lived! My God, how pitiable I looked, how little it took to turn me into a disgusting, cowardly creature! A little sickness and pain, a few weeks of life at the spa, a period of sleeplessness, and I was sunk to the neck in ill humor and despair. I who had heard the voice of the Hindu gods! How good that this evil enchantment was finally lifted, that once more air, sunlight, and reality surrounded me, that once more I heard divine voices, felt reverence and love in my heart!

Attentively I ran through in my mind those disgraceful days, I was troubled and amazed, sad and also a little amused over all the absurdities that had possessed me.

No, I no longer needed to visit the pump room, or the dignified gambling hall, I was no longer at a loss as to how to spend my time. The spell was broken.

And if today, shortly before the end of my cure, I reflect on how this could have come about, if I seek the cause of my decline and all my degrading experiences, then I need only read any page of these notes to see the reason clearly. Not my fantasy and daydreaming, not my lack of morality and civil responsibility was to blame, but exactly the opposite. I had been all too moral, all too reasonable and civic-minded! An old mistake, one I have committed a hundred times and bitterly regretted, is what happened to me this time too. I wanted to adapt myself to a norm, I wanted to fulfill demands that no one at all was making on me, I wanted to be or to play what I simply was not. And so it had happened to me once again that I had done violence to myself and to the whole of life.

In what way had I wanted to be something I was not? I had made a specialty of my sciatica, I had played the role of the sciatic, the guest at the spa, the hotel guest adapting to his surroundings instead of simply being who I was. I had taken Baden, the cure, my surroundings, the pains in my limbs much too seriously, I had got it into my head that through expiation in the form of this cure I had to become well. By the path of repentance, of punishment, of sanctimoniousness, by bathing and washing, through doctor and Brahmin magic, I had wanted to attain what can be attained only by the path of grace.

That is the way it has always been with me. Even that psychology of the baths that I hatched out in the tepid water is a kind of trick, an attempt to do intellectual violence to life; it had to fail and exact revenge. Nor am I, as I imagined for a while, the representative of a sciatic's special philosophy, nor is there such a philosophy at all. Nor is there such a thing as the wisdom of people fifty years old, about which I fantasied in the prologue. It may well be that my thinking of today is somewhat different from that of twenty years ago, but my feelings and my being, my wishing and hoping, are not different, they have become neither smarter nor stupider. Today, as then, I can become a child, an old man, now two years old, now a thousand. And my attempts to adapt myself to the standardized world, to play the fifty-year-old sciatic, remain just as fruitless as trying to reconcile myself to sciatica and Baden by means of psychology.

There are two paths to salvation: the path of righteousness for the righteous and the path of grace for the sinner. I, who am a sinner, have once more committed the mistake of attempting to reach salvation through righteousness. I will never succeed. And it, sweet milk to the righteous, is poison to us sinners, it makes us malicious. I am destined to have to make this attempt, to commit this error, again and again, just as in intellectual matters it is my destiny that I who am a poet must constantly renew my attempts to overcome the world by thought rather than by art. Again and again I take these long and laborious, lonesome excursions, continually make these attempts at reason and end in pain and confusion. But this death is always followed by rebirth, I am always retouched by grace, and the pain and confusion are no longer bad, the wrong paths turn out to have been good, the defeats have been precious, for they have thrown me back on the maternal heart, have made it possible for me to experience grace once more.

And so I will cease moralizing over myself, I will stop storming at my experiments with reason and psychology, at my experiments with the cure, at my defeats and despair, I will no longer bemoan them, I will no longer accuse myself. Everything has turned out for the best. I hear God's voice again, all is well.

Today, if I look around me in my room, No. 65, an amusing thing happens: I experience in anticipation a kind of homesickness at my imminent departure; leaving the room pains me a little in advance. How often here at this little table I have filled pages with my writing, sometimes full of joy in the feeling that I was doing something worthwhile, sometimes full of despondency and disbelief, and yet absorbed in the work, in my attempt to understand and explain, or at least to confess candidly. How often in this easy chair have I read Jean Paul! How often have I lain half the night, the whole night, sleepless in this bed in the alcove, obsessed with myself, quarreling with myself, justifying myself, experiencing my sorrows as an allegory, as a conundrum whose solution and interpretation must sometime be made clear! How many letters have I received and written here, letters from unknown persons and to unknown persons, people to whom my character as represented in my books appeared related, who in question and acknowledgment, in accusation and confession to someone who seems to them related, are seeking what I in my avowals and my poetry seek: clarity, comfort, justification, new freedom, new innocence, new love of life! How many thoughts, how many whimsies, how many dreams have visited me here in this small room! Here on dull and weary mornings I have roused myself for the bath, feeling death in advance in my stiff and aching limbs, reading the handwriting of mortality; here on many a good evening I have spun my fantasies or done battle with the Dutchman. Here on that happy day I read the prologue to my *Psychologia* to my beloved, and saw her happiness over the little token of esteem for Jean Paul, whom she too loves so dearly. And all in all this whole time in Baden, this cure, this crisis, this recovery, this loss of equilibrium, has been for me a momentous epoch.

And what a pity it is that I could not have learned to feel this love and homely sentiment for this little hotel room three or four weeks earlier! But I must accept things as they are. Enough that I can today accept and love and make my own this room and hotel, the Dutchman and the cure. Now that my days in Baden are coming to an end, I see that it is very pretty here, and I believe that I could live here for months. I should really do just that if only to make up for the things in which I have sinned, toward myself, toward my neighbors at table and in the next-door room. Have I not on some utterly dark days even doubted the doctor, doubted the sincerity of his assurances, the hopes that he offered me? Indeed, there would be much to make good. What, for example, entitled me to take umbrage at the private picture gallery of Herr Kesselring? Was I perhaps an arbiter of ethics? Hadn't I myself hobbies that not everyone would approve? And why did I see in that moral gentleman with the wrinkles simply the bourgeois, the egoist, and the presumptuous judge of others? I could just as well have made of him a Roman, a monumental, stylized tragic hero, destroyed by his own harshness, suffering from his own uprightness. And so forth. A thousand omissions would need to be made good, a thousand sins and acts of lovelessness expiated—if I had not just now abandoned the path of expiation and abandoned myself to grace. Well then, let the sins be sins, and let us be happy if we succeed for a while in not piling up any new ones!

When I bend once more over the abyss of the past evil days, I see among the guests, faraway and small, a ghostly image mirrored: Hesse the guest at the spa, pale and disconsolate, with an annoyed expression, sitting in front of his meal, a poor fellow without wit or fantasy, gray with sleeplessness, a loveless, sickly being who does not have sciatica but is possessed by sciatica. Shuddering, I turn away, happy that this fellow is now dead and cannot rise to confront me again. May he rest in peace.

If one takes the sayings of the New Testament not as commandments but as expressions of an extraordinarily profound wisdom about the secrets of our souls, then the wisest saying that was ever uttered, the brief statement of the whole art of living and pursuit of happiness, is "Love thy neighbor as thyself," which, by the way, is to be found in the Old Testament as well. One can love his neighbor less than himself—then he becomes an egotist, a profiteer, a capitalist, a bourgeois, and can, of course, acquire money and power but not a truly happy heart, for the finest, most delicious joys of the soul are locked away from him. Or one can love one's neighbor more than oneself—then he becomes a poor devil full of inferiority feelings, longing to love everything but still full of rancor and discontent toward himself, and living in a hell that he himself daily makes hotter. On the other hand, the equilibrium of love, the ability to love without being at fault here and there, this love for oneself that is not stolen from anyone, this love for others that does not diminish one's own I or do violence to it! The secret of all happiness, all blessedness is in this saying. And if one wishes, one can turn it to its Hindu side and give it the meaning: Love your neighbor, for he is yourself! A Christian translation of *tat tvam asi* (that art thou). Ah, all wisdom is so simple, has been so precisely and unambiguously expressed and formulated for so long! Why does it belong to us only at times, only on the good days, why not always?

IN RETROSPECT

As I write these final pages I am no longer in Baden. I am—with my head already full of new projects and plans —back once more on my steppe, once more in my lonely hermitage. Hesse the guest at the spa, thank God, is dead and no longer concerns us. In his place there is now an entirely different Hesse, a man who, of course, has sciatica, but he has it, not it him.

When I left Baden, the departure was in fact rather difficult. I had formed an affection for all sorts of things and people, an affection I now had to break off—for my room, for my host, for the trees on the riverbank, for the doctor who in my final session once more proved himself splendidly, for the martens, for the pretty and friendly waitresses, Rösli, Trudi, and the others, for the gambling hall, for the faces and figures of many of my fellow sufferers. Farewell, friendly and constantly good-tempered, constantly helpful assistant at the diathermy machine! Farewell, giantess from Holland, and you too, blond-locked hero Kesselring!

My parting from the host at Heiligenhof was especially nice. Smiling, he listened to my thanks, my eulogy of his establishment, then asked me how well pleased the doctor was with me and my cure; and when I told him that the doctor had praised me highly and that I had the prospect of a complete cure, so that I could now leave Baden confidently, my host's smile increased to agreeable roguery, he laid his hand on my shoulder in friendly fashion: "Yes, go your way confidently! I congratulate you. But look, I know something that perhaps you do not: you will be back!"

"I will come back? To Baden?" I asked.

He laughed aloud. "Yes, indeed. Yes, indeed. They all come back, cured or not cured, so far every one of them has come back. Next time you will already be a regular."

I have not forgotten that parting speech. Probably he is right. Probably I will go back sometime, perhaps many times. But I will never be the same as I was this time. I will bathe again, I will be given electrical treatments again, I will again be well fed, become despondent and drink or gamble, but nevertheless everything will be quite different, just as my return home to the wilderness this time has been different from every earlier one. In detail everything will be just the same, everything will be very similar on the whole, however it will be new and different, other stars will preside over it. For life is not a computation, it is not a mathematical sum, but a miracle. So it has been all my life long; everything came again, the same needs, the same desires and joys, the same temptations, I kept hitting my head against the same corners, fighting with the same dragons, chasing the same butterflies, always repeating the same constellations and circumstances, and yet it was a perpetually new game, always recurrently beautiful, recurrently dangerous, recurrently exciting. A thousand times I have been arrogant, a thousand times dead-tired, a thousand times childish, a thousand times old and indifferent, and nothing lasted long, everything kept returning and yet was never the same. The oneness I reverence behind multiplicity is no boring, gray, intellectual, theoretical unity. It is, in fact, life itself, full of play, full of pain, full of laughter. It is represented in the dance of the god Siva, who dances the world to bits, and in many other images; it rejects no representation, no simile. You can enter into it at any time, it belongs to you at every instant, when you know no times, no space, no knowledge, no non-knowledge, when you desert convention, when you belong in love and surrender to all gods, all men, all worlds, all ages. In these instances you experience oneness and multiplicity at the same time, you see Buddha and Jesus moving past you, you speak with Moses, feel the sun of Ceylon on your skin and see the poles rigid in ice. Ten times have I been there in this brief period since my return from Baden.

And so I have not become "well." I am better, the doctor is satisfied, but I am not cured, it can return at any time. Aside from the actual improvement, I have Baden to thank, too, for the fact that I have now stopped persecuting my sciatica so grimly. I can see that it belongs to me, that it was well earned like the beginning of gray in my hair and that it is unwise to try simply to blot it out or remove it by magic. Let us be accommodating, we will win through conciliation!

And if sometime I go back to Baden I will climb into the warm water differently, I will live differently with my neighbors, I will have different worries and different games, write differently in my notes. I will commit new kinds of sins and find my way back to God along new ways, and always I will imagine that I am the one acting, living, thinking, and yet will know that it is He.

When I now look back to the few weeks of the cure, there arises in me, as with every retrospective view, that agreeable illusion of superiority, of understanding and penetration that in youth everyone enjoys so much at each new stage in life. I see the sufferings of my lately departed "I," the bodily pains and the psychic needs, lying behind me; the deadly situation has been survived and the Hesse who a short time ago behaved so comically in Baden seems to me to stand far below today's intelligent Hesse who looks back at him. I see how exaggeratedly Hesse, the guest at the spa, reacted to laughable trivialities, I recognize the droll play of his inhibitions and complexes, and I forget that these trivialities only seem small and laughable to me now because they are no longer present.

But what is big or small, important or unimportant? The psychiatrists consider a person emotionally disturbed who reacts sensitively and violently to small upsets, small irritations, small injuries to his feelings of self-importance, while this same person may perhaps endure with composure pains and shocks that the majority would consider very bad. And a person is considered healthy and normal on whose toes you can step repeatedly without his noticing it, who bears the most horrible music, the most deplorable architecture, the most polluted air without complaint or blame, who, however, pounds the table and calls upon the devil as soon as he loses a trifling sum at cards. In public houses I have very often seen men of good reputation, who were considered normal and honorable, when they lost a game, especially if they considered their partner to blame for the loss, curse and storm so fanatically, so coarsely, so piggishly that I have felt an impulse to apply to the nearest doctor for a certificate of commitment for these unfortunates. There are, in fact, many kinds of standards, to all of which one can allow some kind of validity, but to consider any one of them holy, whether it be that of science or of the public morality of the moment, is something I cannot bring myself to do.

And the same person who can laugh heartily at the self-portrait of Hesse, the guest at the spa, and find this fellow decidedly comic (and quite rightly too) would be very astonished if he should suddenly see someone with his own processes of thought, someone with his own everyday reactions to his surroundings described and analyzed precisely and in detail. Just as under a microscope something otherwise invisible or ugly, a speck of mud, can turn into a marvelous starry heaven, just so under the microscope of a true psychology (something that does not yet exist) every smallest motion of the soul, be it otherwise ever so bad or stupid or insane, would become a holy drama, worthy of devotion, because one would see in it simply an example, an allegorical copy, of the most holy thing we know, of life.

It would be presumptuous if I were to say that all my literary efforts for many years have been nothing but a striving toward that distant goal, a thin, feeble presentiment of that true psychology with universal eye under whose gaze nothing appears small or stupid or ugly but everything is venerable and holy, and yet in some sense that is true.

And if now, bidding farewell to these pages, I survey the whole of my Baden period with one last glance, there remains behind a dissatisfaction, a thorn, a sorrow. This sorrow does not concern my stupidities, my lack of patience, my nervousness, my harsh judgments; in short, any of my human inadequacies and failures, which I know are deeply conditioned and necessary. No, my sorrow, my feeling of emptiness and pain, has to do with these notes, these attempts to record as truthfully and candidly as possible a tiny portion of life. I am troubled and ashamed, this I must admit, not at my sins and vices but simply at the failure of my experiment in expression, at the very meager harvest of my literary effort.

And in fact there is a perfectly definite point at which my disappointment is rooted. Perhaps I can succeed in making this clear by a simile.

If I were a composer, I could without difficulty write a melody for two voices, a melody that would consist of two lines, of two rows of tunes and notes that correspond with one another, complement one another, fight with one another, limit one another, but in any case at every instant, at every point in the sequence, have a most profound interrelationship and reciprocal effect. And anyone who can read music could read off my double melody and always see and hear with every tone its counter-tone, its brother, its enemy, its opposite. Now it is just this, this double voice and constantly advancing antithesis, this double line, that I would like to express in my own medium, in words, and I work myself to the bone trying and do not succeed. I am always attempting it and if anything at all lends tension and weight to my works, it is this intensive concern for something impossible, this wild battling for something unattainable. I would like to find expression for duality, I would like to write chapters and sentences where melody and counter-melody are always simultaneously present, where unity stands beside every multiplicity, seriousness beside every joke. For to me, life consists simply in this, in the fluctuation between two poles, in the hither and thither between the two foundation pillars of the world. I would like always to point with delight at the many-splendored multiplicity of the world, and just as constantly utter a reminder that oneness underlies this multiplicity; I would like always to show that the beautiful and the ugly, the bright and the dark, sin and holiness are always opposites just for the moment, that they constantly merge into each other. For me the highest utterances of mankind are those few sentences in which this duality has been expressed in magic signs, those few mysterious sayings and parables in which the great world antitheses are recognized simultaneously as necessary and as illusion. The Chinese Lao-tse invented several such sayings in which the two poles of life for a lightning instant seem to touch each other. Even more nobly and simply, even more intimately, this same miracle is performed in many sayings of Jesus. I know nothing in the world so deeply affecting as this, that a religion, a teaching, a school of psychology should through the millennia elaborate the doctrine of good and evil, of right and wrong, constantly more subtly and rigorously, making higher demands on righteousness and obedience, only to end finally at the summit with the magic perception that ninety-nine righteous persons are of less value in the eyes of God than one sinner at the moment of repentance.

But perhaps it is a great mistake on my part, yes, a sin, if I believe that I have to labor to proclaim this highest insight. Perhaps the unhappiness of our present world consists just in this, that this highest wisdom is offered cheap on every street, that in every national church, in addition to belief in the authorities, in accumulating money, and in national vanity, faith in the miracle of Jesus is preached, that the New Testament, repository of the most precious and the most dangerous wisdom, can be bought anywhere and is even distributed free by missionaries. Perhaps such incredible, daring, yes, terrifying insights and intuitions as are contained in many of Jesus' talks should be kept carefully hidden and be surrounded by protective walls. Perhaps it would be a good and desirable thing if a person had to sacrifice years and risk his life to learn of one of those mighty sayings, just as he must do for other great values in life. If that is so (and there are many days on which I believe it is), then the latest writer of popular fiction is acting better and more properly than the man who struggles to find expression for the eternal.

This is my dilemma and problem. Much can be said about it, but it cannot be solved. To force the two poles of life together, to transcribe the dual voices in life's melody will never be possible for me. And yet I will follow the dark command within me and will be compelled again and again to make the attempt. This is the mainspring that drives my little clock.

Journey to Nuremberg
(1926)

THE author of these travel reminiscences is not lucky enough to be numbered among those who can give clear reasons for their actions; nor is he lucky enough to believe that such reasons exist either for himself or for others. Reasons, so it seems to me, are always obscure, causality never prevails in life, only in thought. The completely intellectualized man to be sure, one who has altogether outgrown nature, should be able to recognize an uninterrupted causal nexus in his life and would be justified in considering the causes and impulses accessible to his consciousness as the only ones, for he would consist wholly and entirely of consciousness. However, I have never yet encountered such a man or such a god, and with us other humans I permit myself to be skeptical about all ostensible motivations for any action or occurrence. There is no one who acts from "reasons"; people simply pretend to do so and they try very hard, in the interests of vanity and virtue, to convince others that this is true. In my own case, at least, I have been able in each and every instance to determine that the impulses for my actions lie in regions which neither my reason nor my will can penetrate. And today if I ask myself what the real reason was for my autumn trip from Ticino to Nuremberg—a trip that lasted two months—then I become seriously embarrassed; the closer I examine it the more the reasons and impulses seem to branch, split, and divide until finally they extend back into the distant years, not however as a linear causal sequence but rather as a much reticulated net of such sequences, so that finally this in itself unimportant and accidental journey seems to have been determined by innumerable moments in my earlier life.

Only a few of the coarsest knots in this fabric are accessible to me. A year ago when I was in Swabia for a short time, one of my Swabian friends who lives in Blaubeuren complained that I had failed to visit him and I promised that on my next Swabian trip I would make good that omission. Seen from outside, that was the first incentive to the trip. But even this promise had background and collateral reasons, as I later clearly realized. Much though I liked the idea of seeing an old fricnd who would rejoice in my visit, I am nevertheless a comfort-loving man who shuns journeys and crowds, to whom the idea of a trip to a small, remote rural village has little to recommend it. No, it was not simply friendship or even courtesy that caused me to make that promise, there was something beyond that, behind the name "Blaubeuren" there lurked a charm and a mystery, a flood of reminiscences, memories, and enticements. In the first place Blaubeuren is a dear old Swabian country town, the seat of a Swabian monastery school such as I myself had attended as a boy. Further, there are in Blaubeuren and in that same monastery famous and precious objects to be seen, especially a Gothic altar. To be sure, this inducement from the history of art would hardly have been enough to set me in motion. But in the complex of "Blaubeuren" there was the echo of something else, something at once Swabian, poetic, and for me extraordinarily charming: near Blaubeuren in the Blautopf once lived the lovely Lau, and this lovely Lau had swum underground from the Blautopf into the cellar of the Nonnenhof, had appeared there in an open spring, "floating up to her breast in the water" as her historian reports. And it was here in the charming fantasies that linger about the magic names Blau and Lau that my longing for Blaubeuren had sprung up. It was only much later that my reason could catch up and ascertain that it was the sight of the Blautopf and the lovely Lau and her bath in the cellar of the Nonnenhof that were the objects of my desire and that from this source flowed my acceptance of the trip to Blaubeuren. I have always found that not only I but all those enviable mortals who can give reasons for their actions are in truth never prompted or led by those reasons but always by their love affairs, and I have no hesitation in confessing to this particular love of mine, for it belongs among the most powerful and beautiful of my youthful years. When I was young, two female figures of poetry guided my poetic and sensuous fantasies as noble models, both beautiful, both mysterious, both washed round by water, the lovely Lau from "The Gnome" and beautiful Judith of the bath from *Green Heinrich.** I had not thought of either in many years, had not spoken their names, had not reread their stories. And now suddenly while thinking of the word Blaubeuren I saw the lovely Lau again, up to her breast in water, her white arms resting on the stone edging of the cellar spring, and I smiled and knew exactly what the motive for my trip had been. And in addition to the lovely Lau, whom I hardly dared hope to meet in her former residence, there was interwoven with these echoes and fantasies the memory of my youth and its compelling dream world, of the poet Mörike, of age-old Swabian sayings, games, and fairy tales, of the language and landscape of my childhood. Neither my family's house nor the city of my infant years could exercise a similar magic over me, I had revisited them too often, had all too completely lost them. But here in the images evoked by the sound "Blaubeuren" were concentrated all the still-living bonds that linked my heart to youth, homeland, and my people. And all these rela-

---

* "The Gnome" (*Das Stuttgarter Hutzelmännlein*) is a story by Eduard Mörike (1804–1875); *Green Heinrich* (*Der Grüne Heinrich*) is a novel by Gottfried Keller (1819–1890).—Ed.

tionships, memories, and emotions stood under the sign of Venus, the lovely Lau. A stronger magic, of course, could not be conceived.

Meanwhile, all this was still asleep inside me, none of it forced its way into my consciousness, and all that existed at first was a promise—I could fulfill it in two or in ten years. Then one day in spring came an invitation to give a public reading in Ulm. If it had reached me at any other moment, I would have taken care of it in the same way as all the others, with a polite postcard it would have been declined and that would have been the end of the matter. But now the invitation from Ulm came not at a random moment but at a particular one, it came at a time when life was giving me an unusual amount of trouble, when I saw round about me only worries, obligations, and boredom, and no cheerful prospects, and when any thought of change, of movement or flight was naturally welcome. Therefore, I did not write that polite postcard but read the invitation through again, this time already with the dawning thought that Ulm was in the neighborhood of Blaubeuren, and I left the invitation on my desk for a day or two, and then I accepted, on condition that the reading should not take place in the cold winter weather but in the fall or spring. The people in Ulm scheduled it for the beginning of November and I agreed, not however without the small mental reservation with which I treated all far-off engagements, the secret thought: "If it comes right down to it, you can always telegraph your regrets."

Well, it was spring and November was still far away and I did not think much about this engagement; other thoughts and cares preoccupied me, closer, more burning ones, and if now and again I recalled the Ulm affair I thought only with some regret that I had once more let myself be enticed by an occasion whose worth I did not believe in and that would turn out in the end to be a tiresome duty. Singers, virtuosi, and actors whose actual calling it is to appear in public have to get used to the tiresome necessity of obligating themselves six months or a year in advance to appear on a certain day and hour, just as it is also a part of their profession to make themselves independent of mood and whim of the moment and allow their art free play. But for a writer, a quiet village dweller who travels seldom, a man of the study, the thought that on the twelfth of the month after next he must without fail give a public reading in this or that city can be under certain circumstances horrifying. How easily it might turn out that just then was the right time to work, that those would be the favorable hours for which one waits so long in vain—and then in the midst of one's best work one would have to put everything aside for days, pack one's bags, consult timetables, travel, sleep in hotel beds in strange cities, and read one's poems aloud to strangers, poems for which perhaps at the moment one would feel no kinship and which would seem outgrown and trite! And so the poet often has to pay dearly if he allows himself through vanity, desire for gain, or love of travel to be enticed into a public reading.

People engaged in methodical, organized work, who customarily begin their labors at eight and two o'clock, who are prepared on receipt of a telegram to embark on a lengthy journey on the shortest possible notice, for whom a free afternoon means a small paradise, who devote themselves to their relaxations with watch in hand, such men have no inkling of the indolent, unregulated, whimsical ways in which a poet spends his dubious life! Of course there are poets conscious of their duty who with a certain regularity and perseverance devote themselves to work, spending stubborn hours at their desks, beginning at a definite time each morning, men who have schooled themselves to be insensible to the weather and acoustic disturbances from outside as well as to their own moods and indolence, heroic, splendid men, the latchet of whose shoes

I am prepared to unloose, but to emulate them would be for me a hopeless undertaking. As for myself, I believe that no respectable and diligent person would shake hands with me if he knew how little worth time has for me, how I squander days and weeks, yes, months, with what foolishness I waste my life. No employer, no office, no rules prescribe when I am to get up in the morning or when I am to go to bed at night, when I am to work or when I have to rest. My work has no deadline set for it, and it makes the devil a bit of difference whether I take an afternoon for a poem of three stanzas or a quarter of a year. When a day seems to me too beautiful to waste on work, I honor it by going for a walk, painting water colors, or doing nothing. When a day seems to me too gray or too oppressive, too cold or too warm to work, I spend it lying on the couch reading or I fill pages with crayon drawings full of involuted fantasies, or just stay in bed, especially if it is winter and I am feeling achy. If I have mislaid my fountain pen or feel the need to meditate on the relationship between Hindu and Chinese mythology, or if on my morning walk I have met a beautiful lady, then there can be no thought of work. On the other hand, though work is not my strong point and is essentially repugnant to me, the effort to be constantly ready for work is in my eyes a solemn obligation. I have, to be sure, time to do nothing, but I have no time for trips, for sociability or fishing or other nice things—no, I must be constantly near to my workroom, alone, undisturbed, ready at any instant for the possible task. If I am invited to dinner in Locarno tomorrow night, that disturbs me, for how do I know whether tomorrow night may not bring flying one of those rare, beautiful moments when the magic bird sings to me, when the lust for work stirs? For an idler of this sort, who nevertheless likes to have the secret assurance that every day he is prepared for work, there is hardly anything more upsetting than to know months in advance that on such and such a predetermined date in such and such a place he must perform a specific task.

If it were of any importance to me to justify my irregular and wasted life, I could present a few facts by way of exculpation. I could mention that in the moment of actual work, though that may come only a few times during the year, no weather and no problem of health, no irritation, no day, no night any longer exists for me, that then I am as fanatic as a fakir, forgetting the world and myself, throwing myself into the maelstrom of work, out of which I later emerge, exhausted, small, and broken. I could also mention that my squandering of time is not simply due to laziness and disorder but is a conscious protest against the craziest and most holy maxim of the modern world: Time is money. In itself, this sentence is perfectly true, one can easily transform time into money, just as one can easily transform an electric current into light and heat. The crazy and vulgar part of this most stupid of human maxims is simply this—that "money" is unqualifiedly assumed to be a supreme value. But allow me to omit self-justification. I am in fact, despite all apparent proofs that might be adduced to the contrary, an idler, a spendthrift of time, a contented dodger of work, not to mention other sins. Whether I am despised for this or envied, no one except myself knows how dearly I pay for my sins. But enough of that. I do have to say a word, however, about the maxim "Time is money," because it is very closely connected with the story of my journey. My revulsion against that article of faith of the modern world and against the modern world itself, by which I mean machine culture as a whole, is so great that whenever possible I scorn to adapt myself to its laws. While today, for example, it is considered an achievement to travel a thousand and more kilometers in a single day, I consider it unworthy of a human being to endure more than four or five hours in a moving railway carriage, at most, and I require a week for a trip that others accomplish in a day and a night. For the friends who here and there on the journey are my hosts, this can be at times a little bothersome, for if I commence to feel at ease in one place, then I am likely to struggle, often for several days, against traveling farther, against packing, against the whole ugly and exhausting to-do at the station and on the train. Among the rules of life of many wise men, there is this injunction: Live each day as though it were your last. Well, and who would spend his last day breathing soot, lugging bags, struggling through station turnstiles, and performing all the laughable actions that are part of travel by rail? The one nice thing about it is being shut up indiscriminately with other people, but, fine though this can be, after a few hours it usually loses its charm. And should the happy accident occur and you find yourself seated in a railroad carriage next to the person who is destined to be your bosom friend and without whom you could no longer live, you would have to be a bungler if you did not presently succeed in persuading him to get out with you at some attractive station and help you determine whether grass and flowers, blue sky and clouds still exist. I cannot deny that traveling in my fashion does not get a man forward very fast and perhaps smacks of the Middle Ages; should I ever make up my mind to go to Berlin (so far I have succeeded in avoiding that), the trip would require at least twelve days. One has to be completely unmodern in attitude to appreciate this method of travel and to be able to see its great advantages. It has, to be sure, disadvantages as well: traveling my way is rather expensive, for example; on the other hand, my trips have brought me many satisfactions that would have been completely unobtainable by modern methods. And I am perfectly willing to go to some expense for such satisfactions, I value them very highly, since I am in general incredibly pleasure-loving. It is the fate of many people to experience life mostly as sorrow and pain, not only in theory, in a sort of literary-aesthetic pessimism, but bodily and actually. These persons, among whom I, alas, belong, have more talent for experiencing pain than for experiencing pleasure; breathing and sleeping, eating and digesting, all the simplest animal functions cause them pain and distress rather than pleasure. Now, despite all this, following a law of nature, these people feel in themselves an impulse to affirm life, to find pain good, not to surrender, and so they are extraordinarily obsessed with everything that can give them some joy, can cheer them a bit, can make them feel a little happy and warm, and they attribute to all these pleasant things a worth they do not have for the ordinary, healthy, normal, industrious person. This is the way, in fact, that nature brings into being something extremely beautiful and complex for which almost everyone has a certain respect—humor. In those suffering people, in those all too weak, all too helpless, all too pleasure-loving people, searchers for comfort, there arises from time to time what is called humor, a crystal that grows only in deep and enduring pain, but nevertheless belongs among humanity's better inventions. This humor produced by sufferers so that they can bear the pains of life and even sing its praises has, oddly enough, the opposite effect on the others, the healthy non-sufferers, as though it were an outburst of merriment and uncontrolled joy in life; the healthy ones slap their thighs and whinny and then are always taken aback and somewhat offended when from time to time they read some such report as this, that the much loved and successful Comedian X incomprehensibly drowned himself in a fit of despondency.

If a lenient view can be taken of my having so much spare time and jumping from one subject to another, I will immediately get back to my theme. Or if I should not succeed in doing that, just ask yourself: Can there be anything of importance in what a man like me has to say about a journey, a man who rejects railroads and yet uses them, an idler who squanders his days in search of distractions and games, who accepts invitations to give readings though he is extremely skeptical of this activity, and to whom rejection and ridicule of the serious, real, modern, vigorous, diligent life has become a kind of nasty game? No, what such a romantic has to say about a journey can have no sort of relevance, and whoever gives ear to this clown runs the risk that the clown, after the fashion of humorists, will again and again lose sight of his ostensible subject and will have to search for it laboriously. Possibly he is a kind of humorist, and humorists, all of them, whatever they may write, use their titles and subjects simply as pretexts; in truth they all have only a single theme: the extraordinary sadness and, if I may be permitted the expression, shittiness of human life, and amazement at the fact that this wretched life can nevertheless be so beautiful and precious.

This was the situation with my trip: summer had come, the melody of my life at the moment had not become any sweeter, cares from outside beset me, and my old favorite comforts and pleasures, painting and reading, had lost much of their charm, for I was suffering from a continuous pain in my eyes, something that I had, to be sure, known in the past, but which was new in the degree of its severity and persistence. I felt clearly that I was once more at the sorry end of a wish fulfillment and that my life must shortly come under some new sign in order to achieve meaning again. Through many years and with many sacrifices I had succeeded in creating for myself a hermitage where I could sit hidden and completely alone in my den and pursue my games and sins, thought and fantasy, reading, painting, wine-bibbing, writing—and now this wish was fulfilled, I had enjoyed this experiment to the full and my eyes smarted and my work, including reading and painting, had ceased to be happiness, and out of this state would come, once it became unendurable and had roasted me in its fires, some new state, a new attempt at life, a new incarnation such as I had already undergone often before. Now it was a question of tasting my pains to the limit, closing my eyes, making myself small, and accepting fate. From this point of view the trip to Ulm which was to take place at the beginning of November was very welcome. If it brought nothing else, it would, after all, bring change, new scenes, new people. It interrupted the loneliness, it compelled one to participate, to be attentive, it led outward. Very well, it was welcome. I had already begun to make plans. Before the reading in Ulm, I wanted to visit Blaubeuren, unconditionally *before.* I wanted to go there, to the lovely Lau and to my friend, not by any chance bringing with me discouragement and disgust such as often come upon me after public readings. And so I would have to leave at the end of October. But from my village of Ticino to Blaubeuren was a long way, I would have to arrange to cut up this great journey into small, agreeable pieces, to make it enjoyable and digestible. In any case, I determined to make a stop in Zurich, where I had friends and where I could, without exposing myself to the horrors of living in a hotel, indulge myself a little in city life, in music, good wine, cinema, perhaps the theater. On the other hand it seemed to me, the closer I calculated, that the trip would be quite expensive, and the honorarium for the reading in Ulm was not intended for a man who was likely, during a journey, to let days grow into weeks. Therefore, I had no objection when suddenly from Augsburg came another invitation for a reading. Augsburg, as I knew, was only about a two-hour trip on the train from Ulm, and so there would not even be the need for an intermediate stop. I specified that the Augsburg reading should be two days after the one in Ulm, and we reached agreement. Now my journey had already become a bit more important and more probable, for now not only would I see Ulm and Augsburg, those venerable Swabian cities, but from Augsburg I would naturally go on to Munich, where I had so many friends and where so many long years ago I had spent good and happy days.

Provisionally I announced my plans to my friends in Zurich, Ulm, and Munich; enthusiastic answers and invitations added to my desire to travel, also after long consideration it seemed to me not impossible that I could cover the distance from Zurich to Blaubeuren in a single day. In that case, of course, I would have to leave at seven or eight o'clock in the morning and that seemed to me a depressingly early hour for late October, but after all I too could make some small sacrifice; smiling, I wrote down the train times.

In the summer months my principal calling is not literature but painting, and so I sat, insofar as my eyes would permit, very diligently making water colors under the chestnut trees, at the edge of our beautiful forest, paintings of the bright Ticino hills and villages which four years before I imagined I knew more thoroughly than anyone on earth and with which, since then, I have become so much more intimately acquainted. My portfolio of pictures grew thicker, and as gently and unnoticeably as every year, the fields grew yellower, the early mornings cooler, the evening mountains more violet, and I had to mix more gold and red with my green. Suddenly the cornfields were bare, the red earth called for *caput mortuum* and rose madder, and the shocks of corn were golden and pale blond, September had come, and the clarity of the post-summer days began. At no other time of year do I hear the voice of mortality as I do then, at no other time of year do I drink in the colors of the earth so thirstily and so scrupulously, like a connoisseur emptying the last glass of a noble vintage. Also, I had had some small successes with my painting, about which I am somewhat ambitious; I had sold a few pictures, and a German monthly had agreed that someone else's essay about the Ticino landscape should be illustrated by me, I had already seen the proofs of the pictures and had received my artist's fee, and I was toying with the idea that perhaps I might still succeed in escaping from literature entirely and make my living at the more appealing trade of painter. Those were several good days. But when in my joy I overstrained my eyes and could not go on painting, and many signs of autumn began to appear, restlessness overtook me. If it were true that my present life situation was in decline, if I had determined upon change, movement, and travel, then there was no point in waiting so long. Toward the end of September I decided to leave.

Now suddenly there was a lot to do. Going off as early as this meant packing for several weeks, and I had no intention of leading the life of a traveler for all this time but rather of stopping comfortably here and there, perhaps to paint or write. In any case I must take my painting materials with me and a good selection of books. Suits and shirts had to be seen to, buttons sewed on, tears mended, all my chests and drawers stood open. At the last minute it turned out that my black suit for the readings was in bad shape and many things had to be done to it. And before the trunk was closed, another invitation for a reading came, from Nuremberg, with the suggestion that I come there directly from Augsburg. That had to be thought over. Nuremberg fitted excellently into my trip, was the hardly dispensable addition to Ulm and Augsburg for a culture tour of cities. And so I accepted, not for the day after Augsburg but for five days later. This interval would probably allow me to cover the distance between Augsburg and Nuremberg in a dignified fashion.

And now I could leave. Zurich was my first goal. After that I intended to make a reservation at a hotel in Baden, where the healing sulphur springs are, and to spend some time taking a mild cure. But my big trunk had already gone and I was ready to leave with my hand luggage when the September sun began to shine so brightly, the vineyards were so full of ripe blue grapes, that it would have been a sin to travel to cool gray Zurich. And I had not even thought about the grape harvest which I would now miss! To unpack and not go, to creep back once more into the outgrown cocoon I wanted to escape from anyway—that was unthinkable. But in Locarno I had friends I had not seen in a long while. There I could begin my new life without having to say farewell to the sun and the grapes. I traveled to Locarno.

I was returning to a little city and a landscape where years ago I had known intimately every small stream and gully, every fieldstone wall with cracks full of little ferns and wood pinks, a landscape that three times during the war sheltered and comforted me and made me happy and thankful once more. The people of Locarno were in high spirits, Locarno just having been chosen as the location for the diplomatic conference, and the city was hard at work refurbishing and beautifying itself. It was splendid, but if during his stay in Locarno, Herr Stresemann had sat down on one of the pretty benches in the piazza, his suit would have been ruined; they were all freshly done up with oil paint.

I had chosen well, Locarno was a good beginning for my journey. I deprived the statesmen of a number of pounds of sweet grapes by eating them on the sunniest hillsides of Brione and Gordola, and after being alone for so long I enjoyed the pleasure of sitting with friends and talking, expressing in speech and glance those things that come alive in a person minute by minute and that always lose their best and most personal elements on the circuitous path of the pen. In no art am I so much a dilettante and beginner as in that of sociability, but none enchants me more in those rare hours when I can exercise it in beneficent surroundings. Day after day dawned radiant over Tamaro, and if the marvelous little road along the shore of the Rivapiana no longer had the enchantment of loneliness and lostness I enjoyed there twenty and even ten years ago, nevertheless this corner of the lake is still a place of friendly refuge. And as soon as one leaves behind the neighborhood of the hotels and the few most frequented country roads and penetrates into the steep, rough, mountain country, then one is out of Europe and out of time, in the company of stone and bush, lizards and snakes, in a poor but warm and friendly country full of color and little tender charms and amiabilities. Here in past years I studied the lizards, butterflies, and locusts, caught scorpions and praying mantises, made my first attempts in painting and, accompanied by a stray dog named Rio, spent good hot days in cross-country wanderings. Everywhere the fragrance of that time was preserved, everywhere sudden little memories—the corner of a house, a garden hedge—spoke to me of hours of healing contemplation I had spent in the hardest period of my earlier life. Aside from my native city in the Black Forest, this region around Locarno is the only place that has ever given me the feeling of home, and some of this was still with me and gave me cheer.

I stayed four or five days in Locarno, and as early as the third day I felt one of the benefits of travel that I had not anticipated at all. I got no mail! All the worries that the mail brings, all the claims, all the unreasonable demands on my eyes, on my heart, on my mood were suddenly no longer there! I knew, to be sure, that it was only a reprieve and that at my next stop, where I would stay somewhat longer, I would have to have the whole mess, at least the letters, sent after me. But for today, tomorrow, and the next day, I had no mail, I was a human being, a child of God, my eyes and thoughts, my hours and my moods belonged to me, to me alone and to my friends. No publisher warning me, no printer asking for the return of proofs, no autograph hunter, no young poet, no secondary-school student with a request for advice about his essay, and no threatening and abusive letters from some association of Germanic madmen, nothing of the sort, nothing but stillness and peace! My God, being without mail for a couple of days, one sees for the first time what a pile of rubbish and indigestible trash one has to swallow day after day all one's life. Not reading the newspaper for a while is just the same (I have managed that for years now); with a sense of shame one becomes aware of what shabby trivialities one has wasted the morning hours on every day, corrupting one's mind and heart, from the lead article to the stock-exchange list. And how agreeable in lieu of all of this to be able to decide what to think about, what to forget, and what to imagine, according to the whim of the moment! Most important of all: not to be reminded constantly of literature, of the fact that one belongs to a class and profession, a dubious and not very respectable calling, as a result a not highly regarded one, and that in incomprehensible youthful delusion one once committed the error of turning a talent into a profession! Well, I can certainly say that I enjoyed this closed season consciously and thoughtfully, often toyed, too, with the possibility of making this situation permanent, through some chicanery making myself unreachable and without address and so regaining that happiness that every poor bird under the sky, every poor worm in the earth, every shoemaker's apprentice heedlessly enjoys: not to be known, not to be a sacrifice to the idiotic cult of personality, not to have to live in that filthy, lying, suffocating air of public life! Oh, I had often attempted to withdraw from this fraud and had been forced to recognize each time that the world is inexorable, that what it wants from the poet is not poems and thoughts but his address and personality, to honor him, then kick him out, to adorn and then undress him, to enjoy and then spit at him the way a naughty girl behaves with her doll. Once with the aid of a pseudonym I succeeded for almost a year in giving expression to my thoughts and fantasies under a borrowed name, unburdened by fame and enmity, undisturbed by caricatures, but then it was over, then I was betrayed, the journalists came flocking, a gun was held to my head and I had to confess. My brief joy came to an end, and since then I have been Hesse the well-known man of letters, and all I could do to avenge myself was to take pains to write such things as could be enjoyed by only a very few, so that since then I have had a somewhat more peaceful life.

Nevertheless, I was not completely spared from literary reminders. A reader whose acquaintance I made hailed me enthusiastically as the author of *Peter Camenzind*. So there I stood and got red in the face, what was I to say to the man? Should I tell him that I could no longer remember that book, that in fifteen years I had not read it, that it was much mixed up in my memory with *The Trumpeter of Säckingen*?* Moreover, that it was not the book itself I detested but simply the effect it had had on my life; to be exact, that because of its completely unexpected success I had been driven permanently into literature, from which I had not succeeded in extricating myself despite desperate efforts? He would have understood none of this, he would (I knew this from bad experience) interpret my aversion to my literary fame as pretense and coquettish modesty. He would have misunderstood me under any circumstances, and so I said nothing, blushed a little and escaped as soon as I could.

When I continued my journey, determined now to bring my parting with summer and the South to a definite end and to travel uninterruptedly to Zurich, I was able to ex-

* *Der Trompeter von Säckingen* is a sentimental epic poem by Josef Victor von Scheffel (1826–1886).—Ed.

perience another agreeable benefit of travel; to wit, that as soon as one is involved in a trip, saying goodbye becomes easy. At other times, when I left my Locarno friend to go home, I always had the feeling that it would be a long while until we met again, and the parting was always difficult and depressing for me. In this, too, I am a non-modern man, in that I do not disdain and hate feelings and sentiments but rather ask myself: On what do we really live, where do we find life if not in our feelings? What good are a full purse and a bank account, well-pressed clothes and a pretty girl, if they produce no feelings, if my soul is not touched? No, however much I hate sentimentality in others, in myself I love it and pamper it a little. Feelings, the tenderness and easy excitability of emotional vibrations, those are in fact my dowry, with them I must pay my way in life. If I were dependent on my muscular strength and had become a wrestler or boxer, no one would consider that I ought to regard muscular strength as something secondary. If I were good at mental arithmetic and had become the manager of a great office, no one would require that I rate ability in mental arithmetic as something inferior. But what modern times demand from the poet and many young poets demand from themselves is that they hate just those qualities that make the poet, excitability of soul, the ability to fall in love, the ability to love and to glow, to surrender oneself and to experience in the world of feeling the unprecedented and super-normal, that they should hate just these their strong points and be ashamed of them and guard against everything that could be called "sentimental." All right, let them do so; I will not join in, my feelings are a thousand times dearer to me than all the smartness in the world and they alone protected me in the war years from joining in the sentimentality of the smart ones and gleefully reveling in the shooting.

And so I departed with a blithe heart. A farewell of this

sort, if one is not traveling back to his den but out into the world, has nothing oppressive about it; one feels superior to those who are staying behind, one promises without hesitation to return soon, one believes it too, and in any case one is on the way and in the swim. This blithe farewell echoing in my ears was the last of Locarno as I traveled into the St. Gotthard Pass, and I decided not to have my mail forwarded to Zurich but to have it sent on to Baden.

Along this route lie many places that have played a role in my life: Göschenen, Flüelen, Zug, and especially Brunnen, where last summer Othmar Schoek finished the composition of his *Penthesilea*—an afternoon there at the piano in his little room has stayed with me as a radiant memory. I rode past all these and willingly let myself be swallowed up by the city of Zurich. Zurich, of course, is one of those words that has a different meaning for each person. For me it has meant for years something Asiatic, I have friends there who lived for many years in Siam, and at their house among a hundred memories of India, of the sea, and of distant places, I descended, welcomed by the smell of rice and curry, beamed at by a golden Siamese temple cabinet, observed by the still, bronze Buddha. To wander out from this exotic cave into the elegant modern world of music, exhibitions, and the theater, even to the cinema, was for several days once more a pure delight.

Even today I still have the countryman's childlike attitude toward the city. I find it hard to take it all in and I allow myself to be captivated and enthralled by details; in the streetcars I look at the many faces, read the posters, I admire the mechanic or apprentice who rides his bicycle through the crowded streets, hands in pockets, try to recognize the tune he is whistling, I carefully observe the policeman standing in the tumult of a crossing and directing the demented vehicles with his big white-gloved hand, I find myself lured by the advertisements of the cinema theater, look in one store window after another and am amazed at the quantity of books, games, furs, cigars, and other attractive objects, then I drift into the side streets among the fruit and vegetable dealers, second-hand stores, small dingy show windows with pages full of old stamps, then once more I come to a main street and risk my life amid the autos so that I am soon glad to be able to sit down wearily somewhere, not of course in a café or modern restaurant but somewhere in the fish store and second-hand neighborhood, in a smoke-filled little inn where postmen and housemen in smocks sit in front of small glasses of white wine and eat the pretzels or sausage or hard-boiled eggs that are set out in profusion on all the tables. Whether it is in Milan or Zurich, Munich or Genoa, I generally end up in some such place in a rather dingy and moldy side street, in a little tavern whose only decoration is a bowl with two goldfish or a bunch of paper flowers, and on the wall a yellowed photograph of Napoleon III or a suburban athletic club, and where there is something that reminds me of my first forbidden visit to a tavern in my schooldays. There I drink white wine out of a thick stemless glass, good wine, and eat some of the many things lying on the table, ginger cookies covered with caraway seeds, long pretzels, small thick sausages. In these places one hears the common language of the district spoken purely and clearly and can see from the people's clothes and liveries what class they belong to. A chauffeur in a fur coat comes in, drinks a schnapps while standing at the bar, plays the gentleman slapping the host on the back, kicks the dog, wipes his mouth, slams the door behind him; a pale woman with shabby clothes enters, stands humbly for a while near the door, cautiously seeks out the innkeeper's wife, shows an empty bottle under her apron, begins a whispered transaction, is shown out. A young fellow sticks his head in the door and shouts: "Is Robert here?" The host shakes his head: "Today he's at Seventy-five." A servant comes in loaded down with a red plush chair and a potted palm. He leans the chair against the wall, places the palm on the table, seats himself under it, and drinks a double measure of new wine. For reasons I have failed to inquire into, all these actions interest me, I can watch them for a long time, time for a double, time for a triple.

My none-too-refined taste allows me to visit the cinema also. Today I belong among the sincerest and, as I believe, most understanding admirers of Chaplin, I also greatly love the Italian Macista, whereas I avoid the great historical costume films about the courts of princes; they try to be instructive.

I also went to an international art exhibition and was greatly cheered to see how beautiful and powerful the effect of Karl Hofer's paintings was amid the confused mass of modern pictures. Following this, I sat in a café with several painters and writers and in a short while learned all the latest news from the world of art, so for a while was well informed in this field too.

From each of these expeditions I returned contentedly to Siam, rested beneath the Buddha among the Chinese shawls. For a hermit and confirmed solitary, this after all is the finest thing about traveling, to see friends again, to be surrounded by warmth and good will, to chat with someone, to clink glasses with someone. I have never succeeded for long in belonging to a circle, having a place somewhere and sharing in its life, achieving some sort of enduring symbiosis with others. By way of compensation for this, I've always had the good fortune to be able to turn to dear friends for briefer, interim periods and to enjoy the satisfaction of talking openly, without caution and without politics, and giving of myself. That my friends, even those closest friends who have known me in all my madness and eccentricity, nevertheless have remained loyal to me is the single valid justification that I could present for my somewhat comical existence.

And so with these days in Zurich, my traveling was over for a while. I settled myself in the Verenahof in Baden for a fairly long stay, arranged my materials for writing and painting, and found quite enough mail waiting for me, the mail I had evaded for ten days. Now I had to write those postcards again: "My dear sir, My best thanks for your invitation to collaborate with you, but unfortunately . . ." There were invitations to lecture too, even one of interest; I was invited to deliver a lecture on modern Europe's great affection for the East, for India and China. This and that could have been said on the subject, and if the place had not been so far north in Germany and if I had had any talent at all for lecturing, it would have been a real pleasure to exhibit the symptom of this love of Asia in all its simplicity of structure and meaning. But lecturing is not my affair, I had tried it a single time and managed to get by, but on that day I had worse stage fright than on any of the solemn and important occasions of my whole life. No, thank you. "Dear sirs, It was with great interest that I read your invitation to lecture about the West and the East, but to my regret . . ."

A number of manuscripts from young poets also arrived, and in the beginning I promised myself, though with a sigh, in God's name to look through them. But after I was finished with the second day's mail, my eyes too were finished, and I sat there with raging pains and cold compresses. Besides, the letter with which one of these poets accompanied his manuscript was extremely unsympathetic, it dripped with such false and cringing veneration and flattery that reununciation was easy for me. Nevertheless, I wrote each of the three poets a few polite lines saying that because I was suffering from eye strain and had no secretary I could not, alas, read their manuscripts. Then I addressed and stamped the manuscripts and resigned myself to the fact that I must recognize the ten-day rest as fruitless and that once more I must be very careful to spare my eyes. I devoted myself all the more zealously on that account to the Baden cure. I have already described this in another place and consider a repetition useless. I spent many good hours with my doctor, and on many an evening my host, whom I number among my friends, would say: "Herr Hesse, how about a bottle of Pommard?" Also not infrequently I had visitors. My old friend Pistorius, whom I had hardly seen for years, came back and had in the meantime molted and changed no less than I; thankfully I went with him again through his darkly glowing psychic world filled with holy symbols, and I showed him what in the meantime had happened to me and to the seeds over which we had once brooded. Louis the Terrible also appeared one day briefly, suitcase in hand, just for a few hours, he planned to go to the Balearic Islands and paint there, urged me warmly to accompany him, I have heard nothing from him since.

Much quicker than I had expected, the Baden interval came to an end; this time too, as always, I had brought with me much too much to read and to do. Now I had to get to work packing again. It seemed useless to lug all the books and soiled linen with me to Germany, groaning I packed everything I could get along without in my big trunk and sent it home, and on the last afternoon when I was packing my suitcase I found the remaining things would not go in. I had to cram my black suit into a cardboard box and tie a string around it. Moreover, I had slept miserably during the last few nights, and it didn't suit me at all to start traveling again early next morning at seven o'clock or thereabouts and travel straight through to Blaubeuren, as I had announced to my friend there. When I stood there with my damned suitcase and discovered that I had tossed some things into the big trunk that were indispensable for the rest of my trip, at that moment I tasted once more what it means to agree thoughtlessly to obligations. I was supposed to be in Zurich at seven o'clock next morning, but I was still in Baden and had had enough of packing, and I would have liked nothing better than to get back into the sulphur water for another three weeks. Then tomorrow, after a night without sleep (for how could I take a Veronal if I had to be up again at cock-crow?), I was supposed to travel the whole distance to Blaubeuren with a change of trains in Tuttlingen, arrive in Blaubeuren wretched and furious, and all this simply in order two days later to read my poems aloud in Ulm, to unknown people, and then in Augsburg and then in Nuremberg! I had certainly been out of my mind to enter into such plans! No, now I would just travel to Zurich and spend the night there, and in Zurich I would discuss the whole stupid business with my friends, and then three nice telegrams would be composed saying that the Herr Tenor on account of a severe cold could not, alas, come. Well, thank God.

I traveled to Zurich, where I had asked my friend's wife to meet me, and feeling dreadful I sat waiting for her in the station restaurant, sipping a triple Macon, laden with the cardboard box, laden with my travel worries. It was cold, I was chilled and hoarse, I regretted not having stayed in Baden, regretted not having returned long ago to Ticino. Well, Alice came, we rode to her house, the big Buddha looked down in derision while I explained my troubles and doubts. My friend's wife was in favor of my continuing the trip; I would be sorry later on if I gave up in disgust. Disgust indeed, I thought, you more normal people have no notion what it is like for our sort if we have not slept, if the next day we are supposed to get up insanely early, sit for long hours in a train, arrange a program and fulfill obligations. I demurred, and as the dialogue grew sharper, I energetically refused to rise early next morning and catch the train. All right, the opposition gave in. And so I was to get my sleep next morning, after that there would still be time to telegraph.

I sighed with relief, the night and morning had been rescued, my friend came home, we dined, we drank a glass of wine, I permitted myself a Veronal and made my appearance next morning at a reasonable hour, between ten and eleven o'clock. To replace the cardboard box, I was loaned a convenient small suitcase with beautiful stickers from Siam, Singapore, and Java on it, and after lunch, resigned to my fate, I departed for the German border. Now I could very well see, belatedly, that it had been a mistake at the outset to plan the journey to Blaubeuren without a break, and to attempt that stupid heroism of the early morning train. Instead of going straight through to Blaubeuren, I would simply get off in Tuttlingen and spend the night there, thus in God's name arriving a day later than had been agreed at my friend's house and the Klötzle Blei. Resignedly I sat in my compartment, opposite me slept a fat businessman, a blanket over his knees, outside the windows passed a landscape well known to me from my years on Lake Constance, the Rhine and Rhine Falls appeared, the customs man entered and the man who checked our passports, the Hegau Mountains appeared, and old times in which this landscape had been my home filled my mind. We came to the station of Singen, and it suddenly occurred to me that it wasn't right just to pass through here, where friends of mine from the old days were still living. But I could easily understand how I had failed to think of Singen and those friends while I was laying out my travel plans, for I had good reasons for not liking to think of my years on Lake Constance. As I was opening the window and peering out at the station platform, a man in uniform presented himself politely and announced that the train would stop there for forty minutes. Good, I got out and telephoned to town, my friends came running, man, wife, and their son, a college student whom I had last seen as a little boy. So that too was satisfactorily taken care of and when the forty minutes were up I could go on with a clear conscience. Before we came to Tuttlingen, darkness fell, and when the lights were turned on, the businessman, a Saxon, woke up and began to talk. He was discontented, he had come from Italy on business, and in Italy and in Switzerland there was much amiss, above all—. "See here," he said, "you can't fool me, I know precisely, indeed I do. Life is a swindle imposed on us, that's what it is, you can say what you like." I was in complete agreement with the content of his speech but I could not approve his tone, I remained silent and was happy when we arrived in Tuttlingen. Now I was in Swabia, my homeland, and I was going to spend a night once more in a Swabian town. There was a runner from the hotel there, I accompanied him to a good old inn, and shortly before I arrived the gleaming full moon came up over the main street that ran straight as a die through the town. So he too was welcoming me back, that touched me deeply. I found an old, solidly built, dignified edifice with a comfortable room, bathed my still-burning eyes in cold water for a while and ordered chicken soup for supper. It was excellent, and because I did not yet know Tuttlingen it seemed a good idea to take a walk through the city before going to sleep. I turned up the collar of my overcoat, lighted a cigar, and wandered out. I already knew the main street and it seemed to me a poor approximation of the ideal of a Swabian town in the evening, therefore I turned into the first side street I came to, stumbled over some lumber and up a grassy slope; suddenly the moon was there again, reflected in marvelously quiet nocturnal water, and pointed gables poked into the pale sky, far and wide no one stirred, behind a back-yard hedge a dog barked. Slowly I went up and down the road, over a bridge and back again, the cool water's fragrance drifted up to me, the gables were like those in my home town, and while I was thinking of home and of my silly life and lonesome old age the moon came out again small and white in the canyon of the roofs, and at that moment I was visited by a memory of my boyhood. The moment came back to me that had perhaps caused me to become a poet (although I had already written verses before that). This is how it was: In the reader which we twelve-year-olds used in Latin school, there were the usual poems and stories, anecdotes about Frederick the Great and the bearded Everard, and I read all this with pleasure, but among these things there was something else, something marvelous, something completely enchanting, the most beautiful thing that had ever come my way. It was a poem by Hölderlin, the fragment "The Night."* Oh, those few verses, how often I read them in those days; and with what marvelous and secret ardor, and also timidity, came the conviction: That is poetry! That is a poet! What depth, what holiness, what power spoke to me for the first time in the language of my father and mother, how those incredible verses, which for me as a schoolboy were really without content, rang with the magic of prophecy, the secret of poetry!

. . . night comes
Crowded with stars, the astounding one,
Careless of us, resplendently rises
A stranger among mortals
Over the mountain peaks, sad and magnificent.

Never again, no matter how much or how enthusiastically I read as a young man, have the words of a poet so completely enchanted me as those did in my boyhood. And later, when as a twenty-year-old I read *Zarathustra* for the first time and was similarly enchanted, immediately that poem by Hölderlin in the reader came back to

---

* Hölderlin eventually completed this poem and entitled it "Bread and Wine."—Ed.

me, and that first astonishment of my boyish soul confronted by art.

And so this trip to Swabia, born from dark memories of the lovely Lau and the poet Mörike, was foreordained to awaken in me echoes of my early days and to tell me how deeply rooted and inescapable everything is. And if from now on my journey should bring me nothing but disappointments—this moment under the Tuttlingen moon, with the unexpected emergence of the Hölderlin verses, was reward enough.

People of my sort are content with little and yet only with the highest. Amid pain and despair and a gagging disgust at life, always once again for a holy instant to hear a yes to the question of the meaning of this life, which is so hard to bear—though at the next instant we may be smothered once more by the dim flood, that suffices us, from that we can live for quite a while and not merely live, not just endure life, but love and praise it.

From the Hölderlin moon and the sleeping street by the water, I returned to my inn, shaken and also comforted by the unhoped-for encounter with one of the sanctuaries of my youth. For a long time the verses continued to resound into the night, for a long time I continued to hear that voice from the deep well of my youth. Ah, whither had it not enticed me, in all those years, how far away from every road that is valuable and important to the others, the non-elect! How many deep, incommunicable, lonely moments of bliss it had brought me, a nobler humanity than the one we were born to! It had led me into conflict and dissociation from all reality, into ice-cold, unalterable loneliness, into dreadful abysses of self-contempt, into divine exaltations of devoutness. And if today, under the increasing pressure of my life, I take flight in humor and observe so-called reality from its comic side, be it only for the brief period of an intermediate stage, this too is simply an affirmation of that holy voice and an attempt to span for an instant the abyss between it and reality, between the ideal and experience, by means of fragile flying bridges. Tragedy and humor are not opposites, or rather they are only opposites because the one so inexorably demands the other.

If next morning after a late breakfast I found that town of Tuttlingen notably stripped of its magic, the fault was not simply in me and my inability during the morning hours to find anything of interest in the world but rather, so reliable witnesses assure me, in Tuttlingen's being on the whole a somewhat dull city. This did not trouble me, I went nevertheless along the road beside the lake back to those gables, found everything in its place except for the moon and except for the grace of that night hour. And so I had come here at exactly the right moment in an infinitely rare, blessed hour when Tuttlingen had been a mysterious fairy-tale city. Now it was easy to leave the place; I bought a sandwich, found my Siamese suitcase at the station and got contentedly aboard the train, an overcrowded Sunday train which traveled into the beautiful valley of the Danube. I saw Beuron and Werenwag lying in the bright sunlight, longed to get out and examine these enticing places more thoroughly but realized that my friend in Blaubeuren, already disappointed by my failure to appear yesterday, would be waiting for me anxiously, and I compelled myself to sit still. The train plunged into heavy fog, at some bend in the valley the sunny sky disappeared, I could barely decipher the place names on the station platforms. It was gray and misty too in Blautal, where I arrived in the early afternoon. There came my dear friend, one minute late, hurrying along the broad workaday road that leads into little Blautal and to the secrets of Blaubeuren, of which it offers the new arrival no inkling. There we stood and looked each other in the face, neither of us had become handsomer during the years, and I believe that we both felt a deep sincere joy. For me at least, who for twenty years have lived far from my boyhood home, there is something extraordinarily pleasing and warming now and again in seeing that there are actually a few people who were boys when I was a boy, who call me by my schoolboy nickname, and whom I cannot in any way impress. And how moving and touching it is each time to discover that men one knew in their early youth do not change at all! Thus it was with my friend. Our friendship dates from the time when we were fourteen, and he lives in my imagination with the same boyish face of that time, and if he now walks with the care-laden gait of a professor and has a great mustache and a somewhat weary face and the beginnings of gray in his hair, all this cannot deceive me or impress me, he will remain till the day of his death my schoolboy friend about fifteen years old, and no doubt I will be the same for him. To discover this again did me good and in cheerful mood we marched down the dull road into the valley, talking as we went, and arrived without my noticing it in a delightful small city full of thoughtful old houses with carved gables and prosperous roofs, and out of this again into the quiet monastery district. Then suddenly I thought again of the lovely Lau, I reminded my friend of her story and of her stone bath in the cellar of the Nonnenhof and told him that this cellar and this bath were the most important things in Blaubeuren so far as I was concerned, and asked him to take me to see them when he could. But my friend knew nothing about the cellar and the bath, and now I too became doubtful whether the story might not simply be a beautiful invention of Mörike's. Thereupon we met a man and, lo and behold, he was the caretaker of the cloisters, both the conscientious guardian and a connoisseur of the treasures of Blaubeuren. When I explained my quest and described in detail the situation in Mörike's story, his face brightened. Yes, indeed, that cellar existed and a subterranean watercourse connected it with the Blautopf, and as soon as he could he would take me there. We agreed upon an hour the next day and then we entered the former monastery in which my friend lives, were received by his wife and immediately given our midday meal, which she had kept waiting for us. A Swabian potato salad and a fine light Besigheimer wine, and then for the first time I was in Swabia, was in my home country, spoke Swabian myself again, was no longer a traveling gentleman but a brother, no longer a silly hermit but was asked about this and that and given news about fellow students, former teachers, their sons, their daughters. Here at the monastery I encountered a professor who was the son of the director of the Latin school I had attended. Another schoolmate of mine was expected tomorrow, he was now a country pastor and his son was in school here. I watched my host as he thoughtfully ate and smoothed his big mustache and exchanged matter-of-fact, dignified words with his wife, and I saw the little wrinkles around his eyes, but all this made no difference, he was still the boy Wilhelm for me.

I spent two days in Blaubeuren in an annex of the monastery which was horrifying architecturally but became very dear to me. I did not feel well the whole time, the nights were sleepless and I had all sorts of discomforts. I thought with apprehension about the engagement in Ulm, I remembered with longing my den in the South, at times I looked with outright envy at my friend, who held a position, was actively occupied, and every day had duties to perform—but all this went on in my mind in a kind of peripheral fashion and was not really important, whereas everything else was enormously important and beautiful. It was beautiful to meet a few of the monastery scholars, to whom I was a kind of curiosity; for when I had been a monastery student, I had run away at fifteen after a short period of endurance, and I was still remembered in the legends of the institution. But what about this? Were these handsome young fellows with their smooth dear children's faces really as old as we had been when we were students at the monastery school? Was it possible that behind those foreheads and blond boyish haircuts there seethed the same problems we once had, the same longing to indulge in dialectic and philosophy, the same burning ideals? My friend too was of the opinion that today's youth, whose life in the monastery by the way was very much easier than ours had been, were far less beset by problems and that they had an altogether easier time of it. But when he said this, my dear Wilhelm was no longer fifteen, nor was I, there were many wrinkles around our eyes and the gray in our hair was shamelessly visible.

Momentous and beautiful was our first excursion to the Blautopf, under the trees yellow leaves floated on the legendary waters, weir and stream were full of ducks and geese, deep in the earth sat the lovely Lau, smiling up through the blue waters; lonesome and hopeless alongside it stood the touchingly droll memorial to an early king. Everything smelled of home, of Swabia, of rye bread and fairy tales, and once more I was amazed at how little this marvelously alive and really remarkable landscape is known to modern German painters. Lau was hidden everywhere, everywhere there was the scent of youth and childhood, dreams and gingerbread, and no less of Hölderlin and Mörike, and that there were no memorials to them there caused me no regret. It was understandable; Swabia has always had more poets than kings.

And our expedition to the cellar of the Nonnenhof! Our guide led us down an ancient stairway and through a twilit entry vault into a high, handsomely and solidly walled cellar, showed us the points of the compass and where the subterranean waterway ran, and when I could wait no longer and asked about the bath he shone a pocket flashlight into the corner of the solemn room and revealed one of those common crudities, a patch of smoothly laid cement still comparatively new; and so this was Lau's bath! Under this accursed patch of cement rose the secret cool waters in which the lovely Lau had swum, hovering up to her breast! Fortunately the architectural designers had at least left a round hole in the cement covered with a lid, also of cement, which we lifted, and there in the feeble rays of the flashlight the black water shimmered gently until we covered the hole again in silence, the way people cover a desecrated corpse.

We did not raise the question of whether the Swabians and others of today had really been wholly and completely abandoned by the gods, whether they really did not know what they possessed in Lau and Mörike and all these wonders, in which no German district is so rich as Swabia. We left these vexing questions unexamined and were willing to rejoice in what was still to be found in Blaubeuren by way of ancient treasures and heirlooms not covered with cement, and happily there were many of them. We visited and inspected them all with love, the famous altar, the choir stall, the enchanting arches, the chapter hall, the gravestones. And in the night when I dozed off for a meager quarter hour, I did not dream of Lau swimming into her bath and striking her head against the cement cover but of something infinitely dearer that I am not allowed to reveal to anyone. For our group of friends, Blaubeuren was by no means exhausted when we had visited the memorials of more pious times. There were our own Middle Ages that lay closer to us and possessed no less fascination, they were our youth, and now we examined the relics of that legendary time, the ridiculous, dear class photographs in which I, the runaway, was not to be found, and the schoolrooms and dormitories and eating halls and the letters of especially cherished companions of our youth—which must have caused the ears of our friend in Zwickauer Strasse in Altenburg to burn.

In my experience Swabian theologians and philologists have a tendency to be late catching trains but at the last instant they nevertheless do catch them. That's how it went with us, the Middle Ages came to an end with shocking rapidity and I had to leave for the reading in Ulm. We came within a hairsbreadth of missing the train, and for this reason we escaped the solemnity of goodbyes. In the evening twilight I arrived in Ulm.

And now it occurs to me that I have forgotten to mention a small event during my visit in Baden. One day in the doctor's consulting room I met a man from Ulm who invited me to stay at his home, and now he was waiting at the station and with him an old Ulm acquaintance of mine who more than twenty years before had shown me the city for the first time. I was taken to a friendly house full of children and amiable people, there was not a stranger there, I was still in Swabia. On the other hand, the fulfillment of my duty was now upon me. Hardly had I arrived when I had to change and start thinking about my reading, and I did that unwillingly, without being able, even now, to recognize fully the reasons for my attitude. And yet I dare not spare myself the task of sorting out as best I can the causal threads accessible to me.

My dislike of public readings is not only the reluctance of a solitary in the face of social occasions, which can easily enough be overcome from one time to another, but I encounter within me essential, deeply rooted disorder and discord, to put it too briefly and crudely, caused by my distrust of literature in general, a torture to me when reading aloud and even more so in my own work. I do not believe in the worth of the literature of our time. I understand, to be sure, that every period must have its literature as it must have its politics, its ideals, its styles. But I can never rid myself of the conviction that German literature in our time is a transitory and doubtful business, a seed that has grown in thin, badly prepared soil, interesting to be sure, and full of problems, but hardly capable of attaining full, ripe, long-enduring fruits. As a result, I can only consider the attempts of today's German poets (my own included, of course) to produce genuine creations, truly fine works, as in some way inadequate and derivative; everywhere I seem to perceive a trace of the stereotype, the fossilized model. On the other hand, I see the worth of a transitional literature, a poetry become problematic and uncertain, in its conscientious expression of its own shortcomings and the shortcomings of its time with the greatest possible candor. This is the reason I can no longer enjoy and approve many beautiful and well-constructed works of today's poets, whereas I can feel sympathetic toward many very crude and carelessly constructed utterances of the youngest, simply as attempts at unrestrained candor. And this division extends straight through my own little world and literature. I love the German poets of the last great period up to 1850, I love the romantics, Goethe, Hölderlin, Kleist, with my whole heart, to me their works are immortal, again and again I read Jean Paul, I read Brentano, Hoffmann, Stifter, Eichendorff, just as again and again I listen to Handel, Mozart, and all of German music up to Schubert. These works are always perfect, even when they have long since ceased to express our feelings and problems, they are finished creations, exempt from time, at least they are still so for uncounted persons of today. From these works I learned to love poetry, their melodies are as natural to me as air and water, they were the example that guided my youth. Now I myself have known for many years that it is profitless to imitate these splendid models (although I have to attempt it again and again, hopelessly). I know that the value of what we people of today write cannot lie in the possibility of a form emerging valid for our time and for a long while to come, a style, a classicism, but rather that we in our distress have no refuge except that of the greatest possible candor. Between these demands for candor, for concession, for surrender of the self and that other demand familiar to us from youth, for beautiful expression, between these two requirements the whole poetry of my generation swings back and forth in bewilderment. For even if we were prepared for the greatest candor to the point of self-surrender—where could we find the means of expressing it? Our literary language will not provide it nor will the language of our schools, our handwriting has long since become fixed. Isolated, desperate books like Nietzsche's *Ecce Homo* seem to reveal a path, but in the end they reveal far more clearly that there is no path. Psychoanalysis appeared to offer us aid and it has brought advances, but as yet no author, either psychoanalyst or writer trained in analysis, has freed this kind of psychology from its armor of too narrow, too dogmatic, much too vain academicism.

Enough, the problem has been adequately indicated. Now if I, as a writer, am invited to give a public reading and stand with manuscript in hand in front of the audience, I am confronted by this problem in acute form, it turns the papers in my hand into useless trash, it makes my search for candor without consideration of beauty a burning one. Best of all, I would like then to turn out the lights and say to the audience: "I have nothing to read to you nor have I anything to say except that I am struggling to free myself from lies. Help me in this and let us all go home."

Despite this inhibition, I have got through the few public readings to which I have allowed myself to be persuaded almost to the complete satisfaction of the promoters. But each time I have been astounded that the small effort of reading aloud for an hour can exhaust a person so completely, often to the point of collapse. If it were simply an abstract or ideal poet confronting an abstract or ideal audience, then the whole thing would be impossible, the situation would then be purely tragic and could only end with the poet committing suicide or being stoned by the audience. In the world of actual experience, however, everything looks somewhat different, there is room for a little cheating, especially is there room for the old mediator between the ideal and the real—humor. On such evenings I make much use of it, of humor of every kind, especially gallows humor. Let us try to formulate briefly this refraction of the pure rays, this shabby adaptation to reality.

Well, then: A poet who has the profoundest doubts about himself and the worth of his poetic efforts stands before a hall full of listeners, who for their part have not the slightest inkling of the tangled processes in the soul of the respected performer. Now what is it that makes it possible for this poet to read his poems aloud instead of running away and hanging himself? What makes it possible is, first of all, the poet's vanity. Even if he can take neither himself nor his audience seriously, he is nevertheless vain, for everyone is vain, even the ascetic, even the self-doubter. I say this not in order to be coy, and I believe that as far as abstraction from myself goes, if it comes down to that, I am superior to the usual average in Europe: I know better than anyone the situation in which the eternal Self in us examines the mortal "I" and its leaps and grimaces, with sympathy, with derision, with neutrality. Otherwise, how could I come to expose my I to the derision of the less knowledgeable readers? But just because on this point I am more knowledgeable than the average man, often to the verge of the unbearable, just for this reason I can take the vanity of the poet rather coolly into account. It is greater than one would expect from a person inclined to thought, but the belief that gifts for thinking and vanity are mutually exclusive is simply an error. On the contrary, no one is vainer, no one is more set upon echo and affirmation than the intellectual, and in fact he has bitter need of echo and affirmation. This vanity, which in my case is no stronger than with any poet but nevertheless has several horsepower, helps me now in this desperate situation in front of an audience to whom I really have nothing to give, whereas they expect something from me. There is something in me, something that consists two-thirds of vanity, that resists surrender to the people assembled in the hall and confession of its worthlessness. Something in me makes it seem worthwhile to dominate this throng of people, to move them not to deeds, not even to applause, but to attention, to silent listening to my thoughts and poems, whose meaning and intention is diametrically opposed to the meaning and intention of the audience. And so clenching my teeth I make a great effort and since in intellectual matters a single person is always stronger than a crowd, I win the battle. I am listened to silently, I create the impression of a man who actually has something to say. This I can sustain barely an hour, then I must stop, then I am exhausted.

But on the dreary plane of everyday experience, it is not simply my stupid vanity, the animal-like yet cunning passion of my person to assert itself, that helps me; the audience helps me too and so does my relation to it. This is a point on which I am stronger than many of my colleagues. The audience as such is a matter of complete indifference to me. Even if the worst happened between the public and me, if I failed completely and was whistled off the stage—it would matter very little to me. Someone inside me would actively join in the whistling. No, the people in the hall neither make me afraid nor do I expect much from them. I am no longer young, I know all about this. I know rather precisely how many of these auditors later on will make demands on me either in person or by private letter, purely selfish matters. I know the species that kowtows before a famous guest and afterward spews poison on him. I know the species of ambitious people who compliment and honor you to your face, shamelessly and with the strongest superlatives, until they notice that their exertions are not being responded to, and then they quickly turn away. I know the malice with which the intellectually small man rejoices when he sees that public men and men of intellect are also human, have something comic about them, show vanity or embarrassment. All this is well known to me, I am no longer a neophyte who imagines that on his account, because of his particular personality, these people are assembled here. I know it might just as well be a quartet of yodelers, I know that a speech by Ludendorff would attract a hundred times as many people, a boxing match a thousand times. And since I myself live outside middle-class society and participate in it only as a guest, I can consider respect and success in that society (insofar as I have not been drawn into it by my innate vanity) a matter of complete indifference. Here I have all the advantages of the outsider and hermit who lives always with one foot in India, to whom nothing can be given and from whom nothing can be taken away, and I am aware of these advantages.

But the motive force of vanity and my outsider's indifference to the public are not the only things that make it possible, despite the strongest objections and inhibitions, for me to give a public reading now and then. There is, thank God, something else involved as well, something better, the single good there is, namely love. This seems to contradict what I have said about my indifference to the audience, and yet it is true. To be specific, while I save myself from the public through the adroitness born of experience, through the low and somewhat shabby indifference that comes of experience, I turn with just that much greater love, that much warmer zeal, toward the individual person. If this single person whom I love and for whom I can gladly exert myself is really sitting in the hall, perhaps in the guise of a friend, then I simply turn toward him, direct my whole reading just to this one person. If, however, he is not present and there is no sign of him, then I imagine him nevertheless, I conjure him up before my eyes, either by thinking of an absent friend or a beloved, or my sisters or one of my sons, or alternatively I fix upon some face in the hall that is sympathetic. I cling to this face, I love it, I turn all my warmth, all my attention, all my eagerness to be understood in its direction. And this is the talisman that helps me.

In Ulm this was not a difficult matter. Not only were there some friendly and well-known faces in the hall, but also I was in general among friends, I was in Swabia, at home, and so things were not too bad. We met in a very handsome building, the municipal museum, whose director had organized the occasion; he invited me to visit the museum next day, and he and some other people came back to my host's home for a glass of wine and some time together, so nothing I might have said of a problematic kind during my reading had any unpleasant echo. I was very weary and equally happy that it was over.

And now I had almost two days left for Ulm, and I could discover that one's memory of beautiful things, even with people that consider themselves trained to it, is not to be relied on, for as a young man I had once visited this extremely beautiful and unusual city and I had forgotten a great deal. I had not forgotten the city wall or the Metzgerturm, or the cathedral choir or the Rathaus, these images superimposed upon the images of memory differed little from them; on the other hand there were innumerable new scenes which I saw as though for the first time, age-old fishermen's houses standing askew in the dark water, little gnomes' houses on the city wall, proud burghers' houses in the narrow streets, here an odd gable, there a noble portal. Aside from these, however, I was no longer especially receptive to the famous and already established sights; with my old peephole-camera joy I absorbed a mass of details: a Bolognese dog, Swabian faces behind half-curtained windowpanes, miscellaneous knickknacks piled up in the stationer's windows that already hinted a little of Christmas, and—something always fascinating and inexhaustible for me—the store signs. The first and family names of the proprietors and working people in a strange city, to read these is always a necessity and a pleasure for me, just as in the novels I read, names have always been very important and often informative. And it is invariably a strange and interesting experience to come upon a name that I know only from poetry for the first time in real life; thus I felt a small shock when first I saw many years ago the name Arbogast in Alsace, the beautiful legendary name that for years I thought had been invented by Mörike especially for his treasure story. From reading the store signs, one not only learns whether a city is mostly Catholic or Protestant, whether it has many Jews or not, one also learns in particular from the Catholic given names something of the mind and provenance of its population, about their preferences and their patron saints. And everywhere I heard the strong, homely Swabian dialect, everywhere I heard words that I had not heard for a long time. This is like coming upon the chalk or sandstone, the trees and flowers of one's world of memory again, as if one suddenly tasted once more a water, a wine, a food, an apple, a drug which one had not tasted in years and to which a thousand nameless memories cling. I wandered about amid these scents, amid these clouds of nameless memories. Ulm jokes and stories were told to me, in between times I saw my host's children, showed them the fairy tale that I had read aloud the day before; it is in my handwriting with little colored illustrations drawn in the text—during the years of the inflation these illustrated manuscripts helped me to get by. One afternoon we went with Professor Baum through his Ulm museum, which was richly rewarding.

In comfortable rooms filled with beautiful and remarkable objects, I drank coffee and ate cakes with the acquaintance who in my youth had shown me Ulm for the first time. There I became deeply involved with Mörike again, for my acquaintance possessed a quantity of Mörike memorabilia, books in which he had made notes and underscored his favorite passages, and notes about the seeds he planned to plant in his garden next spring, few vegetables and many flowers; an old-fashioned bag of embroidered canvas was produced which Pastor Mörike had once taken with him on his travels. In this house there were many small treasures and they were in the right place. I had come into the house overtired, nervous, and exhausted—for if I hardly know what it means to feel well ordinarily, I am much worse when I am traveling—and in a short time there was a feeling of ease and peace about my heart.

On my last evening in Ulm, while I was going to bed, I fell to thinking of this and that that had happened to me on my Swabian trip, I thought of Singen, Tuttlingen, of Blaubeuren, of Ulm, of the lovely museum, and suddenly it occurred to me how much all this was under the influence of the past, how many of the dead had joined in the conversation, yes, how the liveliest parts had been dictated by the dead. It was Hölderlin in that moment under the gabled houses in Tuttlingen, it was Mörike with the lovely Lau, I had also felt the influence of Arnim and the Guardians of the Crown, it was the builders of all the altars, all the choir stalls, the headstones and the magnificent edifices. And just as on this trip, always and everywhere the dead have been around me—rather, the immortals. And these long-dead men, whose words have been alive for me, whose thoughts have educated me, whose works have made the dull world beautiful and possible, were they not all strange too, sick, suffering, difficult men, creators out of need, not out of happiness; master builders from disgust at reality, not out of acceptance of it? Had the town dwellers of the Middle Ages, who after all were bakers and tradesmen, comfortable, healthy, corpulent people, had they really built these cathedrals, had they really wanted them? Had they not been compelled by the dissatisfaction of the others, the few? And if the real world was right, if our sort were simply neurasthenics, if it would have been better and proper to be a citizen and paterfamilias and taxpayer, to carry on business and beget children, if the factory and thc automobile and the office were really what was normal, true, and reasonable for men—why then did they create such museums? Why did they employ a caretaker to guard the Blaubeuren altar? Why did they make great display cases full of drawings and graphic art and even pay out money through the government for this? Why revere these oddities, this nonsense, these sick games of artists needing reassurance, why collect, watch over, exhibit them, give lectures about them, if there is not something essential in this frivolity, something with meaning, something really deserving to exist? Why were the citizens of Ulm proud of the good state of preservation of their ancient city hall instead of pulling down the old rubbish, building factories and apartment houses in its place? Why did factory owners when they came home from their offices in their automobiles and wanted things to be a bit pleasant, why did they buy with the money they earned in their offices illustrated works on the old monasteries, pictures by dead masters who in their lifetimes had never possessed a hundredth part of what a single picture by them brings today? Why was it that the highest praise I heard in Ulm for any of its modern architecture was that it fitted in so decorously with the pattern of the old streets? And why did everything that belonged to today have to be so ugly? From Zurich to Ulm, insofar as the earth had been altered by the hand of man and built over, there was nothing beautiful to be seen except a few tiny islands of ancient architecture. The rest was stations, factories, apartment buildings, warehouses, barracks, post offices, one as ugly and hopeless as the next, suitable for inciting people to revulsion and suicide.

I have put these questions not to clarify the reasons for this ugliness and hopelessness, I am interested neither in the growth of the population (which should be curtailed by every means, instead of state and society promoting it) nor in economic laws (which were the same at the time the Gothic cathedrals were built as they are today), but I am fascinated simply by the question: Are you, mad poet on your travels, really mad? Are you sick, suffering so from life that often you scarcely want to go on living, simply because you have neglected to adjust yourself to reality "as it once and for all happens to be"?

And once more, although I was prepared to think realistically even at my own expense, I was compelled to reply as I had so often replied before: No, you are a thousand times right in your protest against this miserable "world as it once and for all happens to be," you are right even if you die strangling on this world instead of accepting it.

And once more I felt the lightning flashes between the opposite poles, over the abyss between reality and the ideal, between reality and beauty, felt the swaying of that airy bridge, humor. Yes, with humor it could be endured, even the railway stations, even the barracks, even the literary readings. Through laughter, through refusal to take reality seriously, through constant knowledge of its destructibility, it could be endured. Some day the machines would run amok against one another, the arsenals would discharge their wares, and sometime or other there would be where a metropolis stands today grass growing again and weasels and martens stealing through it. No, one needn't do this comic world the honor of taking it seriously!

The hotel omnibus in Augsburg deposited me in front of a revolving glass door behind which tea music was being played, this witty invention of modern man that absolves him even in his few moments of rest and relaxation from speaking or paying attention or thinking or even becoming conscious. I announced myself at the desk, asked for a room, a porter came with me, everything in view was very modern—restaurant, corridor, coatroom. The boy took me to the second floor, opened the door of the elevator, and suddenly I was in a roomy, ancient palazzo, a feudal hall, silent princely corridors with high imposing doors, over each of which was a carved and painted coat of arms. A door was opened for me, a high bright room appeared, the window opening on a green winter garden. Joyfully I took possession of the most unusual and handsome hotel that I have ever seen in a large German city. The telephone in the room was the one thing that disturbed me, these contraptions are dangerous. Well, if necessary one could always unscrew it or smash it. First of all, I made use of it and announced to my patron that the artist of the evening had arrived. Then I rested a bit, did some unpacking, changed, and ordered milk and cognac to be brought up. I had *Simplicissimus* in my overcoat pocket and in it I read one of Ringelnatz's travel letters, which I enjoy so much; but when there was a tap at the door and they were there to take me to the reading, I noticed that I had been asleep for quite a while. It was dark and cold, I was taken along a broad proud street to a concert hall, this time I did not quite manage to take in the situation completely and to put into operation my customary psychological apparatus, but I soon succeeded in singling out in the crowd a face I could turn to and so I read my things through bravely, occasionally taking a sip of excellent water, and the whole affair was over before I had really got to the point of inwardly protesting against it. Well, that was perfectly all right with me. I hurried into the waiting room, put on my overcoat, and lighted a cigar. Now people began to arrive, I steeled myself for the usual courtesies, was happy at bottom that I knew no one in this city—but there in front of me stood a lady with red cheeks, laughing and saying in Swabian: "You haven't the slightest idea who I am, do you?" It was a woman from the Black Forest, from my home town, who had gone to school with my sisters, and behind her was her daughter, a pretty girl also with blossoming cheeks, and we laughed and decided to stay together for a while. But I soon had reason to notice that I was a bit drowsy that evening: a gentleman put one of my books in front of me with the request that I write an inscription in it for his wife. I had just been thinking about Nuremberg and that now, fortunately, there was only one more city to get through, and so I wrote something in the book and gave it to him with a friendly smile. The man read it and handed it back to me. I had written: "In memory of an evening in Nuremberg"! It had to be erased and changed. Then we went to my hotel for a glass of wine, and the woman from Calw talked about Calw and we discussed all the people of Calw that we could remember, and her daughter sat there and found us old folk droll, and suddenly there was also someone from Neuenberg, and I saw that I was still in the midst of Swabia. It was late when I went up through the princely stairwell to my room. Really it was a simple matter to earn one's bread by readings of this sort. However, it was not bread I lacked but air, and this air, the air of viability, of content, of belief in my calling and my activities, no such air blew in Augsburg either and no such honorarium was paid here. On the contrary (and this is the reason that God has provided tenors and virtuosi with that agreeable plus in self-confidence), if one traveled like a tenor and bard through the cities, as a performer for evenings of literary entertainment, this provided exactly the best opportunity for convincing a conceited artist impressed with his own importance of the opposite, of his dispensability, of the complete meaninglessness of his person and his specialty. Whether the members of the literary club were listening to Thomas Mann or Gerhart Hauptmann or Baron Munchausen or the tenor Hesse, whether a Berlin professor was giving his lecture on Homer or a Munich professor his on Matthias Grünewald, it was all precisely the same, each of these specialties was only one stroke in the plan, one thread in the fabric, and the plan was called intellectual activity and the fabric was called the education industry and neither the whole nor any of the separate specialties had the slightest value whatever. Lord, do not let me lose my sense of humor, let me live a little while longer. And let me participate in some work with more sense, more value, than this country fair. Let me as the least of your servants contribute to Germany's finally closing its national schools, to Europe's energetically working at a reduction in the birth rate. Instead of the money for these lectures, instead of the honor, instead of the flattery, grant me a lungful of breathable air.

Skeptics assert that no one ever yet died of a broken heart. They will also deny that a literary man can die from lack of air. As though a literary man could breathe anything, could distill a pamphlet out of every gas and stench!

Next day the weather was fine and I went out to have a look at Augsburg and realized that this was market day. I have never learned much history but have derived my knowledge entirely from the poets, and so just as through Mörike I was even better informed about the secrets of

Blaubeuren than the professors there, so I had excellent information about Augsburg through my memory of Arnim's *Guardians of the Crown,* about Nuremberg through Wackenroder and E. T. A. Hoffmann. I hardly need give assurances here that Augsburg is a very beautiful city. But one thing appealed especially to me and did me good. In the marketplace, where inspiring quantities of butter, cheese, fruit, vegetables, and so forth were placed on view, I found a sizable number of peasants, and especially peasant women and some children with them, all wearing their old true folk costumes. In my joy I almost threw my arms around the neck of the first one I met and I followed her for a long time among the stalls. Bodices embroidered with small flowers, the odd puffed sleeves tight-laced at the wrists, amusing headdresses—oh, how they recalled my childhood and the cattle market in Calw where hundreds of peasants and their wives, every single one, came dressed in their costumes and where at a distance one could distinguish the peasants from different districts, from the forest or the corn neighborhoods, by the color of their leather breeches!

My last hours in Augsburg were the finest. I had good luck in this city and I had been very unfair to confuse it with Nuremberg the evening before. In addition to all the good and amiable things that had already happened to me, there was a particular surprise in store. In Augsburg there was a married couple who fourteen years before had read one of my books and written to me, and had named their daughter who was born just then after a character in the book, and now this couple came to see me and invited me to lunch and were at loving pains first to provide me with an excellent meal and then by car to show me in a few hours the most important and finest sights in old Augsburg. Even though I was ashamed to owe all this love and attention to a book that today seems to me unbearable, those were nevertheless good hours.

Oh, what beautiful and extraordinary things I saw in that legendary city! In the sacristy of St. Moritz a collection of ecclesiastical vestments of such splendor that one thought one was in Rome, and close by in a chapel four seated bishops, not wooden or stone figures but the mummies themselves, in rich canonicals. For me the most beautiful things were the bronze doors of the cathedral; another sight, however, awaited me inside this venerable church. There I saw a man of countrified appearance with a wide blond beard, dressed in faded green with a knapsack on his back. I saw him first as he was entering the church just in front of me, then I saw him walk searching through the mighty edifice, and then at last he found what he was looking for and kneeled down in front of a chapel, bareheaded, his eyes directed to the picture on the altar, both arms extended wide, with open beseeching hands, and he prayed, prayed with his eyes, with his mouth, with his knees, with his outstretched arms, with his open hands, prayed with his body and soul, blind and deaf to the world, undisturbed by us godless, curious people in the sanctuary in search of bronze and Gothic windows instead of God. This praying man and the women in their peasant costumes are the pictures I garnered in Augsburg for my inner and enduring picture book, not the golden hall, not the proud fountains and burghers' palaces, not the ostentation.

That evening I traveled to Munich and then had several days to rest, to let the confused images settle down in my mind and to regret that I now had to go on to Nuremberg as well. One evening turned out to be quite perilous. I had looked up the director of the Park Hotel, and since he had once known me in other quarters of the world as a friend to good wine he now amused himself by setting before me various carefully selected, aged bottles from his cellar. Toward the end of the evening I, who am, to be sure, a drinker, but not accustomed to large quantities, had to make an effort to pull myself together but managed to get through it. And—unless this was a pleasant delusion induced by wine—suddenly my host and friend from Baden was sitting there laughing and touching glasses with me. With the purpose of furthering my education I went next day to the editorial rooms of a great newspaper, but I did not feel well there and could not stand it for more than a quarter of an hour. But I must not say too much about Munich, I had a bad conscience all the time I was there. A lot of people live in Munich who were once close to me and knew me well, all of whom I liked and should really have visited. But this would have been too much of an undertaking, and what would have happened? Thirty people would have asked me in friendly fashion whether things were going well with me, what I was doing, whether I was content with my life, my health, my activities, and similar painful questions, and I would have had to sit there smiling and nodding my head and that's dreadfully tiring. Nevertheless, I did see some of them whom I consider to be real friends, but not in their homes with their wives, among their children or at their work, but pleasantly together in some cellar or inn in the evening where we could discuss the economic depression and, drinking Waldulmer or Affenthaler, talk about earlier years, about summers on Lake Constance, about trips to Italy, about friends who had died in the war. During these days my mood was not especially good, not only because I had become so very tired of literature and would have given a great deal if I had not had to travel on to Nuremberg, but for other reasons as well.

My journey was slowly coming to an end, in six weeks I had gradually made my way here from Ticino, almost to the last stop, and constantly on the way, without my having thought about it consciously, my heart was filled with the question: What is going to happen now? What have you found out on your trip, what have you achieved?

Will you be able to go back to your work and to your hermitage and sit in your library alone with aching eyes, or will you take up something else? And this question was still unanswered. I had given readings, had enjoyed lively and cordial conversations with friends, here and there had drunk a good wine and had spent friendly hours in a warm and friendly atmosphere; in between times I had forced myself to endure the unbearable, had at moments forgotten myself while looking at ancient architecture (Gothic net-vaults had intoxicated me for hours), also a few times in moments of travel fatigue, after there had been all too much chatter, I had felt a momentary yearning for my distant hermitage—but nothing had changed, nothing had settled itself. I felt the pressure of this situation more and more, and so when I finally completed the trip to Nuremberg, I was not in a receptive and grateful mood and the fact that I went there just the same, that I thought I had to summon up the silly heroism necessary for that instead of freeing myself with a telegram, that was something I now had to expiate. For Nuremberg was a great disappointment to me.

I left on a dismal day, snow and rain intermixed, traveled through Augsburg again, saw the cathedral and St. Moritz looming over the city, then came to a countryside unknown to me and, on the last stretch, a wild, rough, uninhabited landscape with great pine forests, the tips of the trees shaken by the snowstorm. It was beautiful and mysterious but for a Southerner like me it was also oppressive and disturbing. If I go on traveling in this direction, I thought to myself, then no doubt more and more pine trees will show up and more and more snow and perhaps Leipzig or Berlin and then presently Spitsbergen and the North Pole. Dear God, suppose I had accepted the invitation to go to Dresden! It was unimaginable. As it was, the trip was long enough, terribly long, and I was happy when I arrived in Nuremberg. Secretly I had anticipated all sorts of marvels in this Gothic city, had hoped to meet the ghosts of E. T. A. Hoffmann and Wackenroder, but nothing of the sort happened. The city made a dreadful impression on me, for which naturally the city was not to blame but only myself. I saw a truly enchanting old city, richer than Ulm, more unusual than Augsburg, I saw St. Lorenz and St. Sebald, I saw the Rathaus with the courtyard in which stands that incredibly charming fountain. I saw all this and it was all very beautiful, but it was completely surrounded by a big inhuman, business city, with engines chattering here and there and automobiles snaking their way, with everything quivering imperceptibly to the tempo of a different time, a time that does not know how to build net-vaults or erect fountains lovely as flowers in the still courtyards—all this seemed ready to collapse in the next hour, for it no longer had a purpose or a soul. What beautiful, what enchanting things I saw in this mad city! Not only the famous sights, the churches, the fountains, the Dürer house, the castle, but also a great many of those little accidental objects that are actually more important to me. An apothecary shop at the sign of the Globe where I bought a new bath for my eyes, a solid handsome old building that had a stuffed crocodile just out of its egg in the show window together with the shell itself and other such items. But none of it helped. I saw all this only in the exhaust fumes from the damned machines, everything swallowed up, everything vibrating with a life that I cannot believe to be human but only satanic, everything ready to die, ready to turn to dust, longing for collapse and destruction, disgusted by this world, weary of existence without purpose, of beauty without soul. Even the friendliness with which I was received at the literary club, even my sigh of relief as I finished my last reading (for a long time, perhaps forever), even this did not help. It was all comfortless. In the hotel, over-active steam radiators which could not be cooled the whole night through, no possibility of keeping the window open because of the noisy traffic in the streets; also in the room, that base contrivance, the telephone, which, after a sleepless night in raging pain, robbed me of my last hour's sleep in the morning. Men, what makes you torture me so, give me rather a quick death!

Meanwhile, the observer in me accepted all these findings with his usual calm, curious only whether this time the fellow would explode or carry on despite everything. The observer in me (a figure that does not belong to the persona of this narrator) who has nothing to do with the accidental joys and sufferings of the traveling bard except that he takes note of them, this observer was present and at another time will speak in more factual terms of these experiences. Today it is only the traveling tenor who is talking, the accidental man in me who feels and suffers what is accidental.

It was in Nuremberg, where I seemed to myself ninety years old and on the point of death, where I had no other wish but to be buried, it was here that I mainly came in contact with young people. One of them, a secondary-school or college student, caused me embarrassment. He asked that I write something in a book for him, and when nothing occurred to me (what could occur to me in such circumstances?), he proposed that I write a few Greek words, a quotation from the New Testament which appears in one of my books. In twenty years I had not drawn any Greek letters; God knows how this inscription turned out! Another young man, with whom I spent the larger part of those short Nuremberg hours and whose company I enjoyed, was a poet. He had already won my sympathy some time before, partly with a clever essay about me in which he portrayed very well the fruitlessness of my poetic attempts and its cause, and partly too through a little composition whose hero was the poet Grabbe, and which had genuine magic. This young poet went about

Nuremberg with me, sat with me patiently that evening in taverns, though an abstainer himself, and with his amiable face and his small delicate hands at moments he seemed to me an angel appointed to protect me from the worst in this strange city.

Nevertheless, I sat there quite helpless and lost, and only one thing was clear to me, that I must get away as quickly as possible. As it happens, I have a friend in Munich, one of the good reliable friends, to whom I telegraphed that it was impossible for me to stand it in Nuremberg and that he might expect me in Munich on the next express. I crammed my possessions somehow or other into my suitcase, somehow or other got myself out of the hotel and to the station, and rode away from Nuremberg, crushed but happy at my release; the city still seemed to me dedicated to destruction. It was a good train and made no stops on the way to Munich, but it took a very long time and I could hardly endure it until I arrived there, ninety years old, with addled brain, burning eyes, and buckling knees. This was perhaps the finest moment of my journey. There I was in Munich again, still alive, had everything behind me, never needed to give a public reading again. And there stood my friend, big and strong, with laughing eyes, taking my little bag; and avoiding lengthy questions and explanations, he told me we were expected in such and such a wine cellar by our friends. I would have preferred to get into bed, but the wine cellar too was good, I agreed. Various celebrities of literature and criticism were sitting there at a table waiting for us and a truly noble Moselle was served, I heard interesting conversations and discussions and was very contented, for all this did not touch me at all, demanded nothing from me and was simply interesting. I could sit there and look at all those excited clever faces and drink the Moselle and feel sleep approaching, and if I liked, next day I could stay in bed, for a whole day, for a year, for a century, no one could demand anything of me, no railroad train would whistle for me, no lectern stand lighted and adorned with its water pitcher. I did not have to draw Greek or any other kind of letters.

I stayed on for many days with my friend, well outside the city in a country neighborhood, in order to recuperate and to make up my mind about how to arrange my return journey. Here my conscience stirred, or rather my fear of going back home, and I determined to have my mail forwarded to me. The flood of paper arrived and for some days kept me busy, and among all the unimportant items there was also something of interest, there was a fairly long letter from that young poet whose manuscript I had had to send back to him. At that time his too obviously false letter of flattery had made a rather unfavorable impression on me, but now he cheered me by his incomparable candor in letting me know, by home truths selected with power and passion, how unspeakably clumsy, stupid, and repellent I had always seemed to him. Bravo, young brother poet, carry on! Candor, not flowery speech, is what we expect from modern literature.

I was successful in enticing the dearest of my Bavarian friends out of his village in upper Bavaria for a good cordial evening, which I remember with gratitude. Now that I was a private person again, I had a more naïve attitude toward literature and ventured something that I had done only rarely before in my life, I approached some of my colleagues personally. I spent a not unproductive hour with Josef Bernhart; Protestant and Catholic could not approach each other more intimately than we did on that occasion. I spent an evening with Thomas Mann, I wanted to show him that my old love for his kind had not disappeared, and also I had a desire to see how things were going with this man who performed his work so conscientiously and with such dignity and yet seemed to have so profound a knowledge of the ambiguities and despairs of our profession. I sat at his table till late at night and he conducted the occasion handsomely and stylishly, in good humor with a touch of cordiality and a touch of mockery, defended by his beautiful house, defended by his cleverness and good form. I am grateful for that evening too. And now I wanted to see the man who writes the remarkable pieces in *Simplicissimus,* Joachim Ringelnatz, and he was kind enough to join me for an evening, and we drank all sorts of good wine and were happy. When this was over, I went to the trolley-car station and rode home, having had quite enough and ready for bed. However, Ringelnatz's work was only beginning at that hour, he still had to do his music-hall turn, something for which I did not envy him.

In Nymphenburg, I was well looked after and spoiled, could bathe my eyes in cool water all day long or walk up and down under the stately old trees and watch the dried leaves driven along so merrily in the wind, our small brothers the leaves. Often I looked at them in sadness, often I looked at them and laughed. Like them I am whirled along today to Munich, tomorrow to Zurich, then back again, searching, impelled to flee pain, impelled to postpone death a little longer. Why does one defend oneself so, I asked disconsolately. Because that is the game of life, I replied, laughing.

And because laughter seemed a good and very desirable thing, I asked my friend whether there was at that time in Munich one of those genuine classic comedians such as I had now and again seen. Yes indeed, my friend knew one, he was called Valentin and we looked him up in the newspaper and found he was appearing in a small theater in his play *The Robber Knights at Munich.* We went there one evening. Until ten o'clock they had been playing Strindberg in the little theater, then it was Valentin's turn. With a small troupe he was playing *The Robber Knights at Munich,* a marvelous play, an extraordinary piece of nonsense. The purpose of the piece was to give Valentin an opportunity to walk up and down with a long saber and to do and say funny things. Sometimes too it was sad enough to make you weep, for example, the way he sat on the city wall in the cool of the evening, playing his accordion and thinking of his young life, the war, and death. Or when he narrated thoughtfully and at great length a dream in which he had been a duck and had almost eaten a long worm. In this scene the inadequacy of human apprehension in its simplest form was fascinatingly expressed. This tragic situation, too, just like the other one with the accordion, was greeted with roars of laughter, never have I seen a merrier audience. How much everyone likes to laugh! Far from the suburbs, they hurry about in the cold, pay money, wait for long periods, do not get home until after midnight, simply in order to be able to laugh. I too laughed very hard, I would have been glad if the piece had gone on until morning. God knows when I will have a chance to laugh again. And the greater the comedian is, the more terrifying and irremediable his presentation in comic terms of our stupid and terrifying human state, the more one has to laugh! Behind me in the audience sat a young lady who placed both her elbows on my shoulders. I turned around because I thought perhaps she had fallen in love with me, but it was only laughter, she was shaken by it as though possessed by a demon. The memory of Valentin belongs among the treasures of my journey.

But now I had lingered long enough in Munich and at my friend's table. Be a man, I cried to myself, and make up your mind to go. Now it was not the way it had been before in Locarno, it was not easy to say goodbye, I was not traveling out into the world and could not look back with a feeling of superiority on those left behind, now I was going back, into the cage, into the cold, into banishment. Well, yes, the leaf struggles to defend itself in the wind, nevertheless must go where the wind wills. Where will I go now? By how many days will I succeed in postponing my return home? Presumably I will go on traveling for a long time, perhaps the whole winter, perhaps the rest of my life. Everywhere I would finally find this or that friend, would sit over wine for an evening, and here and there my good spirits and the sanctuaries of my youth would meet me at some twilit hour. And everywhere I would be free not just to be sad about the cold wind and the driven leaves but to laugh. Perhaps after all, as I have suspected from time to time, there is something of a humorist in me, in which case I am in a strong position. He has simply not yet developed fully, I have not yet had enough hard times.

On Moving to a New House
(1931)

Moving to a new house means not only beginning something new but giving up something old as well. And now as I move to our new house I can, of course, feel gratitude from the bottom of my heart to the kind friend who gave us this house, I think with thankfulness and renewed friendship of him and of the other friends who joined together to help with the building and furnishing. But to make a statement about the new house, to present it in narrative, to praise it, to sing a song to it, that I would not be able to do, for how is one to compose words and sing songs at the first step of a new undertaking, how is one to celebrate a day before evening comes? At the dedication of a new house we can, of course, cherish hopes in our hearts and urge our friends to carry in their own hearts unspoken wishes for the future of the house and of our lives. However, to say anything about the new house, to give real news about it, to declare any relationship to it, that is something I could do only after a year and a day.

But I can and must, as we move into it, remember other houses which at earlier times gave shelter and protection to my life and work. To each of these houses I am grateful, each preserves countless memories for me and helps in retrospect to give the time I lived there a face of its own. Therefore, just as people at infrequent family gatherings talk about past times and recall the dead, so today I want to remind myself of all the predecessors of our handsome house, call up their images in me, and tell my friends about them.

Although I grew up in old houses of marked character, in my youth I was too little cultivated and far too much concerned with myself to devote much attention or love to the house and the room in which I lived. Though it was by no means a matter of indifference how my room looked at that time, what was important to me about the appearance of a room I occupied was only what I myself had contributed to it. I was neither interested nor pleased by the dimensions of the room, its walls, its corners, its height, its colors, its floor. The things I had brought with me into the room and had spread out, hung up, and set around were what mattered.

The way a twelve-year-old boy goes about adorning his first room and making it his own has nothing to do with taste or decoration; the impulse for this kind of adornment lies much deeper than any matter of taste. Thus, when at the age of twelve I proudly took possession of the first room of my own in my father's spacious house, I made no attempt to divide and conquer the large high chamber or to make it handsome and livable through colors or furniture arrangement, but paying no attention to the position of the bed, the wardrobe, and so forth, I concentrated on a few places in the room which were for me not merely conveniences but sanctuaries. The most important was my standing desk, which I had wanted for a long time and had now been given me, and in this desk the most important thing was the empty space under its slanting lid where I was at pains to arrange a store of more or less secret trophies, things one does not need and cannot buy, things with a memorial value and in part magic properties for no one but me. Among these were the skull of a small animal whose provenance I did not know, dried leaves, a rabbit's foot, a fragment of thick green glass, and many other such things which lay hidden in the twilight of their cave under the lid of the desk, my possessions and my secrets, seen and known about by no one else, more valuable to me than anything else I had. Next in order of importance to this secret treasury was the top of the desk, and here it was no longer a matter of utmost privacy but of decoration, display, and boastfulness. Instead of hiding and protecting I wished to exhibit and vaunt, things had to be pretty and impressive, bunches of flowers, fragments of marble, photographs and other kinds of pictures on display, and my greatest desire was to have a piece of sculpture to exhibit here, no matter what kind, just as long as it was a three-dimensional work of art, any figure or head, and so strong was this desire that I once stole a mark and bought for eighty pfennigs a tiny baked-clay bust of the young Kaiser Wilhelm, a worthless mass-produced object.

This yearning of the twelve-year-old was still present at the age of twenty and among the first things I bought with the money I earned as an apprentice bookseller in Tübingen was a snow-white plaster cast of the bust of Hermes by Praxiteles. I very likely would not be able to endure it in any room today, but at that time I still felt almost as strongly as the boy with his clay bust the primitive enchantment of sculpture, a tangible, palpable imitation of nature, so it can hardly be called a real improvement in taste even if the Hermes was a nobler form than the bust of the Kaiser. I must say too that during my four years in Tübingen I was consistently indifferent to the house and room I lived in. I stayed in the Herrenberger Strasse through all four years in a room that had been arranged for by my parents when I went to Tübingen: a barren, dull room on the ground floor of a barren, ugly house in an unattractive street. Although sensitive to beauty in many forms, I suffered not at all from this dwelling place. To be sure, it was not really a "dwelling place" since from early morning until night I was at work in the bookstore, and when I returned home it was usually already dark and I wanted nothing but to be alone, to be free to read and to do my own work. And at that time I did not yet understand by a "handsome" room an attractive one but rather an ornamented one. I provided plenty of decorations. I had nailed up on my walls more than a hundred pictures of men I admired for one reason or another, some large photographs, some small ones clipped from illustrated periodicals and publishers' catalogues, and this collection grew constantly during those years; I still remember very clearly how I paid with a sigh a rather high price for a photograph of the young Gerhart Hauptmann whose *Hannele* I had read at that time and for two pictures of Nietzsche; one was the well-known picture with the long mustache and upward glance, the other a photograph of an oil painting which showed him outdoors in a wheelchair, with woefully sunken, vacant look. I often stood in front of that picture and studied it. My Hermes was there too, and the biggest reproduction of a picture of Chopin that I was able to find. Besides all this, hung across half the wall above the sofa in the usual student fashion, was a symmetrical arrangement of pipes. I had a standing desk in this room too and in its dark recesses there were still magic, mystery, and treasures, still a constantly accessible retreat from the dull outside world into a magic realm; only now there were no skulls, rabbits' feet, hollowed-out horse chestnuts, and fragments of glass, but, written in copybooks and on piles of loose paper, my poems, fantasies, and essays.

In the fall of 1899 at the age of twenty-two I went from Tübingen to Basel and there for the first time felt a serious vital relationship with the graphic arts: during my Tübingen period what time I had was devoted exclusively to literary and intellectual matters, especially to my involvement, as though drunken or possessed, first with Goethe and then with Nietzsche. In Basel, however, my eyes were opened and I became an attentive and soon a knowledgeable observer of architecture and painting. The little circle of people in Basel that now took me up and helped to educate me was completely saturated with the influence of Jakob Burckhardt, who had died a short time before and who was to occupy in the second half of my life a place that formerly had belonged to Nietzsche. And so during my years in Basel I attempted for the first time to live in a tasteful and dignified fashion by renting a strikingly handsome room in an old Basel house, a room with a great old tile oven, a room with a past. But I had no luck there; the room itself was marvelous but it was never warm although the old oven consumed great quantities of wood, and under the windows from three o'clock in the morning on, milk wagons and market wagons from the Alban Gate rattled over the cobblestones of the apparently quiet side street, making a hellish racket and robbing me of sleep; defeated, I fled after a while to a pretty room in a modern suburb.

And then began the time of my life when I no longer lived in rooms accidentally come by, often moving from one to another, but in houses that became dear and important to me. In the years between my first marriage in 1904 and my moving into the Casa Bodmer in 1931 I lived in four different houses and built one of them myself. I must recall them all today.

By this time I would not have moved into an ugly house or even one of an indifferent character; I had seen much ancient art, had been twice to Italy, and also my life had been changed and enriched in other ways: simultaneously with giving up my former position, I decided both to marry and to live entirely in the country henceforth. My first wife took a great part in these decisions as well as in the choice of the place and the houses in which we were to live. She was determined to live a simple, healthy life in the country, with a minimum of necessities; however, she laid great emphasis on living beautifully as well as simply, meaning in handsome, dignified houses in a lovely landscape with a beautiful view, in short, in houses that were not ordinary but had beauty and character. Her ideal was half peasant cottage, half manor house, a mossy roof under ancient trees, if possible a gushing spring at the front door. I myself had quite similar dreams and wishes and was also under Mia's influence. So what we were looking for was in a sense prescribed in advance. First we searched around Basel in the pretty villages nearby. Then as a result of my first visit to Emil Strauss in Emmishofen, Lake Constance came under consideration, and finally while I was at home in Calw with my father and sister writing *Beneath the Wheel,* my wife discovered the village of Gaienhofen on the Untersee and a vacant peasant house there on a small quiet square opposite the village chapel. I agreed and we rented the house for a hundred and fifty marks a year, which even for that time and place seemed to us cheap. There we began to install ourselves in September 1904, at first with disappointments and the frustrations of long waits for missing furniture and beds which were to come from Basel and which we looked for day after day on the morning ship from Schaffhausen. Then we began to make progress and our enthusiasm grew. We painted the roughhewn beams in the large room on the second floor a dark red; the two rooms on the lower floor, the handsomest in the house, had old paneling of unpainted pine and in addition to the massive stove a so-called "contrivance": a part of the wall above a rough bench consisted of old green tiles which were heated by the fire on the kitchen hearth. This was the favorite place of our first cat, the handsome tom Gattamelata. And so this was my first house. Actually we rented only half the building, the other half consisting of a barn and stall which the farmer kept for his own use. The living quarters in this half-timbered house consisted on the ground floor of a kitchen and two rooms, the larger of which was heated by the big tile stove and served as our living and dining room; rough wooden benches ran halfway along the wall and there it was warm and cozy. The smaller room next to it belonged to my wife, her piano and desk stood there. A primitive board stairway led to the upper floor, where corresponding to the living room was a large chamber with two corner windows from which one could see past the chapel a portion of the lake and shore; this was my study, containing a big desk I had had built which I still have today, the only piece of furniture from those times; once more I had a standing desk as well and all the walls were lined with books. To enter, one had to pay careful attention to the raised beam that formed the doorsill; anyone overlooking this would strike his head on the low frame of the doorway, something that happened to a good many. Young Stefan Zweig on his first visit had to lie down for a quarter of an hour and recuperate before he could speak, he had come in too quickly and enthusiastically for me to be able to warn him. On this floor there were also two bedrooms and above it all a big attic. There was no garden with this house, only a small patch of grass and two or three meager fruit trees, and a border I dug along the house for red currants and a few flowers.

For three years I lived in this house and during that time my first son came into the world and many poems and stories were written. In my *Picture Book* and elsewhere there are many scenes from our life of that time. Something that no later house could give me made this farmhouse precious and unique in my eyes: it was the first! It was the first refuge of my young marriage, the first legitimate workshop of my profession, here for the first time I had a feeling of permanence, and for that very reason occasionally a feeling of imprisonment, of being hemmed in by boundaries and obligations. Here for the first time I indulged in the beautiful dream of creating and achieving in a place of my own choosing some kind of home, and it took shape with meager and primitive means. Nail after nail I drove into those walls, and they were not nails I had bought but came from the packing cases of our move, nails that I had one after another hammered straight on our stone doorstep. I stuffed the gaping cracks in the upper story with oakum and paper, and painted them over with red, I fought for the few flowers against the bad soil beside the house, against dryness and shade. The arranging of this house was done with the fine pathos of youth, with the feeling of our own personal responsibility for our actions and in the belief that it would be for our whole lives. We attempted in this peasant cottage a simple, candid, natural country kind of life, un-metropolitan, unfashionable. The ideas and ideals we pursued derived as much from Ruskin and Morris as from Tolstoy. In part it was a success, in part a failure, but for both of us it was completely sincere, everything was carried out with loyalty and devotion.

Two pictures, two experiences, stand out sharp and clear in my memory when I am reminded of this house and the first years in Gaienhofen. The first is of a warm and sunny summer morning, the morning of my twenty-eighth birthday. I woke up early, startled and almost frightened by extraordinary sounds, ran to the window and there below stood a country orchestra of wind instruments, collected by my friend Ludwig Finckh from a couple of neighboring villages, playing a march and a chorale, and the horns and the keys of the clarinets sparkled in the morning sun.

That is one of the pictures that goes with the old house. The other also has to do with my friend Finckh. This time too I was wakened from sleep but it was still the middle of the night, and under my window stood not my friend Finckh but my friend Bucherer, who told me that the little house that Ludwig Finckh had just bought and furnished for his young wife was in flames. Silently we went up through the village and there the sky was blood-red and the quaint little witch's house that had just been enlarged, painted, and furnished was burning up to the last shingle, and its owner was on his honeymoon and tomorrow would arrive to bring his bride to that house. The heap of ruins was still smoldering and smoking when we had to be on our way to meet our friend and greet him and his wife with the sad news.

By degrees and without regret we said farewell to our farmhouse, for now we had decided to build a house of our own. Various considerations had entered into this decision. In the first place, external circumstances were favorable, and with our simple, frugal way of life, money had been laid aside each year. Then too for a long time we had yearned for a proper garden and for a more open, higher location with a wider view. Also, my wife had been sick a great deal, there was a child, and such luxuries as a bathtub and a hot-water heater no longer seemed so completely unnecessary as they had three years before. And, so we thought and said, if our children were to grow up here in the country it would be nicer, more proper, if they did so on their own ground, in their own house, in the shadow of their own trees. I no longer know how we justified this notion to ourselves, all I remember is that we were quite serious about it. Perhaps there was nothing behind it but the sentiment of middle-class householders, although this had never been strong in either of us—but in the end we had both been corrupted by the fat years of our first success; or perhaps in this, too, there lurked some peasant ideal? I never felt very sure of my peasant ideals even at that time; deriving from Tolstoy as well as from Jeremias Gotthelf and reinforced by a fairly lively movement current in Germany of flight from the city and life on the land, a movement with moral and artistic foundations, these fine but ill-formulated articles of faith were alive in our minds, just as they came to be expressed in *Peter Camenzind.* I no longer know exactly what I understood by the word "peasant." Today in any case I believe that I know nothing with greater certainty than that I am the exact opposite of a peasant, that is (according to my native type), a nomad, a hunter, an unsettled lone wolf. Well, at that time my thinking was probably not very different from what it is today, but instead of the opposites "peasant-nomad" I felt and formulated the opposites "peasant-city dweller," and by being a peasant I understood not only remoteness from the city but especially the closeness to nature and the safety that characterize a life led not according to reason but according to instinct. That my country ideal itself was only a proposition of reason bothered me not at all. Our inclinations always have an astounding knack of masquerading as philosophies of life. The error of my life in Gaienhofen then was not that I entertained false ideas about peasants and so on but that in part I consciously struggled toward something quite different from what my true nature demanded. How far I allowed myself to be guided in this matter by the ideas and wishes of my wife Mia I cannot say; however, her influence in those early years was, as I see only now in retrospect, stronger than I would have admitted.

In short, it was decided to buy land and build. An architect friend of ours from Basel was at hand, my parents-in-law provided the larger part of the building cost as a loan, land was to be had cheap anywhere, I believe a square meter cost two or three groschen. And so in our fourth year on Lake Constance we bought a piece of property and built a pretty house on it. We chose a location well outside the village with a free view over the Untersee. One could see the Swiss shore, the Reichenau, the spire of the Constance Cathedral, and behind it the distant mountains. The house was more comfortable and larger than the one we had left, there was room in it for children, maid, guest; drawers and closets were built in and we no longer had to bring water from the spring as before, there was running water in the house and under it a wine cellar and a root cellar and a darkroom for my wife's photography, and many conveniences. After we moved in there were disappointments and worries, the cesspool was frequently clogged and dirty water stood in the kitchen sink and threatened to overflow while I and the hastily summoned master builder lay on our stomachs in front of the house and poked with sticks and wires into the drainpipes we had dug up. On the whole, however, it turned out well and gave us pleasure, and if we conducted our daily life as simply as before there were still a number of small luxuries of which I had never allowed myself to dream. In my workroom was a built-in bookcase and a big folding desk. All the walls were covered with many pictures, we now had several artist friends, we bought some things and received others as gifts. Instead of Max Bucherer, who had moved away, two painters from Munich now lived nearby in the summer, Blumel and Renner, whom we liked and whom I still count among my friends.

I had thought out an especially fine and luxurious heating system for my study, a big green tile stove in which coal could be used for slow combustion. We took great pains with it and once during its construction sent back to the factory a whole wagonload of tiles because they were not quite the beautiful green that I had had in mind and had ordered. But it was just this oven that showed me the shadow side of all conveniences and technical improvements: the thing heated well, to be sure, but when the weather turned stormy it generated gas which it was unable to expel and it would then explode with a noise I can still hear today and the room was suddenly full of coal gas, smoke, and soot, one had to get the coals out as quickly as possible, extinguish them and then hurry off on a two-hour walk to Radolfzell to fetch the potter, and then for many days there was no heat and the study was useless. Three or four times this happened and twice I left immediately after the accident: hardly had the wicked explosion occurred and my room filled with smoke when I had packed my suitcase and rushed off, summoning the potter in Radolfzell and traveling from there by train to Munich, where as associate editor of a magazine I had things to do anyway. Nevertheless, this misbehavior was exceptional.

Almost more important to me than the house was the garden. I had never yet had a garden of my own and it followed from my principles of country living that I myself must lay it out, plant it, and tend it, and this I did for many years. In the garden I built a shed for firewood and gardening utensils; working along with a farmer's boy who advised me, I staked out paths and beds, planted trees, chestnuts, a linden tree, a catalpa, a row of beeches, and a quantity of berry bushes and pretty fruit trees. The fruit trees were nibbled at and destroyed during the winter by rabbits and deer, all the rest flourished beautifully, and at that time we had strawberries and raspberries, cauliflower, peas, and lettuce in superfluity. I also laid out a seed bed for dahlias and a long alley on both sides of the road where some hundreds of sunflowers of remarkable size flourished and at their feet thousands of nasturtiums in all shades of red and yellow. For at least ten years in Gaienhofen and in Bern, alone and singlehanded I planted my vegetables and flowers, fertilized and watered my beds, kept the paths free from weeds, sawed and split all the required large quantity of firewood. It was fine and instructive, and yet in the end it became severe slavery. Playing at being a farmer was fine so long as it was a game; when it turned into a chore and a duty, the pleasure in it was gone. In his book Hugo Ball, on the basis of my very sparse communications on the subject, has revealed the meaning of this Gaienhofen episode, although he has been a little too harsh and unfair toward my friend Finckh. There was more warmth in our friendship, more innocent fun, than he allows.

Moreover, how drastically our souls rework the image of our surroundings, falsify it or correct it, how much the pictures of our memory are affected by our inner life is demonstrated with disconcerting clarity by my recollection of the second house in Gaienhofen. Even today I have the most precise image of the garden of this house, and inside the house I clearly see my study with its roomy balcony in all its details, and I could name the place where each of my books stood. But my memory of the remaining rooms, twenty years after leaving the house, has become remarkably hazy.

And so we were properly accommodated for life and settled in, peacefully at our front door stood the one tall tree on our property, a mighty and ancient pear under which I had built a wooden bench; busily I arranged my garden, planting it and making it pretty, and already my oldest boy came trailing after me with his child's spade. But the eternity for which we had built did not last long; I had exhausted Gaienhofen, there was no further life for me there, I frequently went on short trips, the world out there was so wide, and finally I went as far as India in the summer of 1911. Today's psychologists, obsessed by baseness, called something like this "flight," and of course this element was present among others. But it was also an attempt to gain perspective and an overall view. In the summer of 1911 I went to India and came back at the very end of the year. But none of this was enough. In time there were added to our unspoken inner discontents outer ones as well, the easily argued problems between man and wife: our second and third sons were born, the eldest was already of school age, my wife at times felt homesick for Switzerland and also for nearness to a city, for friends and for music, and gradually we came to regard our house as being on the market and our life in Gaienhofen as an interlude. In the year 1912 the matter came to a head when a purchaser for the house was found.

The place we now wanted to move to after eight years in Gaienhofen was Bern. Of course we did not want to live in the city itself, that would have been a betrayal of our ideals, but we wanted a quiet country house in the vicinity of Bern, perhaps one like the marvelous old estate my friend Albert Welti, the painter, had been living in for some years. I had visited him several times in Bern and his handsome, slightly unkempt house and grounds far outside the city had pleased me very much. And if my wife through memories of youth already had a great love for Bern and its way of life and for old Bern residences, then for me the fact of having a friend like Welti there influenced my decision.

But when we actually decided to leave Lake Constance for Bern, everything had become quite different. A few months before our move our friend Welti and his wife died in quick succession, I went to his funeral in Bern, and it turned out that if we really wanted to move there the best thing would be to take over Welti's house. We rebelled inwardly against this inheritance, which smelled too much of death, and we searched for another place in the neighborhood but found nothing that suited us. The Welti house was owned not by them but by a patrician family in Bern and we were able to take over the lease, together with some household furnishings and the Weltis' wolfhound Züsi.

The house on Melchenbuhlweg near Bern, above Castle Wittigkofen, was really in every respect the realization of our old dream, which had become more and more firmly fixed in our minds since our days in Basel, the ideal house for people like us. It was a country house in the Bern style, with the rounded Bern gable, which in this particular house because of the marked irregularity of its proportions had something especially winning about it, a house which in the most agreeable fashion, as though especially for us, combined a mixture of peasant and manorial features, half primitive, half elegant and patrician, a house dating from the seventeenth century with additions and interior rearrangements from the time of the Empire, surrounded by venerable trees, completely overshadowed by an enormous elm, a house full of marvelous nooks and crannies, sometimes of agreeable, sometimes uncanny sort. A large section of farmland and a peasant house went with it, which was rented out to a tenant farmer from whom we got milk for the kitchen and dung for the garden. Our garden, laid out on the south side of the house, sloped downward in two severely symmetrical terraces with stone steps and encompassed several beautiful fruit trees; some two hundred steps from the house was a so-called "bosquet," a little grove consisting of a few dozen old trees, among them splendid beeches, the grove standing on a little hill that commanded the neighborhood. Behind the house, water spouted from a handsome stone fountain, the big veranda toward the south was overgrown with a giant wistaria vine, from there one looked across the neighborhood and many wooded hills to the mountain chain, all of which was visible, from the Thun foothill region to the Wetterhorn, with the huge mass of the Jungfrau group in the middle. House and garden are fairly accurately described in my fragmentary novel *The House of Dreams*, and the title of this uncompleted work is a memorial to my friend Albert Welti, who gave this name to one of his most remarkable paintings. Inside the house there were many interesting and cherished things: old, pretty tile ovens, furniture and paneling, elegant French pendulum clocks under bell jars, old full-length mirrors with greenish glass in which one looked like the portrait of some ancestor, a marble fireplace in which I made an open fire on every autumn evening.

In short, we could not have imagined anything we would have liked better—and yet from the beginning it was shadowy and unhappy. The fact that this new existence of ours had begun with the death of both the Weltis was like an omen. And yet at the beginning we enjoyed the advantages of the house, the incomparable view, sunset over the Jura, the good fruit, the old city of Bern where we had friends and where we could hear good music, only everything was a little resigned and subdued; it was not until many years later that my wife admitted to me that from the very outset in the old house, which had enchanted her as it had me, she had often felt fear and oppression, yes, something like a dread of sudden death or of ghosts. Now there slowly developed the pressure that changed my then way of life and partially destroyed it. Not quite two years after we moved came the world war, for me came the destruction of my freedom and independence, there came the great moral crisis on account of the war that compelled me to find new foundations for my entire thought and work, there came the serious, protracted illness of our youngest, our third little boy, there came the first premonitions of my wife's emotional illness —and while I was overstrained by my official duties because of the war and grew more and more morally desperate, everything crumbled away that had till then constituted my happiness. In the latter part of the war period I sat in that remote house with no electric light, often without kerosene, in the darkness, gradually our money disappeared, and finally after prolonged bad times, my wife's illness erupted, she was in sanatoriums for a long time; in the neglected, much too large Bern house, it was hardly possible for me to maintain a household, I had to board my children out, for long months I was alone in the desolate house with a single faithful maid and would have long since departed if my war job had allowed it.

Finally, when in the spring of 1919 this war job was over too and I was free again, I left the haunted house in Bern in which I had lived for almost seven years. The parting from Bern, by the way, was not difficult. It had become clear that from now on there was morally only one possibility of existence for me: to put my literary work ahead of everything, to live only for it and no longer to take seriously money troubles or any other consideration. If I did not succeed in this, I was lost. I traveled to Lugano, spent a few weeks in Sorengo, sought for, then found in Montagnola, the Casa Camuzzi and moved there in May 1919. I had only my desk and my books sent on from Bern, for the rest I rented furniture. In this last of my houses up to now, I lived for twelve years, during the first four all the time, from then on only in the warmer seasons.

This pretty and rather odd house which I am now leaving has meant a great deal to me; it was in many respects the most original and beautiful of any I have ever owned or inhabited. To be sure, I owned none of it whatever nor did I have the whole house, but rented only a small apartment of four rooms. I was no longer lord of the manor, father of a family with house and children and servants, who calls to his dog and cultivates his garden; I was now a little, penniless, literary man, a threadbare and rather dubious stranger who lived on milk and rice and macaroni, who wore his old suits till they were threadbare and in the fall brought home his supper of chestnuts from the forest. But the experiment which was the point of it all succeeded, and despite everything that was difficult in those years, they were beautiful and fruitful. It was like waking from a nightmare that had lasted for years, I inhaled freedom, the air, the sun, I had solitude and my work. In the very first summer I wrote in quick succession *Klein and Wagner* and *Klingsor's Last Summer*, and in doing so sufficiently relaxed my inner tensions so that in the following winter I was able to begin *Siddhartha*. And so I had not been destroyed, I had pulled myself together again, I was still capable of work, of concentration; the war years had not, as I had half feared, destroyed me intellectually. Materially speaking, I would not have been able to survive those years and do my work if it had not been that several friends stood by me constantly and loyally. Without the support of my friend in Winterthur and my dear friends from Siam, it would not have worked, and a particularly great office of friendship was done me by Cuno Amiet by taking in my son Bruno.

And so I have lived for the last twelve years in the Casa Camuzzi; garden and house appear in *Klingsor's Last Summer* and in other of my compositions. Dozens of times I have painted this house and drawn it and probed its complex, whimsical forms; especially in the last two summers, by way of farewell, I have made drawings from the balcony, from the windows, and from the terrace of all the views and many of the amazingly beautiful corners and walls of the garden. My palazzo, the imitation of a baroque hunting lodge, sprang from the whim of a Ticino architect some seventy-five years ago, it housed a whole series of other tenants, but none stayed as long as I have and I believe none loved it more (and smiled at it as well) and made it truly his adopted country as I did. The product of an extraordinarily luxurious taste and a delight in building a house that circumvented or overcame difficulties in the terrain, this half-stately, half-droll palazzo has a variety of aspects. The door of the house opens pompously and theatrically on a princely stairway leading down into the garden, which with many terraces, stairways, scarps, and ramparts continues until it loses itself in a ravine where splendid old examples of all the trees native to the South are to be found, grown together and interlaced with wistaria and clematis. From the village itself the house is almost entirely hidden. From the valley below as it peers out over the quiet wooded ridge, it looks with its spiral staircases and little towers exactly like a country castle out of one of Eichendorff's novels.

Much has changed here during the twelve years, not only in my life but in the house and garden too. The lordly old Judas tree at the foot of the garden, the largest I have ever seen, which year after year bloomed so luxuriantly and in the fall and winter looked so strange with its violet-red pods, fell victim to an autumn storm. Klingsor's great summer magnolia, close to my little balcony, whose ghost-like, giant white blossoms grew almost into my room, was cut down at a time when I was away. One spring when I returned from Zurich after a long absence, my honest old front door had actually disappeared and its place was walled up, I stood in front of it bewitched and as though in a dream and found no way in: they had done a little rebuilding without saying anything to me about it. But none of these alterations changed my affection for the house, it was more my own than any of the earlier ones, for here I was not a married man and father of a family, I was alone and at home, here I fought my way through the discouraging, harsh years after the great shipwreck in a situation that often seemed completely hopeless, here for many years I enjoyed the deepest solitude and suffered from it too, I made many poems and pictures here, comforting soap bubbles, and grew more attached to all this than I had been in any setting since my youth. In gratitude to this house I have painted it often and celebrated it in song, in many ways I have tried to recompense it for what it gave me and what it meant to me.

Had I remained alone, had I not once more found a life companion, very likely I should never have left the

Casa Camuzzi, although in many respects it was inconvenient for an aging and no longer healthy man. During the fairy-tale period I was often bitterly cold and I endured all sorts of other woes. And so now and again during recent years an idea formed itself, though I did not take it seriously: perhaps I might after all move again, buy or rent a house, or even build one, where I would have a more comfortable and healthy refuge for my old age. These were wishes and thoughts, nothing more.

Then the lovely fairy tale came true: on a spring evening in 1930 when we were sitting in the "Arch" in Zurich, chatting, the conversation came round to houses and to building, and my occasional wish for a house was mentioned. Then my friend B. suddenly laughed aloud and shouted: "You shall have that house."

This seemed to me a joke, a pleasantry over wine in the evening. But the joke has become serious, and the house about which we playfully dreamed at that time now stands there, awfully big and beautiful, and it is to be at my disposal for life. Once more I am undertaking to settle myself anew and once more it is to be "for life," and this time presumably it will be so.

There will be time to write its story later on; after all, it has barely begun. Today something else is in order. We will touch glasses and look our good and generous friends in the eye and thank them. We will empty our glasses to them and to the new house.

Notes on a Cure in Baden
(1949)

It has been twenty-five years since a kindly doctor first sent me as a patient to Baden, and the time of that first Baden cure must have found me inwardly prepared for and capable of new experiences and ideas, for it was then that the little book *A Guest at the Spa* was written, which until recently, even in the illusionless bitterness of old age, I have thought of as one of my better books and have remembered with unalloyed sympathy. Stimulated partly by the unaccustomed leisure of hotel life at the spa, partly through new acquaintances among men and books, I attained during those summer weeks of the cure a mood of contemplation and self-examination, midway on the road from *Siddhartha* to *Steppenwolf*, a mood of objective observation of my surroundings as well as of myself, I took a playfully ironic joy in observing and analyzing the passing moment, I was at a point of suspension between careless indolence and intensive work. And since these observations and playful representations of the life of the cure and the hotel, the casino concerts and idle wanderings, were after all somewhat trivial and inconsequential, my desire to think and write soon focused on another, both weightier and merrier subject—myself—on the psychology of the artist and literary man, on the passion, the seriousness, and the vanity of writing, which, like all art, attempts the apparently impossible; and the result, when it is successful, never corresponds to or even resembles what the writer has striven for and attempted, but makes up for that by sometimes turning out to be attractive, amusing, and comforting, just like ice flowers on the window of a heated room in winter in which we no longer behold a battle between opposing temperatures but landscapes of the soul and dream forests.

Only once, to be sure, in the last twenty years had I reread the book about the guest at the spa that emerged at that time, and this for the purpose of a new edition after the war years of destruction, and in the course of this reading I had the experience familiar to all artists and writers, that by no means do we have sure and steady judgments about our own productions, that in memory they can alter astonishingly, grow smaller or more beautiful or worthless. In this new edition *Guest* was to appear in one volume with *Journey to Nuremberg,* which was closely associated with it both in theme and in time of composition, and as I set myself to rereading the two small works I had not *Guest* but *Journey to Nuremberg* in mind as the better and more successful, and this judgment, the reason for which I was unable to reconstruct, was so firmly entrenched that I was seriously surprised and in a sense disappointed when at the end of my reading I had to conclude just the reverse, that of the two so similar sketches *Guest* was by far the more valuable and appealing; so much so that for a while I even seriously considered leaving *Journey to Nuremberg* completely out of the new edition of my works. In any case, the result of this careful rereading was the discovery, on the whole a cheering one, that decades before I had written not only a tolerably candid but a merry and enjoyable piece, something I could no longer accomplish today.

Since this discovery, time has slipped by again, it passes marvelously fast for old people, the years of old age in comparison with the solid, sturdy years of the past have the wearing quality of cheap, poor cloth made of cellulose, and now it is twenty-five years since I made notes on my first visit to Baden. Moreover, I must admit that every time I returned to Baden those notes caused me some anxiety, for on several occasions it has happened that one of my fellow guests has just read the book and immediately wants to talk to me about it, and being accosted thus and forced to endure conversation has become more repellent and vexatious to me over the years. This aversion, like my hunger for quiet and solitude, had steadily increased during the last years, I was infinitely sick and tired of "being on people's tongues," it had long since ceased to be a joke or an honor but was indeed a misfortune, and if from time to time I leave my once-so-well-hidden habitat, as for instance to take the cure in Baden, I do so among other reasons out of fear of and revulsion against the visitors who continually stand at my front door and respond not at all to my pleas for mercy whether quiet or angry, who creep around the outside of my house and often pursue me into the most private and hidden corners of my vineyard. They have taken it into their heads to ferret out the eccentric, to confront him, to trample on his garden and his private life, to goggle through the window at him at his desk, and to destroy completely by their chatter the remainder of his respect for human beings along with the remainder of his faith in the meaning of his existence. This tension between the world and me had long been building and growing, and since the invasion from Germany, foreseen for years, actually began, it has become an almost unbearable distress. I have endured hundreds of such attacks and intrusions with sweet or sour mien, but three times in the course of the recent weeks of the invasion I confronted and spat at visitors whom I found strolling about in my garden as though it belonged to them. No patience, no weariness, is so deep that it will stand anything; no pot is so big that it will not sometime run over.

So it was a kind of flight when I decided once more upon a cure in Baden. I had been there many times, always in late autumn. The baths and the softly stupefying, measured course of the hotel days, the early waning of the brief November light, the rest and the agreeable warmth of the half-empty building seemed to me desirable; I would either, as often before, relax and do nothing but follow routine, or as on other visits I would fill up the sleepless night hours by writing verses in bed and in doing so attain a higher degree of wakefulness than ever by the day; in any case, it was a change, and in the climate of age and decline this can at times be a not inconsiderable inducement. I decided to go, and my wife, for whom the nearness of Zurich was more of an attraction than the baths, agreed. We packed, sparing neither books nor writing materials. Off we went, and once more I moved into the comfortable old hotel which since my first cure had so often welcomed me back and calmly witnessed my transformation into an aging and then into an old gentleman. I had long since become a part of the furniture of aged guests, the hoary-headed ones who are smiled at with consideration and respect, and this time too I had moved up in the ranks, once more some of the very old regulars whom I had often encountered here had died. In their places in the dining hall now sat other ancients, and of course there were also some new faces among the personnel who did not greet the returning regular with the confident smile of recognition.

Over two and a half decades I had had many experiences in this building, had reflected and dreamed and written a great deal. In the drawer of my little hotel desk the manuscripts of *Narcissus and Goldmund*, of *The Journey to the East*, and of *The Glass Bead Game* had lain, hundreds of letters, of diary pages, and some dozen poems had been composed in the rooms I had occupied here, colleagues and friends from many countries and many periods of my life had visited me here, I had had many companionable drinking evenings and also many subdued bread-and-water days, times of intoxication with work and times of weariness and aridity. In this building, as in the whole town, there was hardly a corner without memories for me. People who acknowledge no homeland often cherish for such places, rich in old memories, a certain self-mocking but not untender love. On the third floor there was that bright room with three windows in which I had written the poems "Night Thoughts" and "Reflection," the former on the night after the first newspaper reports of the pogroms and the burning of synagogues in Germany. And in the other wing of the building a few months before my fiftieth birthday *Poems from a Sickbed* had taken shape. And downstairs in the hall I had received the news of my brother's disappearance and in the same place a day later the announcement of his death. Now for many years I had always occupied the same room in the oldest part of the building, and it would pain me if on my return the blue-red-yellow flowered wallpaper was not still there. But it was, together with the desk and the reading lamp. Gratefully I saluted this little pseudo-home.

Everything promised to be peaceful and comfortable. To be sure, among the regular guests whom we met in the hotel was a lady who for a number of years had visited there just as I had and who a number of times earlier had inexorably trapped me in long, one-sided conversations; but she knew me now, for on my last visit there had been a little scene between us which I felt justified in regarding as definitive. We avoided her and if on occasion I found myself in her neighborhood unaccompanied, I went in search of someone else with such haste and desperation that hardly anyone would have had the heart to stop me.

As reading matter we had brought Dostoevsky's *The Idiot* with us and had already begun it. It was just as exciting as it had been thirty years before, but this time anticipation was occasionally disappointed in that the book seemed to have lost something, during the years, in substance and content and the worthless people and silly hour-long conversations seemed to have increased. If we live long enough, it will probably come to the same point with the book as it did long years ago after the first two readings: aside from the unforgettable figure of the Prince, nothing will remain in memory but Rogozhin and the two women, and among the scenes the opening one in the railway carriage, the two in Rogozhin's gloomy house, the talkative night party on Lebedev's terrace, and the terrifying scene in which the two young women spit at each other and the Prince stays behind with Natasha. One will remember that in between there are conversations that run for hundreds of pages—which, nevertheless, after a long time one will want very much to read. We were both captivated again by the flickering, quivering atmosphere of the novel, and it suited this mood exactly when one evening after dinner my wife came into the room and said: "There's a murderer rushing up and down out there in front of the door."

"I must see him," I said, and hurried out.

Sure enough, a man was walking up and down, restless and trembling in great excitement, through the corridor and vestibule, a young man obviously a foreigner, but it was not the Oriental and Jewish look that struck me—this type I know well and find sympathetic; what distinguished him like a sign and had suggested the word "murderer" to my wife was simply his emotional state, a slightly disturbing kind of unease, of feverish agitation. But a murderer he was not, I knew that at my first sight of him; rather, perhaps, a suicide; the agitation and restlessness of his movements would have fitted with that, and yet it was not probable. Probable and almost certain was only the fact that this "murderer" was someone in a condition of great excitement, someone under pressure and in distress; probably and almost certainly he also had his eye on me, and this less in the hope of help or counsel than for the sake of conversation. I went slowly past him and had a look at him, first with a feeling approaching sympathy, but then more and more with dread. For this I saw was someone who wanted to and had to speak, perhaps because he had something on his heart that made it hard to breathe, perhaps only because he had been alone longer than he could bear, and now the pressure from inside was more than he could master. I lost my way in a side corridor and was assailed by misery, for I was almost completely certain that as soon as I returned he would speak to me, he would burst out at me, and I was actually frightened of this. For in my condition at the time, a state of great disillusionment, of flight from people and of deep doubt about the meaning and worth of everything I had lived and worked for, nothing could terrify me more and bring me closer to despair than an attack by a man who was looking for precisely all the things I could not give: faith, sympathetic response, receptive attention to his questions or complaints or accusations. Our tactical situations were too unequal: I was weak, weary, on the defensive, and also certain, in advance, of defeat; he, however, was young and strong and had behind him the strong motive power of his fever, his excitement or rage or neurosis or whatever one wished to call it. I had every reason to be afraid of him. But I could not linger forever in the halls and galleries and I could not expose my wife, who was waiting for me in my room, to the possibility that he would burst in and terrify her. In God's name, I had to get back. This frantic "murderer's" impulse to talk or to complain or to attack was a state of mind that I knew very well, over years and indeed decades many people had come to me in this feverish condition, either because they suspected a special quality of understanding in me or simply because I had accidentally crossed their path. I had listened to many complaints, confessions, wild arguments, explosions of dammed-up suffering and resentment, and not infrequently it had turned out to be a valuable experience for me, a strengthening confirmation or a useful insight. But now, at this stage of my difficult and impoverished life, when each approach by a new person, each intrusive new acquaintanceship, was experienced as a burden and a danger, now such an attack by a stronger and tougher man was deeply repugnant, it summoned up everything in me for defense and repulsion, and I returned to my room with indignant stride and an expression that presumably promised no friendliness at all. Sure enough, he stepped forward and now for the first time, as he turned toward me in the pale light of the lamp, I saw his face, which had been in half shadow before, an excited but good face, young and open, but also determined and full of willful purpose.

He said he was, like me, a guest in the hotel and that he had just read my *Guest at the Spa* and that it had so greatly excited and irritated him that he absolutely had to talk to me about it.

I explained briefly that for my part there was not the slightest need for conversation, that on the contrary I was in flight from an invasion of conversation-hungry persons who had become extremely burdensome. As expected, he did not yield, I had to promise to listen to him next day, but I begged him to be content with a quarter of an hour. He saluted and went away, I returned to my wife, who resumed her reading aloud from *The Idiot,* and as the friends of Rogozhin, Hippolyte, and Kolia went on with their lengthy discourses, most of them seemed to me to resemble the stranger in the vestibule.

When I went to bed, it became obvious that the stranger had already won the game: I greatly regretted that I had not listened to him at once that evening, for now the prospect of the next day and the obligation I had undertaken weighed upon me and spoiled my sleep. And what had the man meant when he said that reading my book had "irritated" him? For he had used this expression. Presumably, then, he had run across things in my book that he found indigestible and repulsive, about which he would demand an explanation or against which he would protest. So I was busied for half the night, and that half of the night belonged not to me but to the stranger. I had to lie there and construct ideas about him, I had to sketch out what he would perhaps say and ask, I had to lie there and torment myself by recapitulating from memory the approximate content of the book, *A Guest at the Spa.* Here too the sinister stranger had the advantage; he knew, from recent reading, the book which I had written twenty-five years ago and had last reread a number of years before. It was only after I had attained some clarity about what my attitude in the forthcoming conversation would be that I succeeded in thinking about something else and finally falling asleep.

The next day came and with it the afternoon hour for which we both were waiting, the stranger and I. He arrived and we sat in the same vestibule where the night before his threatening figure had suddenly appeared. We sat opposite each other at a very beautiful old gaming table with inlay work, in the middle of its round surface a chessboard with squares of light and dark wood; in happier days I had sometimes played chess at that table. Though it was daytime, this room was not much brighter than it had been the evening before, but it seemed to me that I now saw the face of my opponent properly for the first time. The way I felt in this situation, I would really have welcomed being able to find his face unsympathetic, it would have made my defensive position easier. But the face was altogether sympathetic, that of a smart, educated Jew, a Jew from the East who had been piously reared and had actually been a pious man well versed in the Scriptures, who had, however, on his way to becoming a theologian and rabbi developed doubts and turned about, for he had had an encounter with truth itself, with the living spirit. He had been terrified and inspired, he had had, presumably for the first time, an experience that I had had several times in my life, he was in a spiritual condition which I had learned to recognize in myself and in others, that of awareness, of insight and knowledge, of spiritual grace. In this condition one knows all, life looks one in the face like a revelation, the insights of earlier stages, the theories, the teachings and articles of faith, have fallen away and been carried off like spray, the tables of the law and the authorities are broken. It is a marvelous state, the majority of people, even the spiritual seekers, never experience it. To my part too it had fallen, I too had been touched by the miraculous gale, I too without lowering my eyelids had dared to look truth in the eye. To this highly favored young man, as I discovered after two exploratory questions, the miracle had appeared in the form of Lao-tse, for him grace bore the name of Tao, and if there was still anything like a law or a morality for him it was the command: Remain open to all things, despise nothing, condemn nothing, let all the rivers of life flow through your heart. For anyone who attains it, especially for the first time, this state of mind has the character of absolute finality and is closely related to a religious conversion. All questions seem answered, all problems soluble, all doubt banished forever. This finality, however, this victorious "forever," is an illusion. The doubts, the problems, the battle will go on, life unquestionably has become very much richer but not a bit less difficult. It was at this point that the disciple of Lao-tse seemed to stand: still borne aloft and wholly transformed and renewed by his experience of freedom and grace, he was obviously already pursued by shadows and on the point of plunging headlong from blessed exaltation back into the world of conflict, and to this plummeting fall I was accessory.

For now a book had fallen into the hands of this highly favored young man, my *Guest at the Spa;* he had read it and it had become a stumbling block to him, for with it the infinite opening-out had encountered limits, the universal affirmation had met resistance; he had read a book, a silly and very inadequate book, and this reading had breached his lofty blessing, his experience of a universal harmony; an egocentric, carping, and arrogant mind had spoken to him from the book, he had not been able to summon up the superiority and amusement to fit this disturbing voice into the great harmony, he could not answer it with laughter; he had hit upon this stone and stumbled over it, this book instead of cheering him had tormented and angered him. What had especially angered him was the arrogance with which the author from his artist's viewpoint, from his puritanism of taste, had carped and argued about the public's joy in "kitsch" in films, without being able to conceal the fact that he himself in his deepest emotional life took pleasure in this kitsch and sensuality. And almost sillier, yes, offensive, was the manner and tone with which the author had talked about the Hindu conception of oneness; he seemed to be presenting it as something to be believed literally and swallowed whole as a student accepts the multiplication table; he, the author, appeared to be offering it as dogma, as authoritative truth, whereas for the initiated the Tat Tvam Asi must be at best a beautiful soap bubble, a deceptively iridescent play of thought.

This was approximately the content of our conversation, which as agreed did not last much over a quarter of an hour. It was carried on almost entirely by him, for I put up no resistance nor did I call his attention to the fact that if one opens oneself to everything, then one should not get so angry over a book that one has to beat the author about the head and ears. Nor did I point out during that quarter of an hour that my book like any poetic creation did not consist merely of content but rather the content was relatively unimportant, just as unimportant as the possible intentions of the author, that the important thing for us artists was whether, as a result of the intentions, meanings, and thoughts of the author, a pattern woven of language stuff, of language yarn, emerged whose immeasurable worth stood far above the measurable worth of the content. I did not say this, because during our "conversation" it never occurred to me and because as long as my partner was talking about my book with his fine passionateness, I had to admit that he was completely right. He was speaking, to be sure, simply of the content, the rest had not touched him. During that quarter hour I would have been ready to disclaim the book or retract it if that had been possible, for not only was this reader's criticism completely justified insofar as it concerned the thoughts in the book, but I was genuinely grieved that it had caused vexation to a noble and pure spirit.

Silent and oppressed, I looked now at the face and hands of my critic, hands that were not shrunken and gray like mine but, like his voice and his whole vital presence, young and flexible and full of strength, now I looked at the handsome colors and ornamentation of the wood in the gaming table at which we two players sat and which presumably would still testify to the good taste and joyous spirit of its long-forgotten creator when even my young partner had become old and withered and tired of words and meanings.

My wife had not been present at this parley, it would have kept the man from expressing himself freely. Now, however, when the quarter hour had been exceeded, she appeared and sat down with us, and with this protection I, who had hardly opened my mouth during the whole meeting, uttered a few words which were perhaps soothing and conciliatory.

Happy though I was to say goodbye and useless though a continuation of the meeting would have been, nevertheless it hurt me to the heart that I had had nothing to give or to show to this genuine seeker except the mask of weary age, which reduces to unimportance judgments about oneself and one's books and even defense against such judgments. I would have been happy to offer him something pleasant so that at least a little bit of cheer would have remained with him from this quarter hour, which I felt to have been so deadly.

And it was days and nights before my depression from this meeting lessened and I could comfort myself with the thought that the stiff silence and unresisting withdrawal of the old man would serve the young one, as soon as he again participated in the Tao for reflection and meditation, just as fruitfully as would any other attitude I might have adopted toward his appeal.

For Marulla
(1953)

Dear little sister! Yesterday they buried you in the old cemetery in Korntal, probably the place that has lost least, in these unholy days, of the spirit and fragrance, the quietude and dignity, of the once "holy" Korntal.

On our father's grave the fir tree, which I had seen only once when it was young and small and had not seen again, had grown into a tall, stately tree. A few days ago it had to be felled and its roots dug out so that the grave would have room for you too, and that was the right thing to do, for this is your place, beside our father, whose lonesome old age you served and comforted at the cost of much sacrifice.

These long years of service left their mark on you and earned you a particular kind of respect from us Hesse children, and among the sacrifices you unhesitatingly made is presumably the renunciation of that other love and companionship that would have suited you as it does every well-raised young woman. Even the virginal and almost nunlike character of your later life showed the influence of our father. If that pious man during his years in Korntal after our mother's death radiated such peace and cheerful, serious dignity, if he became as unforgettable as a patriarchal figure from Biblical times to so many who knew him at that time, and even to many who knew him only by sight and from a distance, your sacrifice, your presence, your foresight and care, your company and collaboration, especially in the years of his blindness, played an important part. "An early Christian" is how Bishop Wurm described him to me once, and on another occasion he wrote that our father was one of the two persons most worthy of reverence that he had encountered in all his life.

Now Father has been dead for almost four decades, Bishop Wurm too, and most of those who knew our father and revered him; on Father's grave moss has grown and the lofty fir tree, it too has now had to make way, and you, dear sister, have returned home to him. All of you have left me alone, my brothers and sisters, so that for a while your memory may be kept fresh, and the memory of our parents and of the fairy tale of our childhood. Often in the course of my life I have done honor to this memory and erected small memorials to it, in many of my stories and poems I have tried to preserve something of that fairy tale, not really for the sake of readers but essentially only for me and for you, my five brothers and sisters, for only you could understand the countless secret signs, tokens, and playful references, and with each recognition and rediscovery of our common experience you have felt that same rather painful warmth around the heart that I felt in conjuring up the irrecoverable.

And if today in my thoughts beside your grave I remember those stories and poems, I feel not only a somewhat painful joy but something else, a torment, a dissatisfaction with myself and my stories, yes, something almost like remorse or bad conscience. For in those writings there is almost always mention of only one sister, although I was so happy to have two. Even in earlier times I have occasionally been taken aback by this. In many cases, to be sure, this combining of two sisters into one is nothing but a simplification, an economy or convenience resulting from an incapacity, a lack in my talent, which has always prevented me from writing stories concerning many persons. This is principally connected, I have always felt, with a complete lack of dramatic talent and dramatic temperament. But naturally, in the course of decades of fruitless struggle against this lack, I have found excuses, extenuations, yes, vindications for my incapacity.

Once a great poet of the Far East, after examining a schoolboy's poem in which there was mention of "several plum blossoms," uttered the dictum: "*One* plum blossom would have been enough." And so it seemed to me that it was not only permissible and excusable to turn two sisters into one in my stories, it was even perhaps an advantageous consolidation. Except that this agreeable manner of explaining away the problem usually did not stand up very well under self-examination, and for good reason, for the *one* sister in my stories is, for readers who know us personally, really always Adele and not Marulla; moreover, your name, Marulla, occurs in my writings, I believe, only a single time, in the story of the beggar, while Adele's name the reader meets often.

Not that I feel I owe you a justification or a plea for forgiveness; nothing of the sort would have been needed between us. Indeed, it was natural and proper that Adele should be closer to me, especially in the earlier days, for it is natural and proper that a precocious youngster should seek and prefer friends older than himself, and especially in our childhood the two years' difference between Adele and me were just insignificant enough not to cause difficulties in our friendship and yet sufficiently important so that an occasional gentle mothering of the boy, so fond on other occasions of playing the Knight, could only increase affection.

In spite of the one sister of my stories, however, you two were not by any means a symbol nor was only Adele dear, interesting, and important to me, on the contrary even in the early years of my life I saw and felt both of you always as sharply individualized figures, and with the years this differentiation increased steadily in precision and charm. We were six brothers and sisters and all our lives very devoted to one another, and we found in the differences of our characters and temperaments, as is understandable in any fairly well constituted family, even more joy and fun and more occasions for increased love than in what we all had in common. As a matter of fact, as we grew up and became older, some of us discarded much of what was common to us through our upbringing, and our brotherly and sisterly love suffered not a bit thereby.

We might perhaps have been compared to a sextet, the combined play of six voices from six different instruments, only there was no piano and no first violin, or rather, they were there of course, but they did not stay in the same hands, each one of us was from time to time the principal player: each one when he was born, when he endured trials and tribulations, at his engagement and marriage, even more at times of danger and threatening or suffered sorrows. It may be that each one of us younger children—I am not sure of this—on occasion envied the radiant warmth, the merriness and attractiveness which were native to Theo and Adele, or the friendly casualness of Karl, but each had his own gifts and abilities to contribute, even our dear youngest Hans, who, if it had not been for that assault by a bestial teacher and a premature and unlucky choice of profession, would no doubt have had a happier life. For—of this too I am uncertain, it is only a perhaps—if we summoned up the strength and flexibility to withstand life, nevertheless all of us were sensitive and discriminating enough to be just as vulnerable to self-doubt, anxiety, and desperate suffering as our Hans.

Compared to Adele, the creature of fantasy with her love of festivity and great hunger for beauty, you were soberer, cooler, more critical, but always ready for fun. If you did not have the animation and marvelous enthusiasm of Adele, by way of compensation you were more foresighted and more precise in your judgments, less easily blinded or carried away, and more exact in your verbal and written expression; in this the training and example of our father are evident. Your wit found appropriate descriptions for many people and many events. Toward the world of fantasy and art your attitude was not inflexible but reserved, what was beautiful was dear to you, but you did not like to be flattered by it, seduced or taken by surprise. What was only beautiful, only pleasing, was open to suspicion in your eyes, it had to have the value of truth as well.

It sticks in my mind that once you told me or wrote me what you thought about poetry. My memory of it is not precise but it was something like this: at times you prized and greatly loved a real poem, but you did not think that a valid idea was automatically made better by being formulated in verse instead of in prose and you could believe even less that a bad, muddled, halfway idea was made better or more complete by being dressed up in verse. When I wrote a poem to you and sent it for your last birthday, the only poem I have been able to squeeze out in these late, barren years, fortunately I was not thinking of that judgment of yours. I wasn't trying to impress you with beautiful poetry, just show you that I was thinking of you and had taken some little pains on your account. But later, when my rather muddled and awkward verses had been sent off and I remembered again what you had said, I was a bit ashamed, and then was happy when my gift nevertheless met with a kind reception.

Once—this is something I must confess today—I was a little angry at you, a little disappointed in you, and in this I was altogether in the wrong. It was on that journey to Nuremberg which I described in a sketch of the twenties, at a critical and often miserable time of my life before it had undergone catharsis through *Steppenwolf*. You were in Munich at the time and in the heavy oppression of those days, after I was through with the Nuremberg engagement, it was a comfort to know that in Munich not only old friends were awaiting me for an evening of drinking but you were there too, one of us, someone from the beautiful, holy, early morning of life. I came there jostled and driven by stormy currents through the narrow straits my life had to traverse at that time and I hoped, from meeting and talking with one of the few people closest to me, an intimate from childhood, for something beautiful and impossible, for an otherwise unattainable degree of understanding, yes, of protection and rescue, for something that no one could really give me and that no one would have been able to represent. And when I found you in Munich at home and pretty much contented, not lacking in joy at our meeting but neither disposed nor inclined to adopt the role of a confidante toward me, I drew back, disappointed and rebuffed, and on this occasion we attained no real cordiality. What I was seeking from you for a moment at that time in Munich no one could have given me, not even Adele, not even our father or mother. But I was caught in my dilemma and only later, a good while later, was I able to understand and be thankful that you maintained your quietude and distance and declined to follow me into the wasteland of my confusion.

It was lovely to have you as a guest in Montagnola, once for several weeks during one of Ninon's trips; we lived there very quietly and in general cheerfully with each other and when in the evening you read aloud to me, translated passages from English texts, reported to me clearly and concisely about something you had read at my request, then I could picture the life you had lived with our father during the years of his widowhood, as helper and comrade. Alas, at the end of one of these visits there came to us that which united us completely, intimately, and profoundly for the rest of our days—the news of Adele's death—after which we two were the last of the brothers and sisters. From then on, we were again completely together, even during your very long and severe period of suffering, although we were able to see each other again only a single time.

It was in this last period of our closeness, too, that something fell away and lost importance, something that had always disturbed and separated us a little. It was my being a writer, or rather my standing in public life, the to-do about fame, the throngs of genuine and false admirers who were a burden to you often enough. Adele had taken this more lightly, it had indeed given her some fun and flattered her to have a famous brother, it was a bit of finery and festivity for her. But you in your noble sobriety took a very critical view of this fame, this public life, these celebrations and admirers. Of course you knew what I thought about these things, but you saw me and my life to an ever-increasing degree eaten up and impoverished by this rampant monster, you saw me imposed on by duties that sucked out and robbed me of my own private life. And it was just this, my very own wholly private life, to which you were devoted and which you would gladly have shared more completely than was possible. Famous or not, I was your brother, and as a sister you were fond of me, and if fame took me away from you and the narrower natural circle of my nearest, you quite properly saw in this a loss for you as well as for me. And you were able to accept this distressing loss, to understand that I could not escape it, that I not only had to write my books but also had to accept as well as I could the pleasant as well as the burdensome consequences of my scribbling.

There was one thing of great importance that I never thoroughly discussed with you, any more than I did with my other sister and brothers. I mean the faith in which we were raised and which we six did not all retain. Adele, you, and Hans, each one of you in your way, remained true to the faith of our parents, and I have reason to believe that your own faith was closest to that of our father and the most open to formulation, yes, it was more or less completely expressed in your catechism and the beautiful hymns of the seventeenth century, with some small additions from Spener, Bengel, and Zinzendorf.

What I could never seriously talk out with our parents, the history of my criticism and my doubts about this faith and my gradual finding of my way in an extra-confessional piety drawn from Greek, Judean, Hindu, and Chinese sources as well as from Christian ones—this one might think would have served as a proper subject of conversation with you. But that conversation never took place. There was a reluctance, a prohibition in the way; a respect for the conviction of others and a disinclination we all shared for proselytizing made this impossible, and deeper still was the feeling that one must not shake or jar that which was unqualifiedly common to us all. And so we brothers and sisters created a beautiful, patient state of peace above the dogmatic abysses and we lived within it. Had your Christian faith and my world faith been put in naked confrontation, they would have had to part like water and fire, like yes and no. But what as largely unformulated faith guided your life as well as mine like an inner compass was nevertheless something common to us both, probably it was good that we felt it to be holy and untouchable.

I have taken leave of you, Marulla, without believing in that reunion of which you were certain in your last pain-racked dreams. But I have not lost you, you are with me as are all my dearest dead. Just as Adele or Mother has been with me at times, no doubt to warn me against forgetting in everyday life the divine and solemn, so you above all will stand by me if I am in danger of falling into imprecision, or uttering untruths through haste, through playfulness, through fantastic waywardness. Then you, so I believe and hope, will throw me a glance from within your circle of virginity, of order, and of incorruptible truthfulness, incorruptible even through brotherly love.

Events in the Engadine

(1953)

Dear friends:* The longer one works at it, the harder and more ambiguous the labor with language becomes. For this reason alone I shall soon no longer be able to record anything at all. And so before I tell you about my experiences in the Engadine we must really reach an understanding about what we mean by "experience." During the relatively short period of my conscious life, this word like so many others had lost a great deal in value and importance, it is a long downhill road from the golden worth it had, say, in the works of Dilthey to the devaluation by the journalist who tells us how he "experienced" Egypt, Sicily, Knut Hamsun, or Miss X the dancer, whereas perhaps he has not even seen and recorded these matters well and honestly. But if I am to carry out my wish and attempt to reach you by way of the circuitous path of the written word and printers' ink, I shall have to blind myself a bit and try to maintain the fiction that my archaic speech and way of writing still have the same validity for you that they do for me, and that an "experience" for you, as for me, is more than a fleeting sense impression or a chance event among the hundred accidents of everyday life.

A different matter, which has nothing to do with language or with my craft, is the way old people experience things, and here I may not and must not allow myself fiction or illusion but must stick to what I know: a younger

* "Events in the Engadine" is a circular letter addressed to Hesse's friends.—Ed.

or youthful person has no conception of the way old people meet experience. Essentially there are no new experiences for them, they have long ago had their share of appropriate and predetermined primary experiences, and their "new" experiences become always rarer, are repetitions of what has been met with several times before or are new strokes on an obviously completed painting, they cover past events with a new thin layer of color or varnish, one coat on top of ten, on top of a hundred earlier ones. And yet they signify something new; though they are not of course primary, they are genuine, for they bring with them among other things self-confrontation and self-examination. A man who sees the sea or hears *Figaro* for the first time gets a different and usually stronger impression than one who does so for the tenth or fiftieth time. To be specific, the latter has for the sea and for music less eager but more experienced and sharper eyes and ears; he registers not only the no-longer-new impression differently and with more discrimination than the other, but he inevitably recalls in it the earlier impressions; he both renews his experience with the sea or *Figaro* in a new way and also encounters his earlier self, his youthful eyes and ears, whether with a smile, with ridicule, superiority, compassion, shame, joy, or remorse. In general, it is appropriate to advanced age to feel toward earlier ways of perceiving and experiencing more sympathetic or abashed than superior, and especially the productive person, the artist, when he encounters his lost prime of life with its potency, intensity, and productivity, very seldom has the feeling, "Oh, how weak and silly I was at that time!," but rather the wish: "Oh, if I only had some of the strength of those days!"

Among the experiences destined to be appropriate and important to me, next to human and intellectual ones, are those of landscape. In addition to the landscapes that were my homeland and belong to the formative elements of my life—the Black Forest, Basel, Lake Constance, Bern, Ticino—I have adopted a few, not very many, characteristic landscapes through travel, wandering, painting, and other studies, and I have recognized them as essential signposts; for example, upper Italy, Tuscany in particular, the Mediterranean Sea, parts of Germany, and others. I have seen many landscapes and almost all of them have pleased me, but only a very few were destined by fate to be deeply and permanently satisfying, gradually blossoming into little second homelands, and probably the most beautiful of these landscapes and the one that has made the most powerful impression on me is that of the Upper Engadine.

I have been in this mountain valley perhaps ten times, occasionally just for days but more often for weeks. I saw it for the first time almost fifty years ago when as a young man I spent a vacation in Preda above Bergün with my wife and my boyhood friend Finckh, and when it was time to return home we decided to take one more strenuous walking trip. Down in Bergün a cobbler put new nails in the soles of my shoes and the three of us started off with our knapsacks through Albula by way of the long, beautiful mountain road and then by the much longer valley road from Ponte to St. Moritz, a country road without automobiles but with countless tiny one- and two-horse carts in an unceasing cloud of dust. In St. Moritz my wife said goodbye and traveled home by train. Then, while my friend, who was upset by the altitude and slept badly at night, grew constantly more silent and irritable, the uppermost valley of the Inn appeared before me, despite the dust and heat, like a prevision of paradise. I felt that these mountains and lakes, this world of trees and flowers, had more to tell me than it was possible to absorb and assimilate at this first meeting, that sometime or other I would be drawn back here, that this severe mountain valley so rich in forms, so solemn and harmonious, was important to me, had something valuable to give or to demand from me. After spending a night in Sils Maria (where I am writing these notes today), we stood on the bank of the last lake in the Engadine. In vain I urged my travel-worn friend to lift up his eyes, look across the lake to Maloja and toward the Bergell, and see how incredibly noble and beautiful this scene was; it did no good, and he said irritably, pointing with outstretched arm into the immense depths of space: "Oh, come now, that's a perfectly common theatrical effect." Whereupon I proposed to him that he take the country road to Maloja while I would follow the footpath on the other side of the lake. That evening we sat on the terrace of the Osteria Vecchia, far apart, each of us alone at a little table, and thus we ate our meal; it was not until next morning that we made up and went happily springing down the shortcuts of the Bergell road.

The second time was a few years later when I went to Sils for a meeting with my Berlin publisher, S. Fischer, just for two or three days, and stayed as his guest in the same hotel that I have revisited each summer during the last few years. This second stay left only a few impressions. I do remember, however, a fine evening with Arthur Holitscher and his wife; we had a great deal to say to one another in those days.

And then there was another experience at that time, a sight that on each successive visit has been more precious and important to me and has touched my heart: the rather gloomy house pressed close against a rock wall where Nietzsche made his home in the Engadine. Surrounded by the bright and noisy world of sport and tourism and big hotels, today it stands there defiantly, looking somewhat annoyed and disgusted, arousing awe and sympathy, an urgent reminder of the lofty image of man which the hermit set up even in his false doctrines.

After that, years passed without my seeing the Engadine again. These were my years in Bern, the sad war years. Then at the beginning of 1917 when I was ill from war work and even more so from the general misery of war and was urgently ordered by my doctor to go away, a Swabian friend of mine who was in a sanatorium above St. Moritz invited me to come there. This was in the middle of winter, the bitter third winter of the war, and I became acquainted with the valley from a new side, with its beauties, its ruggedness, its powers of healing and comfort. I learned to sleep again, I regained my appetite, I spent days on skis or skates; after a while I could stand conversation and music again, I could even work a little, at times I climbed alone on skis to the Corviglia shelter, which no cable car went to at that time, and usually I was the only one there. And in February 1917 I spent an unforgettable morning in St. Moritz. I had gone there on an errand and as I entered the square in front of the post office a man in a fur cap came out of the post-office building, in front of which a large crowd of people had assembled; the man began to read aloud from a dispatch that had just arrived. The people thronged around him, I too ran over toward him and the first sentence I could understand was: *"Le czar démissiona."* It was the news of the February Revolution. Since then I have ridden or walked through St. Moritz a hundred times, but seldom without thinking of that place and that February morning in 1917 and of my friends and hosts of that time, all of whom have long since died, and of the jar and shock to the soul that I felt when after a short period of being a patient and a convalescent in the peace of Chantarella the voice of that public crier, warning and exhorting, called me back to the present and to what was happening in the world. And so it is everywhere I go in this region, everywhere former days and my own face and my own self look back at me, the self that long ago had these very scenes before his eyes; I meet the man of less than thirty who cheerfully carried his rucksack so many kilometers through the August heat, and the man twelve years older who at a grave crisis, awakening from the suffering of the war, tortured and aged, found up here a brief interval of recuperation, of renewed and strengthening contemplation; and then there is that later stage in my life when in this dear mountain valley I was skiing companion to Thomas Mann's youngest daughter, patron of the recently built Corviglia cable car, sometimes accompanied by my friend Louis the Terrible and the latter's clever dachshund, at night the silent laborer at the manuscript of *Narcissus and Goldmund.* Oh, what a secret rhythm of remembering and forgetting takes place in our soul, secret and cheering as well as disturbing, even for one acquainted in some measure with the methods and theories of modern psychology! How good and comforting it is that we can forget! Each of us knows what his memory has stored up and can control. No one of us, however, can find his way in the monstrous chaos of what he has forgotten. Sometimes after years and years, like buried treasure or a wartime shell plowed up by a farmer, some fragment of what has been forgotten, pushed out of the way as useless or indigestible, comes to light again, and at such moments (in *Narcissus and Goldmund,* one such vital moment is depicted) all the multitudinous, precious, splendid contents of our memory seem to us like a little pile of dust. We poets and intellectuals depend a great deal on memory, it is our capital, we live on it—but if an intrusion of this kind from the underworld of the forgotten and discarded takes us by surprise, then what is recovered, be it pleasing or not, has more weight and power than our carefully preserved memories. At times I have considered the idea that the impulse to wander and to conquer the world, the hunger for what is new and yet to be seen, for travel and foreign lands, which is familiar to most people of imagination, especially in their youth, is also a hunger for forgetfulness, for the banishment of whatever has been oppressive, for the masking of familiar scenes by as many new scenes as possible. The inclination of old age, on the other hand, toward fixed habits and repetition, to the constant search for the same locations, people, and situations, would then be a striving to hold on to the possessions of memory, a never-satisfied need to assure oneself of what has been stored up in memory, and perhaps too a wish, an unadmitted hope, that this treasure store should increase, perhaps one day there would be the rediscovery of this or that experience, this or that encounter, this or that scene or face that had been forgotten and lost, to add to the contents of memory. All old people, whether they know it or not, are in search of the past, of the apparently irrecoverable; the past, however, is not irrecoverable, not absolutely gone, for it can, under certain circumstances, through poetry for example, be brought back and forever retrieved from the realm of what is gone.

Another way of recovering the past in a new guise is meeting people again whom one had known decades ago and not seen since they were so very much younger. A friend of mine once lived in the Engadine in a very charming, comfortable house with pine paneling and soapstone ovens; he was the magician Jup, the friend of Klingsor. He often entertained and spoiled me in princely fashion when I was still a skier and a regular visitor to the Corviglia shelter. At that time there were three charming children playing in his house, two boys and the youngest, a girl, who struck one immediately because each of her eyes was bigger than her tiny mouth. I have not seen the magician himself for decades, he no longer visits the mountains, but a few years ago I happened to encounter his wife again and at her house saw the now-grown children: a musician, an undergraduate, and the girl, who was still distinguished by her enormous eyes and tiny mouth; she had become a striking beauty and talked with enthusiasm of the Paris professor with whom she was studying comparative literature. She was present too in her mother's house on the afternoon when our friend Edwin Fischer played Bach, Mozart, and Beethoven. Ever since the time in Bern when as a quite young man this musician played for me his settings of my Elizabeth poems, he has again and again turned up, each time at a different stage in life, and our cordial friendship on each occasion has been continued and strengthened.

So with each return here the beloved past came to greet me and still does, irrecoverable perhaps but capable of being conjured up. To measure against it the present and my present-day "I" brings joy and pain, cheers and shames me, makes me sad and comforts me. To see the slopes which once I used to climb effortlessly afoot or on skis, the least of which would not be negotiable for me today, to think of the friends with whom I shared many of my Engadine experiences and who have now been resting for a long time in their graves hurts a little. But to summon up those times and friends, in conversation or in lonely thought, to leaf through the rich album of memories (always with the faint hope that perhaps a lost, forgotten picture may turn up again and outshine all the rest) is a joy, and as one's powers decrease and the little walks from year to year grow shorter and more difficult, so on the other hand, on coming back each year, this joy of remembering and adding to the thousandfold fabric of memory becomes constantly greater. My life companion Ninon has had a part in it, ever since a skiing winter almost thirty years ago, for since then I have never come up here without her, and she has been with me on those evenings in the magician's house, with S. Fischer, with Wassermann and Thomas Mann, and two years ago she was present at the grand reunion with my schoolmate from Maulbronn, Otto Hartmann, the cheeriest and noblest representative of good Germanism and good Swabianism of all my friends. It was a high holiday, our friend made us the present of a day out of his short vacation; we took him by car to Maloja and up the Julier, the mountains stood crystal-clear under the high August sky and, heavy of heart, I said farewell to him that evening. But our rather hesitantly expressed hope that we might perhaps see each other again was fulfilled: a few days before his death he was once more my guest in Montagnola *dona ferens;* I have told you about this in a memorial letter.

And now I have come up here this summer by a new route because on the day of our trip the road in Bergell was buried by a rockfall, the bridges were destroyed, and we had to take a new circuitous route by way of Sondrio, Tirano, and Poschiavo and the Bernina Pass, a lengthy but extremely beautiful trip whose thousand scenes soon became confused in my mind and began to vanish; what I have retained best is the impression of the hundredfold pleated and terraced hills of upper Italy covered with vineyards, a scene that in my earlier years would have been of scant interest to me. At that time it was the uninhabited, untamed, wild, and preferably romantic landscape I was eager for; only much later, but more with every passing year, have I become fond of and interested in the interaction of man and landscape, the shaping, manipulation, and peaceful conquest of the landscape through farmland and vineyard: terraces, walls, and paths clinging to the hillsides, outlining their shapes, peasant cleverness and peasant diligence in the silent, stubborn war with the destructive wildness and caprice of the powers of nature.

The first important encounter of the summer was human and musical. For years the cellist Pierre Fournier had been a summer guest in our hotel while we were there. In many people's judgment Fournier stands first in his field; in my view he is the purest of all cellists, a virtuoso equal to his precursor Casals, and perhaps his superior in artistry because of the severity and precision of his playing as well as the taste and uncompromising quality of his programs. Not that I would always entirely agree with Fournier on the matter of these programs; he plays lovingly many composers whom I could dispense with without pain, Brahms, for instance, but the music of Brahms is serious and can be taken seriously whereas the famous old man once played in addition to genuine music all kinds of ostentatious and silly stuff. Fournier and his wife and son were for years known to us by sight and we had often heard him in concert, but at the hotel we had left each other in peace, had only nodded at a distance and pitied each other when one of us saw the other besieged by the curious. This time, however, after a concert in the Rathaus in Samaden, we happened to become better acquainted, and he generously offered to play for me some time in private. Since he was leaving soon, this chamber recital had to occur on the following day, and it happened that this was an unlucky day for me, one of ill health, of irritability, weariness, and depression such as even at the stage of age's pseudo-wisdom can fall to our share from our surroundings and the unmastered desires of our own hearts. I almost had to force myself to go to the artist's room at the appointed hour in the late afternoon; because of my sadness and bad humor it seemed to me that I was taking my place unwashed at a festive board. I entered, was given a chair, the master seated himself, tuned his instrument, and instead of the atmosphere of weariness, disillusionment, dissatisfaction with myself and the world, I was immediately surrounded by the pure and austere air of Sebastian Bach, it was as though I had suddenly been lifted up out of our mountain valley, which on that day had lost its magic for me, into a much higher, clearer, more crystalline mountain world that expanded all the senses, called to them and sharpened them. What I had been unable to do throughout the day—take the step from the commonplace into Castalia—the music did for me in an instant. For an hour and a half I sat there listening to two solo suites by Bach, with brief pauses and little conversation between, and the powerful, precise, dry playing of the music was like bread and wine to a starving man, it was nourishing and cleansing and it helped my soul regain its courage and its breath. That province of the spirit that I had built for myself as refuge and rescue, when I was drowning in the filth of Germany's shame and the war, threw wide its gates once more and received me to a great festival, solemn and serene, such as is never quite realized in the concert hall. Healed and thankful, I went my way and I was sustained for a long time after.

In earlier days I often attended similar ideal musicales, I have always had a close and cordial relationship with musicians and have made many friends among them. Since I have been living in retirement and can no longer travel, these happy times have naturally become few in number. Besides, in the appreciation and judgment of music I am in many respects demanding and conservative. I did not grow up with virtuosi in concert halls but with chamber music, and the finest was always that in which one could participate oneself; in my boyhood I took my first steps in the realm of music with the violin and a little singing, my sisters and especially my brother Karl played the piano, Karl and Theo were both singers, and if in my early youth I got to hear the Beethoven sonatas or the lesser-known lieder of Schubert performed by amateurs whose interpretation was no virtuoso display, still it was not without profit and reward if, for example, I heard Karl next door straining and fighting for a sonata; and when he finally "had" it I could share his feeling of triumph and the rewards of battle. Later, to be sure, in the first concerts by famous musicians that I heard, I sometimes succumbed to the magic of virtuosity as though to intoxication, it was overwhelming to hear great experts smilingly master technical problems with apparent effortlessness, like that of an artist on the tightrope or trapeze, and there was an almost painful sweetness if in suitable passages a little emphasis and high polish were added, a yearning vibrato, a melancholy dying diminuendo; but this kind of enchantment did not last so very long, I was healthy enough to perceive how limited it is and to look behind the sensuous charm for the work itself and the spirit of the master, not the spirit of the dazzling conductor or soloist. And with the years I became perhaps oversensitive to the magic of technical expertise and that tiny excess of power, passion, or sweetness that it adds to a work, I no longer loved witty or dreamy conductors and virtuosi but became an admirer of objectivity; at all events, for years I have been able to accept exaggeration on the ascetic side much more readily than its opposite. Now my friend Fournier completely satisfied this attitude and preference.

Shortly after that, another musical experience with a droll and cheery conclusion was to come my way at a recital by Clara Haskil in St. Moritz. Aside from three Scarlatti sonatas, the program was not quite what I would have wished: it was an altogether fine and noble program, but except for the Scarlatti there was not one of my favorite pieces. Had I had my way, I would have chosen two other Beethoven sonatas. And then the program announced *Bunten Blätter* by Schumann, and I whispered to Ninon just before the beginning of the recital how sorry I was that it was not *Waldszenen* that awaited us instead, they were finer or at any rate much dearer to me, and it was of great importance to me to hear my favorite shorter piece by Schumann, *Vogel als Prophet*, as many times as possible. The recital turned out to be beautiful, and I forgot my much too private preferences and wishes, but the evening was auspicious over and beyond that.

The artist, who was enthusiastically applauded, gave us an encore and behold, it was precisely my beloved *Vogel als Prophet*. And as with every hearing of this noble and mysterious piece I remembered the time I first heard it, I saw the Gaienhofen house and my wife's room with the piano, the face and hands of the player, the face of a dear guest, a long, bearded, pale face with sorrowful dark eyes, bending far over the keys. Shortly afterward this good friend and sensitive musician took his own life. One of his daughters continues to write to me off and on and she was happy to hear from me fine and affectionate things about her father, whom she had hardly known. And so for me this evening in a concert hall filled with a rather worldly audience was also a little festival of reminiscences of an intimate and precious kind. In the course of a long life one carries around with him a great deal that can only be extinguished with one's own death. The musician of the sad eyes has been dead for almost half a century, but for me he is alive and at times very close, and the *Waldszenen* piece about the bird, if I hear it after a period of years, is always, over and above its particular Schumann magic, a source of memories, of which the piano room in Gaienhofen and the musician and his fate are simply fragments. Many other notes are struck too, going back to boyhood, when from hearing my older brothers and sisters play the piano, many a small Schumann piece became lodged in my head. Also I have never forgotten the first picture of Schumann that I saw in childhood; it was in color, a probably no longer acceptable color print of the eighties, in a child's card game of the portraits of famous artists with an enumeration of their principal works; Shakespeare, Raphael, Dickens, Walter Scott, Longfellow, and others have had for me all my life the faces they had on those colored cards. And that three-handed card game with its pantheon of pictures and works of art arranged for the young and for simple folk may perhaps have been the first stimulus for that conception of a comprehensive university of literature and the arts of all times and cultures which later was to bear the names of Castalia and *The Glass Bead Game*.

In the decades of my relations with this mountain valley, the most beautiful birthplace of a great river known to me, I have naturally been able to observe the advances of mechanization, the inroads of speculation, the deluge of strangers, changes almost as far-reaching as in the neighborhood of my Ticino habitat. Even fifty years ago St. Moritz was no more than a busy little city of foreigners, and the old leaning church tower seemed even at that time to look down troubled and senile on the crowd of barren business structures, as if aware of more profitable uses for its meager plot of ground, and ready at any moment to succumb to the laws of equilibrium and collapse. However, it stands there today unchanged, calmly maintaining its balance, while many of the brutal, oversize buildings built for speculation around 1900 have already disappeared. But everywhere in the limited space between St. Moritz and Sils and even deep into Fex the parceling and exploitation of the land proceeds, the building of big and small residences, the infiltration of a foreign population increasing faster every year. A great many of these houses are inhabited only a few months, indeed often only a few weeks during the year, and this always growing number of new residents in the valley community remain in large measure strangers to the old residents whose homeland they are buying up; even those well disposed are not there very much, never experience the bitter times of winter, the avalanches, the melting snow, and have hardly any part in the often serious problems and needs of the community.

It does one good occasionally to visit by car places that have changed little or not at all in the last decades. My walks no longer extend very far, but by car my wish to see these places can be gratified. Thus for years I have wanted to visit again the places in these mountains where the first walking trips of my youth began, the Albula Pass and Preda. This time the trip went in the opposite direction from my original journeys on foot, and that dusty little road between St. Moritz and Ponte, on which so many amusing carts were once driven, was no longer recognizable. But beyond Ponte, which today is called La Punt, we were soon in a silent austere world of rock in which I recognized, one after another, shapes and locations from earlier times; at the top of the pass I sat for a long while on a grassy hill away from the road, and in looking at the long, bare, multicolored mountain ridges and little Albula (whose pretty name always puts me in mind of *animula vagula blandula*), I remembered things from the 1905 summer of wandering. The bare stone ridges and boulder fields stared down unaltered, and for a little while we had that feeling, beneficent and admonitory, that a stay at the seashore or in the mountains away from people and civilization can give, the feeling of being outside time, or at any rate living in the kind of time that counts no minutes, days, or years but only geological milestones separated from one another by millennia. This was a fine feeling, alternating between a timeless, primeval world and the brief epoch of one's own life, but it fatigued one too, to realize that everything experienced and able to be experienced by humans seems so transitory and unimportant. After our rest on the height I would have preferred to return to the hotel, I had let myself in for enough and more than enough of conjuring up the past. But there was tiny Preda too, those few houses at the entrance to the tunnel where in my early days as a still-childless married man I had spent some weeks of my vacation. And then, calling much louder, was the image in my memory of a little mountain lake, deep green with dark blue peacock eyes. I wanted to see it again, and we had of course arranged to drive back by way of Tiefencastel and the Julier. Soon we were among the first pines and larches and I began to detect even on this side of the pass small signs of time and civilization; during another stop the stillness of the valley, which had been total, was broken by the persistent noise of a motor which I took for an excavator or tractor, but it was only a mowing machine in the field below, looking tiny in the distance. And now the lake appeared, Lake Palpuogna, its smooth, cool, green surface reflecting the forest and mountainside, the three wild dark precipices looming high above. It was as beautiful and enchanted as in former times, except for the lower end of the lake, where there had been damming and all sorts of improvements, and the number of cars parked along the road. But on coming to Preda I felt my receptivity to old memories and my joy in revisiting old scenes disappear completely. I had thought of pausing to look up the little house we once lived in and to inquire about the people who owned it. But I no longer wanted to do that, it seemed pointless to learn that old Nicolai and his relatives were long since dead. Also it was one of the first hot days of this cool, rainy summer and no air from the heights reached here. Quite possibly too, forgotten things from the time of my youth and my first marriage stirred in me; not only travel fatigue and summer heat distressed me and made me sad, but just as much a feeling of unease and remorse at many passages in my life, sorrow at the irremediability of everything past and gone. I rode on through little Preda without stopping, though I had really wanted to visit it again, and merely hurried our return home. While attempting a mental examination of that unease and remorse, I hit upon no particular sins or omissions in my earlier life, for they were forgotten, but I did experience once more that curious, dull, and never to be mastered feeling of guilt that can attack men of my generation and my kind if they think of the time before 1914. Whoever has been awakened and shaken by world history since that first collapse of the peaceful world will never be entirely free from the feeling of complicity, although it is more appropriate to the young, for age and experience should have taught us that this question is the same as that of our share in original sin and should not disquiet us; we can leave it to theologians and philosophers. But since within my lifetime the world in which I live has changed from a pretty, sportive, somewhat self-indulgent world of peace to a place of horror, I will no doubt suffer occasional relapses into this state of bad conscience. Presumably this feeling of shared responsibility for the state of the world, which those who have it sometimes like to interpret as a sign of an especially sensitive conscience and a higher humanity, is only a sickness, or, to be specific, a lack of innocence and faith. The completely well-balanced person will not hit upon the arrogant idea that he must share responsibility for the crimes and sicknesses of the world, for its inertia in peace and its barbarity in war, unless he is important and influential enough to be able to increase or lessen its suffering and guilt.

During this Engadine summer I was fated to have another and unexpected encounter with the past. I had not brought much reading matter with me, had had only my letters forwarded. And so I was surprised one day when a package from my publisher arrived without having made the circuit by way of Montagnola. It contained a new edition of *Narcissus and Goldmund* and as I was looking at it, examining paper, binding, and jacket and already wondering to whom I could give it so as not to weigh down my luggage, it occurred to me that I had not read it since its composition, or rather since the proofs of the first edition some twenty-five years before. Twice I had lugged the manuscript of this novel from Montagnola to Zurich and from there to Chantarella, I also remembered two or three chapters that had cost me troubled and sleepless nights, but the whole thing had become a little foreign and unfamiliar, as is the way with most books and their authors in the course of passing years, and I had never felt any need to renew the acquaintance. Now, as I was casually leafing around in it, it seemed to challenge me and find me willing. So *Narcissus and Goldmund* became my reading matter for some two weeks. It had been one of my more successful books, it had been, as the disagreeable expression has it, "on people's tongues," and the tongues of the people had not always given thanks and praise; on the contrary, next to *Steppenwolf* the good *Narcissus and Goldmund* is the book of mine that has elicited the greatest number of reproaches and outbursts of indignation. It appeared not long before Germany's last era of warriors and heroes and it was to a high degree unheroic, unwarlike, weak, and, as people told me, conducive to an unprincipled lust for life; it was erotic and shameless, German and Swiss students favored burning it and banning it, and the mothers of heroes, invoking the Führer and the Great Time, expressed their indignation in terms that were often more than discourteous. But it was not these experiences that had led me to avoid rereading the book for two decades; that had come about unintentionally from certain changes in my way of life and work. Formerly I had had to reread my books when I received proofs of new editions, and had also on these occasions reworked them somewhat and especially shortened them. But with the increase of my eye troubles I came to avoid this work as much as possible, and for a long time it had been taken over by my wife. I had, to be sure, never lost a certain love for *Narcissus and Goldmund,* it had come into being during a fine and vigorous period, and the curses and buffetings it had endured spoke for, rather than against, it in my heart, as was the case too with *Steppenwolf*. But the picture of it that I carried in my mind had like all memories changed and faded in the course of time, I no longer knew it well, and now that I had long since stopped writing books I felt free to devote a week or two to restoring this picture and correcting it.

It was a friendly and beneficent reunion, for nothing in the book evoked regret or remorse. Not that I was in complete agreement with everything about it, naturally the book has shortcomings; it seemed to me, as with almost all my writings when I reread them after a long time, a bit too long, a bit too talkative, perhaps the same thing is said too often in somewhat different words. Nor was I spared a recurrent and rather shaming insight into my lack of talent and ability; this reading was a self-examination that once more showed me clearly my limitations. It struck me again most forcibly that most of my longer works of fiction do not, as I believed during their writing, present new problems and portraits of new people in the way the true masters do but only repeat variations of the few problems and types congenial to me, though at new stages of life and experience. Not only was my Goldmund contained in embryo in Klingsor but even in Knulp, just as Castalia and Joseph Knecht are in Mariabronn and Narcissus. But this insight did not pain me, it meant more than simply a reduction and curtailment of my self-esteem, which before, to be sure, had been appreciably greater; it meant something good and positive as well, it showed me that in spite of many ambitious wishes and efforts, on the whole I had remained true to my nature and had not abandoned the path of self-realization even at times of crisis and constraint. And the cadence of the writing, its melody, the rhythm of its rise and fall were not alien to me nor did they smack of the past or of faded periods of my life, though that lightness of flow was something I could not duplicate today. This kind of prose was still suited to me, and I had forgotten nothing of its main structure or substructures or of its phrasing, none of the playful touches; it was the language far more than the content of the book that I had retained true and undistorted in my memory.

But for the rest—how incredibly much I had forgotten! It is true that I did not come upon any page or sentence that was not immediately recognizable, but on hardly any page or in any chapter could I have said in advance what I would find on the following page. Small details had been stored up in my memory, such as the chestnut tree at the monastery gate, the peasant house with the dead bodies inside, Goldmund's horse Bless, also more important things such as some of the conversations between the friends, the nocturnal excursion "into the village," the horse race with Lydia. But forgotten, incomprehensibly forgotten, was most of Goldmund's experience with Master Niklaus, forgotten the pilgrim-fool Robert, forgotten the episode with Lene and how on her account Goldmund killed for the second time. Some of what I had remembered as successful and beautiful disappointed me a little. Some places which had given me trouble during the writing and with which I had not been fully satisfied were hard to find, and when found seemed all right.

During this reading, which I performed slowly and carefully, events connected with the composition of the book also came back to me. I shall share one of them with you since some of you were probably present when it happened. It was toward the end of the twenties, I had promised to give a reading in Stuttgart because I wanted to visit the home of my youth, and I was the guest of one of my friends there who is now no longer living. At that time *Narcissus and Goldmund* was almost finished in manuscript and, not very intelligently, I picked out and brought with me to read aloud the particular chapter that contains the account of the plague. It was listened to with respect; at that time this description was especially important and precious to me, and my stories of the Black

Death seemed to make an impression; a certain solemnity spread through the hall, or perhaps it was only the silence of discomfort. But when the reading was over and "the inner circle" met at a favorite tavern for supper, it seemed to me that Goldmund's wanderings through the Black Death had powerfully stimulated the life instinct of the audience. I myself was still completely absorbed in the chapter; for the first time, and not without hesitation, I had presented in public an example of my new way of writing; I was still involved with it and had most unwillingly accepted the invitation to this friendly supper gathering. And now, whether rightly or wrongly, I had the feeling that those around me were heaving a sigh of relief after listening to my story and were throwing themselves with redoubled zest into life. There was a wild, noisy contest for seats, for waiters, for menus and wine cards; there were smug, laughing faces and jovial greetings all around, and I heard the two friends on either side of me raising their voices against the uproar to order their omelets with liver or ham; it seemed to me that I had got into the midst of one of the drinking bouts where Goldmund, amid the throng of those eager to live, attempting to dull the fear of death, drains his cup and succeeds in prodding the hysterical merriment to ever-greater heights. But I was not Goldmund, I felt lost and rejected and disgusted by this merriment, it was impossible for me to stand it. So I sidled to the door and slipped away and out of sight before anyone could miss me and bring me back. That was not smart or heroic behavior, as I knew at the time, but it was an instinctive reaction that was not to be overcome.

After that, I gave public readings once or twice again because I had given my word, but that was the end of it.

* * * *

And now this Engadine summer too has slipped away

while I have been making these notes, it is time to pack and depart. Writing these few pages has cost me more trouble than they are worth; I haven't the knack of it any more. A bit disappointed, I travel home again, disappointed over my various physical disabilities, but even more because, despite all my effort and a great expenditure of time, I have not been able to produce anything better than this circular letter, which after all I have owed many of you for a long time. At least something beautiful is in store for me, something very beautiful, my trip home by way of Maloja and Chiavenna, the always enchanting journey from the cool clarity of the mountain heights into the summer-hazy South, to Mera and the bays and the little cities, to the garden walls, olive trees, and oleanders of Lake Como. I will breathe this fragrance once more with gratitude. Take care and farewell!